Nation or the Empire

Indian Civilians at the Crossroads

Satyaki Nath

frontpage

frontpage
www.frontpagepublications.com

First published 2015

Frontpage Publications Limited
Level 2, 13 John Prince's Street, London W1G 0JR, United Kingdom

Frontpage
Level B, 76 B B Ganguly Street, Kolkata 700012, India

British Library Cataloguing in Publishing Data
A catalogue record for this book is available from the British Library

ISBN: 978 93 81043 16 5

Printed in India
By Intricate Solutions, Sadhana Chamber
76 B B Ganguly Street, Kolkata 700012, India

To

Sri Gadadhar Chattopadhyay

Content

Acknowledgements

I am fortunate to have worked under the tutelage of Sri Devi Prasad Pande, Member Traffic, Railway Board, India. His motivation helped me to recover from the pitiable state that I was languishing in. I cannot repay his debt. I am obliged to Sri Asim Kumar Maitra for the meaningful discussions and his guidance. I record my whole-hearted thanks to Sri Radhey Shyam, General Manager, South Eastern Railway and Sri Prabhat Sahay, Additional General Manager for allowing me to take up the work. I owe sincere thanks to Sri Manoj Pande, Sri Gopal Krushna Mohanty and Sri Suchitto Kumar Das for their indulgence and support. No amount of thanks is adequate to Sri Basudev Roy. He rather owns many of the ideas that the book is based on. Our morning walks at Alipore Agri Horticultiural Society Garden were really invigorating both physically and intellectually. Arguments went back and forth and many ideas actually evolved during the course of walk. Thanks are also due to Sri Vijay Kumar, Sri Gunanand Jha and Sri Parashuram Singh for showing interest in my work. Sri Pramod Kumar Jena is my senior colleague and elder brother rolled into one. He stood with me throughout the difficult time. I have also been benefitted from consultation with Sri Soumitra Majumdar. Encouragement from Sri K V R Murthy, Sri Prabhas Dansana, Sri Mukul Jain, Sri Ajay Shankar Jha and Sri Sharat Bhatia deserves special mention. I owe thanks to Sri Madan Mohan Maity and Sri Dipankar Bhattacharya with whom I discussed many issues related to this work.

My work spanned little over two years. There were many occasions during this moderately long period when I nearly flagged off. I am thankful to all who sustained me moving. They all are members of the proverbial Indian Railway family. I acknowledge my thanks to our departed colleague Sri Vivek Kumar Sahay from whom I received avuncular indulgence. I remain grateful to mysenior colleague Sri Swarup Kumar Gupta but for whose firm support I would have faltered. His inspiration has been truly invaluable. I am grateful to Sri Prabir Kumar Chatterji and Sri Partha Sengupta who encouraged me to continue the work. My work did not fail to receive the usual encouragement from Sri Swastik Misra. A talk with him many a times boosted my sagging morale. Sri Prithviraj Bose, Sri Krishnendu Mukherji, Sri Arvind Veluswamy, Sri Swapan Sarkar, Sri Asish Nag and Sri Indranil Mukherji are as passionate about the project as me. Sri Pranab Deb,Sri Sopan Dutta, Sri Prabir Kumar Ghosal and Sri Samir Kumar Dasgupta have helped me in managing the documents and pictures that appear in the illustration.

Bulk of the documents that I used for the work was available at National Library, Kolkata. The Library officials have been extremely helpful and courteous. I wish I could name all of them but space becomes the constraint. I shall certainly fail in my duty if I do not record my thanks to some of them. I can never fully acknowledge the help extended by Sk Alimuddin and his reprographics team. Sri Partha Bose and the old news paper section have ungrudgingly provided me whatever document I looked for. Sri Meher Singh on many occasions, albeit without disclosing the secret, found out the book which was otherwise 'not found'. Here at National Library I came to know Sri P T Nair and lately benefitted from his guidance. Other libraries that I have frequented for this work are National Archives, New Delhi, Bangiya Sahitya Parishad Library, Kolkata, Calcutta University Library and Visva-Bharati Archives, Santiniketan. I do not intend to forget the assistance that I received at all these places.

Last but not the least I am thankful to Sri Abhijit Mazumder of Frontpage Publications for agreeing to publish my work. My understanding with him grew quite fast. My college friend Sri Partha Sarathi Pal is most excited about the work and provided vital clues. I received good deal of support from my family members as well. My uncle Sri Sabyasachi Nath designed the cover page. Sri Nitya Ranjan Nath, another uncle who resides at Potomac for over five decades, read a part of the manuscript and quickly provided valuable guidance. So did Pratyay my cousin who himself is a student of history. He read the entire write-up and encouraged me to publish the work. Sri Anjan Dutta, my uncle read part of the manuscript with lively interest and shared his observation. My parents had always approved whatever academic activity I have pursued and there was no deviation on this occasion also. It is not customary to thank one's own spouse for assisting in such endeavour. Hindu custom implies that the wife co-authors the book her husband. My wife allowed me to spend the weekends at libraries and enjoyed lively discussions with me. My children Shoumili and Soumabha, though complained occasionally, were quite considerate.

15 August 2014

Kolkata

Satyaki Nath

Preface

The starting point of taking up the project is perhaps reading Partha Chatterjee's book 'The Prince and the Sannyasi'. The independent conduct of the Indian judge in the third decade of 20th century interested me. At that time the republic was in the horizon. A question occurred to my mind as to how the Indian officials conducted in the service a couple of decades earlier. The Empire, they were serving, was at its zenith. My residency near National Library, Kolkata afforded just the right opportunity. One sultry Saturday afternoon I reached the library more for breaking the monotony of routine work. Composing a book was nowhere in my mind. A title search of 'Indian Civil Service' produced a formidable list. The first few books I read were the memoirs of eminent British Civilians. Gradually the scope expanded as I looked for government documents. However, all along I was drifting without any specific idea to work on. Things crystalised slowly and I started jotting down. It was not before reaching the end that I could finalise the topic.

In this book I have tried to capture the condition of the Indian members of Indian Civil Service. The period covered is from 1855 when open competition was introduced for recruitment, to the First World War. During the period the service was greatly aspired by British youths. University graduates predominantly from Oxford and Cambridge joined in large number. There was no open competition during the war years and when the competition resumed British youths started losing interest. The diarchy introduced subsequent to Montague-Chelmsford reform diminished the attraction of the service. British youths resented to work under Indian ministers and a sizeable number of British Civilians retired prematurely in the 1920s. The first sixty years of the open competition, it appears, was perhaps the period of fiercest test.

Along with the majority of British candidates competed Indians whose number grew slowly. The competition was very uneven and the Indians were placed at great adversities. The test was conducted only at London and was based on British educational curricula. The qualifying age was altered on a number of occasions to the detriment of Indians. All these barriers were, however, successfully overcome by outstanding Indian individuals. They joined the ruling aristocracy in rather awkward condition of serving their motherland administered by foreign rule. My attempt has been to find out their experience and conduct in the service.

Note on Spelling

Spelling of Indian names during imperial period was so different and diverse that it warrants some clarification. I have used the name as it appears in the government documents and tried to maintain consistency throughout the book. The only conscious departure has been at times of quoting where I have reproduced the names without any alteration. Arabinda Ghose may appear most puzzling who, while appearing in the open competition was Aravind Ackroyd Ghose (AAG). He evaded the riding test and was denied the appointment. He joined Baroda State Service and transformed to Arabinda Ghose. Starting his spiritual life he became Aurobindo. Though the words Muslim, Mahomedan and Mohamedan all mean the same community, Mahomedan was most frequently used during the period. I have used the same word unless when quoting from original.

List of Illustration

CHAPTER I
PIONEERING ZEAL

During the mighty imperial rule marked by European supremacy, Satyendranath Tagore was the first Indian to have joined the coveted Indian Civil Service in 1863. Satyendranath, the second son of Debendranath Tagore and grandson of Dwarkanath Tagore, was born in Jorasanko Thakur family, Calcutta (now renamed as Kolkata) on 1 June 1842. Satyendranath's father Debendranath, commonly known as *Maharshi*, was a religious philosopher and one of the founders of Brahmo Religion. Maharsi spent most of his time in the Himalayas away from the family in a spirit of detachment. In January 1842, Prince Dwarkanath, grandfather of Satyendranath, sailed for Europe to adapt to western way of life. A distinguished citizen of Calcutta, identifying himself with all the public movements of the day, Dwarkanath, before proceeding to Europe, was felicitated by his fellow citizens at Town Hall, Calcutta on 8 January 1842. Dwarkanath emerged as a civic leader, simultaneously expanding his business activities in alliance with the British traders. On his return home, Dwarkanath met with considerable opposition from the Brahmin Community who wished to excommunicate him for transgressing caste rules whilst in Europe. Refusing to perform *prayaschitta*, Dwarkanath lost no time in resuming his various public activities. He directed his initiative towards promoting female education and encouraging medical studies. Three years later he made his second trip to Europe. Dwarkanath did not return from this trip and finally died in London in August 1846. This time Devendranath stuck to his conviction and displayed extraordinary courage. Despite the advice from his friends and relatives he refused to take part in any rites which seemed to him idolatrous. He was left all alone but stood firm. He performed the last rite according to a form which he himself had prepared for the occasion. Satyendranath inherited this familial characteristics and courageously overcame superstition then prevalent among the Bengalees against sea travel to England. At the time, he and his friend Manomohan proceeded to England they had barely crossed their teens.

Task ahead of the young men to proceed to England to compete for the Indian Civil Service was, indeed, very difficult. It is Manomohan Ghose or Menou, as his friend called him, who insisted on the difficult undertaking and accompanied Satyendranath in the voyage. Manomohan's father Ramlochan was a Sub Judge at Krishnanagar who once came to know that appointments in the Company's Civil Service had been thrown open to Indians. Ramlochan might have had high hope of his son, Manomohan. The boy, by that time, was also matured more than his age, and started making plans of fulfilling his father's long cherished dream. The examination was, however, conducted only at London for which one had to reach the alien land crossing the sea against social taboo. Finishing his education at Krishnanagar, Manomohan joined Presidency College, Calcutta where a friendship soon developed with Satyendranath. Very soon, Satyendranath became interested in his friend's idea and all plans thereafter were made jointly. On 28 March 1862, both Satyendranath and Manomohan sailed for England by 'Colombo', a P & O Company's steamer. *Hindoo Patriot*, a Calcutta based news-weekly, reported on 24 March 1862 that 'two young Natives will proceed to England by the next mail steamer for the purpose of competing for the Civil Service Examination. They are very respectfully connected. One of them is the grandson of Baboo Dwarkanath Tagore and the other the son of Baboo Ramlochan Ghose, the pensioned Principal Sudder Ameen of Nuddea (now Nadia). We trust many more will follow their example'.

Prince Dwarkanath, while touring Europe, was accompanied by his nephew, medical attendant, servants and cook among others. The journey of his grandson though undertaken in company of his friend Menou, was un-chaperoned. Both Satyendranath himself and his father Devendranath wrote to Rakhaldas Halder, a proponent of *Brahmo Samaj*, who was in London studying at the University College of London, seeking assistance for lodging arrangements. At that time, Satyendranath's cousin Gyanendra Mohan Tagore was also in London with his family. Both the friends had earlier experience of sea travel but faced the initial discomfort. Hardly had they reached Madras, 'only four days away from home',[1] Satyendranath wrote to his elder brother 'that monster sea-sickness has devoured us'.[2] Cribbed in their cabin, they could hardly enjoy the splendid beauties of Indian Ocean. The duo gradually recovered from this helpless situation and after a journey of 40 days reached Southampton on 2 May 1862. Gyanendra Mohan received them and the two friends stayed for few days with the family of Gyanendra Mohan in London. Here, they came in contact with Hodgson Pratt, a retired Bengal Civilian. Pratt guided the young Indians and they shifted to Windsor staying with the family of Dr Giles. The arrangement in Giles' house was almost like a hostel. Giles himself taught English and other teachers gave them lessons in Arabic, Sanskrit and French. The friends often met Edward Ryan, the Civil Service Commissioner. Ryan had served Bengal as Chief Justice and was known to the Calcutta residents. Even today his portrait adorns the wall of the Asiatic Society of the city.

In many ways, the friends' undertaking was more formidable than a pure academic test. Sea travel was a taboo in those days among caste Hindus with risk of social exclusion. In an alien land six thousand miles away, they had to live, torn off from all family relationship and friends. Both the friends were married and left behind their wives in India. The examination curriculum was not suitable to Indians and no countryman had ever made any endeavour either. Climate condition with cold winter and fog often created problem for acclimatisation. Their task was thus greatly difficult but equally strong was their youthful resolve, aspiring to secure a role in the administration of their own country. Misfortune as it was, the country under foreign yoke did not offer any greater role to its natives in the government. On 2 December 1862, by which time they had spent seven months in England, Manomohan wrote, reflecting the emotional crises he was passing through, that 'I am no longer the same in body or mind. If the task we have willingly undertaken had not been imposed upon us by the interests of a nation, I should not have it worth my while to sacrifice my body and mind for its accomplishment. Whether after all the sacrifices, we shall succeed or not, is a question that yet remains to be solved; but whatever the result may be, nothing will deprive us of the satisfaction of having honestly done what was in our power...Satyendra is every day getting healthier and stronger, and I wish I could say the same regarding myself. We work every day for nearly eleven hours, but I am sorry to say that if one day I work very hard, I am laid up for the next two days; Satyendra manages to keep very good health in spite of all this drudgery'. Manomohan received an encouraging letter from the rebel poet Michael Madhusudan Dutt. 'I am glad you and our little Indra[3] are getting on well'[4] wrote Madhusudan who himself was in London at that time, pursuing legal study. 'Remember my boys that the eyes of our nation are on you',[5] the poet attempted to motivate the young men by succinctly pointing out the importance of their mission.

Civil Service Examination was completed in July 1863, in which 219 candidates competed for 60 appointments, all but two being European. After the examination, the two friends set out for a continental trip. When they were holidaying in France, the result was announced. Though Satyendranath stood 43rd in order of merit, he was rather unhappy over the failure of his friend. Satyendranath returned to England and joined University College of London for his probationary training. Studentship at this College was nothing memorable for Satyendranath. Interaction with the Vice-Chancellor was also very rare. He had, however, Charles Schawnan as his fellow student who in course of time became one of the active members of 'India Group' of the Parliamentarians. Satyendranath successfully cleared the final examination in 1864. On this occasion, *Hindoo Patriot* proudly informed the nation that '...We are glad to be able to announce that Baboo Satyendranath Tagore has successfully passed the second examination. He is now a pucca Civilian'.[6] Satyendranath reached India in November 1864, leaving behind his friend Menou in England who wished to compete further.

Manomohan, however, was unlucky as in the year 1864 the marks allotted to Sanskrit and Arabic were reduced to 375 each from 500 earlier. He attempted twice (or thrice?) and remained unsuccessful. Thereafter, he enrolled for the Bar and returned to India in November 1866 as a Barrister. Before leaving England, Manomohan summarised his experience in a letter dated 29 January 1866 to *Hindoo Patriot*. 'In persevering to the last for the Civil Service, I have done my duty, and I am not sorry that I have not met with success, for I know that the time I have spent in studying for this examination has not been spent in vain. I shall rejoice to see some more of my countrymen come over to this country to fight for the prize which I have lost, and nothing will give me greater happiness than to help them with personal experience of the examination and to see them successful in gaining an object for which I have myself fought vainly, but I trust, not dishonourably.'

The story of the first native Civilian permeated into every corner of the whole country. *The Bengalee*, a leading newspaper, reported on 16 September 1863, that...'To us and our Countrymen at large, Baboo Satyendranath Tagore's good fortune is an event of the largest signification, and one for unalloyed congratulation. Already the news has travelled with the flash of lightning to all parts of India and there is in consequence of rejoicing and thanks giving in every Indian heart in which a narrow selfishness has not extinguished the capacity to feel exalted at the brightening of national prospects'. Calcutta citizens arranged a public gathering to congratulate the first native Civilian. It was held at Belgachia Villa, Calcutta with participation of eminent persons of all community. Satyendranath called on Viceroy Lord Lawrence and Sir Cecil Beadon, Lieutenant-Governor and sailed for Bombay in November 1864, the Presidency he was allotted. This time of course, his family allowed taking his wife Jnanadanandini with him.In the service, Satyendranath was denied the more attractive executive line and spent his time in judicial assignments. He consorted well with his European colleagues and never complained of serving the Empire. But what pleased him immensely was the genial welcome extended by native community of Bombay Presidency. The distance and language barrier which separated Bombay and Bengal Presidencies, all dissolved in a moment. Native community found in Satyendranath, their ethnic representation. The issue of posting at despicable locations and frequent transfer troubled the native community as much as it did Satyendranath himself. He resigned prematurely from service perhaps with a sense of dejection due to his ability not being acknowledged by imperial administration.

Indian students were encouraged and started reaching England for competing, initially from Presidency cities of Calcutta, Bombay and Madras (renamed as Mumbai and Chennai respectively) and from other towns afterwards. On 3 March 1868, Surendranath Banerjea started for England for taking part in the examination with two of his friends Romesh Chunder Dutt and Behari Lal Gupta. Apprehending disapproval of the plan to cross *kala pani* by their family members, arrangement was made in secret and was known to Surendranath's father only who had extended all help. The trio passed the night preceding their departure at the house of Manomohan at Cossipur, and before the day break they started for the steamer at Chandpalghat. Tickets were booked for 'Surendranath Banerjea and his two friends' in an attempt to suppress the identity of the passengers. Chandra Sekhar Gupta, father of Behari Lal reached Chandpalghat and tried to dissuade his son, only to be turned down by the resolute young man. Chandra Sekhar, Head Assistant of the Currency Office, Calcutta despaired endlessly and returned home with the supplication 'whatever you do my son, do not marry a bibi'.[7] They reached Southampton after a voyage of nearly five weeks and met W C Bonnerjee who was informed in advance by Manomohan. Womesh Chandra, who was studying law, took them to London and put them up at a boarding house.

So great was the interest of Manomohan in encouraging his countrymen to visit England, that poet Michael Madhusudan Dutt nicknamed him 'Protector of Indian Emigrants proceeding to Europe'.[8] Manomohan next motivated his brother Lalmohan to proceed to England and compete for the examination. Lalmohan unfortunately could not fulfil his brother's dream and also came back to India as a Barrister. The glorious moment for Manomohan perhaps came when his only son Mahimohun competed successfully in the year 1890. The boy had initial education at the St Xavier's College, Calcutta and was sent to England in 1885 at the tender age of 12.

In September 1890, the proud father made a tour to England in company of his son who joined Balliol College, Oxford for his probationary training. Two other Indian students, Kiran Chandra De and Mohini Mohun Ghattack, who were going to compete for the examination, also accompanied. Manomohan's desire of touring 'Nilghery' in company of his son, however, remained unfulfilled. In October 1896, the day he was preparing to start from his native place Krishnanagar to Calcutta on the way to Madras, to see his son, who was a member of the Madras Civil Service, a fatal stroke of apoplexy carried him off the world. Successful in legal practice, Manomohan was considered to be a veritable terror to moffusil magistrates. His zeal 'in endeavouring to recruit such magistrates from among the ranks of his own countrymen'[9] was apparently not in consonance with his tireless attack on tyrannical British judicial administration. Advocating appointment of Indians to high administrative posts, the ardent nationalist perhaps rightly diagnosed the system malaise and its real cure.

In unveiling the portrait of Manomohan Ghose in Calcutta on 29 January 1898, Satyendranath Tagore, referred in feeling terms to the undying friendship and the distinguished career of his brother pilgrim. Manomohan with his success in legal profession and national politics never had any reason to regret his failure at the Civil Service Examination. No one was, however, more correct than Palmer, the teacher of Manomohan in Calcutta, who observed the early traits of his student, and used to say of young Ghose that 'he carried a very old head on a pair of young shoulders'.[10] Notwithstanding his forthright attack on British racial discrimination and strong contribution to the incipient nationalism, Manomohan had significant number of friends in Anglo-Indian community. His European friends might have been second to their native counterpart in number but certainly not in eminence. In London, a move was initiated for a memorial in honour of Manomohan. Sizeable amount was raised, and spent on a special library at the Bethune College, Calcutta, named 'M M Ghose Memorial Library'.

Indian youths honoured the words of Manomohan and tenaciously overcame the adversities. Four Indian candidates succeeded in the open competition of 1869. One of them, Romesh Chunder Dutt ranked as high as third in the list. Their hard work did not cease with the selection and they pluckily fought for the privileges that their European colleagues availed. No sooner had the result been announced, Civil Service Commissioners received a complaint that but for Romesh, the age indicated by the other Indian candidates, while applying for the open competition was in variance with their actual age. An investigation immediately followed which cleared Behari Lal of the controversy. Surendranath and Sripad Babaji of Bombay faced the misfortune and were disqualified for being above the prescribed upper limit of age. Surendranath was not to accept the unjust order lying down and his fight testified the tenacity and fearlessness of the young lad. Both Surendranath and Sripad were reinstated in the service by an order of King's Court. Sripad returned to India in 1872, a year later than his other three Indian colleagues and was posted in Bombay Presidency. Romesh, Behari Lal and Surendranath remained together in the same province of Lower Bengal. Surendranath on joining the service was appointed as Assistant Magistrate in Sylhet district of Lower Bengal. He could barely complete a year in the service before a fresh controversy broke out. A judicial statement more in the nature of a routine one signed by the young native Civilian turned out to contain misrepresentation of facts. The statement containing the names of absconded convicts was prepared by the subordinate office clerk that Surendranath signed without further verification. The list containing a wrong name was thus tarred with a black brush. This would not have attracted much attention under ordinary circumstance, but the relation between Surendranath and his superior, the District Magistrate, had strained by this time. The innocuous statement thus presented the District Magistrate an opportunity to implicate the young Civil Servant. He brought the matter to the notice of Calcutta High Court with suggestion that it be further probed. In course of time, Sir George Campbell, Lieutenant-Governor of Bengal constituted a commission to inquire into the case. The investigation concluded to have found in the case a multitude of irregularities that Surendranath had committed. Surendranath was held responsible for charges varying from want of application of mind, accuracy and conscientious discharge of duty to falsehood and palpable abuse of judicial powers. Sir George Campbell felt strongly that the high standard of honour and morality laid down for the European members of the service should not be relaxed for Indian Civilians. Such gross and persistent dereliction from truth and honesty in work and conduct, Campbell observed, could not be viewed leniently. He, therefore, recommended the dismissal of Surendranath from the hard-won service which the Secretary of State promptly ratified. Surendranath proceeded to England but on this occasion met with very indifferent response from the Secretary of State. Failing to reverse the order of his removal, Surendranath decided to complete his study of Law which he had earlier undertaken at Middle Temple. A further shock, however, was awaiting him. Citing his removal from the Civil Service, the Benchers of Middle Temple declined to call him to the Bar. Surendranath returned to the country in September 1875 thoroughly dejected and it was his wife's bright and cheery countenance that lifted his spirit. Native sympathies were with him and Pundit Ishwar Chandra Vidyasagar offered him the post of Professor of English in his Metropolitan Institution. Surendranath started the career of teaching. Very soon he brought out the newspaper *The Bengalee*, as its editor.

Surendranath's compatriot Sripad Babaji was posted in the Bombay Presidency and mainly served in judicial administration. Sripad served admirably well displaying his independence of mind. His career was, however, cut short by his premature death in 1889. Though their activities lay in different spheres, Romesh, Behari Lal and Surendranath were linked by the closest ties of friendship and affection throughout their life. Romesh and Behari Lal were pioneers in the hitherto un-trodden path of Indians entering the Bengal Civil Service. Romesh served mostly in executive side while Behari Lal followed the judicial line. Surendranath felt that the position of his friends was difficult, and their anxieties were great. 'But they excelled in those high qualities which should distinguish all pioneers',[11] Surendranath confirmed. He felt that, 'when in their careers a conflict occurred between the claims of the service and those of the nation, they preferred the latter'.[12] Surendranath, a leading nationalist in his time, had no doubts in declaring that his 'friends exalted the interest of the motherland above the sectional concerns of the class to which they belonged'.[13] In the year 1880, Behari Lal was the Presidency Magistrate of Calcutta and had the criminal jurisdiction over European subjects as well. Native judges in the districts did not possess the authority and Romesh, while carrying out district assignment, felt the discrimination. The two friends corresponded on the issue and Behari Lal made up his mind to rectify the anomaly. When Criminal Procedure Code was being revised in 1882, the Bengal Government routinely asked its officers for comments. In response, Behari Lal submitted a note on 30 January 1882, citing the 'anomalous position of an Indian District Magistrate or Sessions Judge, appointed to a position of authority but unable to exercise that authority'.[14] This note was forwarded by Sir Ashley Eden, then Lieutenant-Governor of Bengal to Government of India. Ilbert, the Law Member of Lord Ripon's Executive Council, in consultation with local Government authorities, prepared a Bill which soon invited a great deal of controversy as Europeans strongly opposed to give up their right to be tried by a non-European judge. Behari Lal's name reached every corner of the Empire and the nation split in two parts on racial line. Ripon eventually had to reconcile to the European argument, modifying the scope of the Bill, much to the chagrin of Indian community.

Behari Lal's colleague Romesh, assertive and proud of his ethnicity, was a man amongst rulers and a prince among his peers. While in service, Romesh through his ability and zeal had made his presence felt. His superiority both in intellect and administrative acumen was observable in every gathering that he attended. Romesh was placed in charge of several important districts and was the first Indian to be promoted as Commissioner of a Division, first Burdwan and then Orissa. While serving as the Commissioner of Burdwan, he was elected a member of the Bengal Legislative Council. It was a strange coincidence that the 'three friends' who sailed together for England and returned as successful civilians, viz. Romesh, Behari Lal and Surendranath sat together in the Bengal Legislative Council. Surendranath, as a non-official member, of course had the unlimited latitude to conduct himself. But it was Romesh, who through his independent conduct bemused his friend. No fetters could bind Romesh as he declined to move in the usual official groove. He, along with another official member, Henry Cotton, had for once voted against the government in Bengal Legislative Council. His upright attitude caused flatter in the official benches which naturally contrived hard to displace him. The atmosphere darkened further and the intervention of President of the Council became imperative. On this occasion, Sir Charles Elliot, Lieutenant-Governor, reacted extraordinarily asserting that he welcomed independent outlook of the members. His countenance of Romesh's conduct extirpated the controversy and silenced the aggrieved official element in the Council. No less aggrieved was Romesh himself as he felt that the colonial administration did not acknowledge his abilities.

In a letter dated 24 September 1893, Romesh confided to his brother Jogesh that he was risking his official career by supporting the Indian National Congress in their demand for separation of the Judicial and Executive services. He was acutely aware that his conduct might deny him the *pucca* commissionership. But the allure of promotion and career prospect had long ceased to appeal to him. Continuous injustice had effectively dulled his emotion and made him indifferent. On numerous occasions, Romesh had been passed over by his juniors, lending credence to his belief of lacking the trust and confidence of the Government. On the other hand, he also felt an intense joy for serving the interest of his country. In this state of mind, Romesh was not averse to the idea of collaborating with his colleagues Sir Richard Garth or Reynolds, to press for a reform in the system of imperial administration. As 19th century was drawing to its end, Romesh resigned from the service in 1897, a move that technically un-muzzled him. He had barely completed the qualifying twenty-five years' service that earned him pension. It was supremely rewarding that the nation had keenly watched the activities of its son and acknowledged his contribution. Romesh was invited to preside over the annual session of the Indian National Congress at Lucknow in 1899. An enlightened and liberal Indian Prince, the Maharaja of Baroda, did not falter to discover the capable man. Sayaji Rao Gaekwad acknowledged the abilities of the Indian administrator and offered Romesh the post of Dewan-ship which he gladly accepted.

Surendranath devoting his initiative in teaching and journalism emerged, in course of time, as the leading politician of the nation (in Making!). His relationship with his friends, sharing both joy and sorrow, was never affected by any event. In 1883, Surendranath was sentenced for imprisonment for defamation of Court. Behari Lal was then serving as the Presidency Magistrate of Calcutta. When he heard the sentence of imprisonment of Surendranath by Calcutta High Court, Behari Lal lost no time. He came straight to the Presidency Jail to see his friend. Sympathy, so open and undisguised on part of so high an officer of the Government, perhaps implied 'tacit disapproval of the judicial sentence of the Highest Court in the land'.[15] Behari Lal's visit to the Presidency Jail soon became talk of the town and the Anglo-Indian newspapers never missed the opportunity to highlight the incident. But these little things never disturbed the equanimity of Behari Lal. With his confidence undimmed, Behari Lal became an officiating Judge of the High Court in British India.

Behari Lal continued his Government service for another decade since Romesh had stepped down. He finally retired from Indian Civil Service in March 1907, and joined Baroda state as Legal Remembrancer in September 1909. Romesh was the Dewan of the State and the re-union with his friend greatly comforted him. Both the friends were living together, and Behari Lal nursed his friend when Romesh suddenly fell ill in 1909. Behari Lal was with his friend, till Romesh breathed his last. A couple of months before his death, Romesh wrote a letter to Surendranath greatly recognising the patriotic service of his friend. Amazing was the letter penned by a 'sun dried bureaucrat',[16] bearing the marks of crisp observation, steeped in oriental emotion which read as under:

'What a wonderful revolution we have seen within the life time of a generation! What a change in the thoughts and ideas of a nation and what a noble part you have played in leading that change. One by one, all our fellow workers are dropping round us, - Bonnerjee is gone! Anandamohan is gone! Lalmohan is gone! And we too shall soon pass away. But the History of India of 19th century and early 20th century will cherish the names of a band of patriotic workers–none nobler, truer, none persistent and more patriotic than yourself.'[17]

Chapter II

INDIA UNDER THE COMPANY

East India Company

The term 'Civil Service' was first used by the East India Company as a name for its establishment of non-military or civilian employees in India, to distinguish it from its military, maritime and ecclesiastical establishments. The Company was incorporated by Queen Elizabeth by way of *Letters of Patent* on 31 December 1600. The Company titled 'The Governors and Merchants of London trading into the East Indies'[1] was a body of merchants given certain rights and privileges to carry on their trade and manage their internal affairs. These privileges continued under fresh Charters and Acts of Parliament. In 1698, on the authority of an Act of Parliament, a new Company titled 'The English Company, trading in East Indies'[2] was formed. For a short period, these two companies competed with each other to the detriment of the interest of both. The competition did not continue for long as the trading houses realised its futility. Profitability overshadowed all other considerations and the companies closed their rivalry entering into agreement of co-operation. Amalgamation was thus agreed and all other arrangements suitably fell in place. The two Companies merged themselves and vested the management on a Court of Managers of an equal number of Delegates from each body. The Company thus formed, came to be known as 'The United Company of Merchants of England Trading to the East Indies'.[3] The shorter title 'The East India Company'[4] was, however, confirmed as late as 1833.

In the initial years, Surat emerged as the chief establishment of the Company in India. By 1643, factories were established at other locations of Eastern Coast in Masulipatnam and Madras which were considered to be the nuclei of pushing the Company's trade into the interior of the country. Three distinct zones of Bombay, Madras and Calcutta were subsequently made into Presidencies, under the jurisdiction of President and Council, with fortification to protect against external aggression. All the settlements or factories, as they were called, within each area, carried on their business under the direction of and in subordination to the President or Governor and Council at the Presidency or Head Quarter. A Chief or a Manager headed the whole establishment of a factory and had a seat in the Council at the Presidency. Under the Royal Charters and Acts of Parliament, the Company was given some power to raise and equip troops for defensive purposes. Thus the Company's service fell into two classes of Civil and Military. Civil service was further graded into writer, senior writer and factor. For appointment as writer, the candidate had to write out his petition in his own handwriting and submit along with it evidence of age and testimonials about his qualifications. The Court referred the petitions to its Committee of Correspondence on whose report selection was made. The selected candidates were given a long printed indenture to sign drawn up in a form approved by the legal advisers of the Company. Among many other articles in this bond, the writer had to sign certain agreements and conditions between Company and himself. These were embodied in an accompanying document known as 'Covenant' which was the origin of the term 'Covenanted Servant'. The Covenants practically embodied their condition of service, rights and obligations.

These civilian employees of the Company were originally traders. Subsequent to the *Battle of Plassey*, the character of the Company changed and its trading operations were supplemented by territorial dominion. Eventually the Company ceased its trading activities and governance became its soul job. The merchants thus transformed into administrators. A decade had hardly passed and by the year 1765, the use of the term 'Civil Servant' was well-established. The same was mentioned in the new Covenant which the Company brought into force in that year. Lord Clive, as head of the Government, used the term in his letters to the Directors of the Company in 1765 and 1766.

After the Battle of Plassey, in 1760 Mir Kasim Ali Khan ceded to the Company three districts of Burdwan, Midnapore and Chittagung so the rent might defray the cost of defence of Bengal by the Company's army. At this point, Company's servants had nothing to do with the civil government except the ceded districts of Burdwan, Midnapore and Chittagung where they were gradually establishing a creditable standard of maintaining peace and prosperity. This system of dual government created great deal of conflict as Company's servants were peremptorily forbidden to ascertain any public authority over the officers of Nawab's Government. Lord Clive, who resumed the office of the Governor of Bengal in May 1765, was primarily engaged in establishing the Diwani, the control of revenue administration through Company's servant since Nawab and his ministers still had the authority of civil administration. It was, however, not practicable to replace the Indian and Persian collectors of revenue by the Company's servants who lacked the local knowledge and expertise. As a feasible remedy, English officers were associated with the Indian staff to supervise their work. By way of adopting superior surveillance and making amend of abuses of official power, it was hoped that a sound and vigorous administration would be gradually established. In 1772, this state of dual authority, however, came to end when the Company's decision to undertake the management of revenue system by the agency of Company's men was communicated to Warren Hastings, the first Governor-General of Bengal. Through the next three decades, the Company successfully established the civil administration of its territory which continuously expanded through subsequent annexation.

British Parliament and Indian Affairs

British Parliament's first interaction with India came in 1641, when East India Company laid a petition before the House of Commons. In 1698, by way of an Act, the Commons themselves created a new Company to which the King was to grant a charter. Since then all the Company's charters were incorporated in the Acts of the Parliament. The interference of Parliament in Indian affairs was at its peak between 1767 and 1793. During this period, the operations of the Company were twice subjected, in 1772 and 1781, to a rigorous examination by the Parliamentary Committees. Three Acts of major importance were passed viz. the Regulating Act of 1773, the India Act of 1784, and the Charter Act of 1793. This period was also the time when successive Governor-Generals built the foundation of civil and judicial administration in India. As Parliament through its enactments tried to increase its control over the activities of the Company, the Governor-Generals by their own initiative built the framework of civil administration. Communication, in those days, was tardy, allowing the head of the Government in India to act independently. When Government asked for instructions from the Board in England, it was unlikely to receive any before a year had elapsed. Governor-General in India was accordingly often compelled to act without orders, and for that reason he was more apt to do so even when it was not so urgent. On many occasions strong men like Lord Wellesley presented the Directors with a *fait accompli*, and then asked for its sanction for subsequent accomplishment.

The Regulating Act of 1773 provided for a distinction between the civil and commercial function of the Company. Collectors and Company officials, engaged in revenue and judicial administration, were prohibited from participating in commercial transactions, and thus function of governance was delinked from commercial trade. The scenario, subsequent to the disruption of Mughal Empire, greatly altered and eventually the Company got involved into Indian politics. The Company, taking part in Indian politics marked with diversities, soon realised the need for administrative co-ordination among the three different Presidencies. The Act, therefore, elevated the position of the Governor of Bengal to Governor-General compelling other Presidencies to seek its consent for 'war and peace'.

Pitt's Act (1784) treated the Company's Indian territories as 'imperial dominion' without any avowal of British sovereignty over the area. It emphasised and enlarged the supreme control of the Governor-General. The Company was allowed to carry on both commercial business and civil administration. Safeguard against abuse of power by Company's civil officials were, however, made stricter, defining acceptance of gift or act of insubordination as punishable misdemeanour. The minimum age of recruitment of writer was fixed as 15 year and maximum 18 year which was subsequently raised to 22 year by the Charter Act of 1793. The same Act contributed to the development of an *esprit de Corps* in civil service by forbidding entry of outsiders in the covenanted cadre. It was resolved that henceforward all posts with payment over £ 500 a year would be reserved for the Company's new 'Covenanted Service'. By that time, Company's service had become the dumping ground for friends and relations of the Directors and those connected with them. Jobs were distributed without reference to qualifications, and soon evil had assumed such proportions as to lead even to needless multiplication of offices. The Court had to intervene, directing the Government of Bengal in 1785, not to yield to pressure of influential persons at 'home'. Governor-Generals were distressed with recommendations from British aristocracy for employment of their favoured ones. Cornwallis's conviction and innate strength enabled him to withstand the pressure. He did not relent to the request of the Prince of Wales and even the Queen. With his intimate friend Dundas, he was equally firm, reminding him of injury to the public interests conceded through grant of such request. Through his stern and uncompromising attitude, Cornwallis was certainly able to check the evil to a great extent, though absolute extermination could not be achieved. Final success came perhaps through the protracted correspondence he zealously pursued with the Court of Directors. Appointment from outside covenanted service was statutorily forbidden by the Act of 1793. It provided that all vacancies in the civil line of the Company's service in India, below the rank of members of the Executive Councils, should be filled up from amongst the Civil Servants of the said Company only. The Act legislated that actual residence in the country for a period, varying with the amount of the salary of the post in question, would be an abiding requisite. Promotion of Covenanted Servants was linked to seniority and emoluments were elaborately defined. The Act of 1793 thus marked the beginning of a new regime. The authority of the Governor-General was also further enlarged authorising him to visit a Presidency and take charge of it with the assistance of the Council. Governor of the Presidency was on such occasion temporarily superseded as Cornwallis did in Madras in 1791. The Presidency Governors generally resented, albeit helplessly, such interference. But the Governor-General found it no easy matter either to impose his authority on them.

Company Directors and their Patronage

When in 1813, the renewal of the Company's Charter came up in the House of Lords, Lord Granville proposed that appointment to Indian Civil Service be given to the successful candidates selected in a competition open to the boys educated at the great English Public Schools. His voice, however, was drowned in the loud advocacy of the members at the Parliament arguing that the Company's system had produced all the able civilians who had given evidence before the Parliamentary Committees. The Charter Act took away the monopoly of the Company's trade in India thus radically changing its character. Merchant class and Bankers who formed the major stock holders of the Company consequently lost interest, and the retired Indian officials acquired these stocks and the subsequent control over the Company management. The Company was reduced from its commercial activity to become a patronage bureau. As Parliament was the authority to determine the continuity of patronage system, the Directors gave plenty of appointments to the families of political influence.

The Directors, prior to 1794, made their nomination on personal or political grounds and on some instances resorted to sale of their patronage as a legitimate supplement to their small official salaries. The practice earned so much of bad name for the Company that by Dundas' Act, it was stipulated that every Director within ten days after his selection would take an oath that they would not receive any perquisite, enrolment, fee, present or reward for any appointment. Newspaper reports, however, kept on appearing with stories of corruption in appointment. It generated so much of public rage that in 1809 a Select Committee was appointed by the House of Commons to inquire into the allegations of corrupt practices related to the nomination.

At the same time, ascendancy of Anglo-Indian families in stock holding of the Company helped the nomination process from degenerating further. Directors with their Indian experience and clear insight could look more sharply into the qualities required for Indian Civilians as they maintained the glory of the Empire in the Asiatic colony.

In 1833, Company's Charter again came up for revision. The monopoly of English trade with China, which had been left to the East India Company in 1813, was taken away from it. On the question of appointment, Macaulay, the Secretary to the Board of Control, desired to rearrange the system. His proposal for a fourfold nomination by the Directors from which the successful candidates would be selected by competition was greatly resented by the Directors. Their influence contrived so much that Macaulay's plan lay in a pigeon hole at the Board of Control, until the Parliament could be induced to effect repeal in 1837.

Governor-Generals in India

As Parliament devoted attention in framing regulation to assist establishment of Company's Government in India, the successive Governor-Generals through their initiative transformed these regulations into actions in founding the structure of civil administration. Warren Hastings, the first Governor-General, while taking on responsibility,recognised the importance of district as a unit of civil administration. In districts, the Covenanted Servants entrusted with collection and revenue settlement came to be known as Collectors. Judicial administration of the district was, however, dealt by two courts, one each for civil and criminal jurisdiction. Collector presided over the Civil Court and supervised proceedings of the Criminal Court. Thus the same incumbent was entrusted with the authority of Executive as well as Civil and Criminal justice. At the Presidency level, a Council of Revenue was created, with Hastings as President and the Councillors as Members. Appellate Courts of Civil and Criminal justice were established at Calcutta, the headquarter of the Company's Government. Hastings' attempt to introduce civil administration through government official, though successful to a reasonable extent, could not totally eliminate age-old administration run by the local influential land-holders. This form of local administration was so deep-rooted that it clashed with the legitimate system. The Zaminders and aristocrats resisted for a time, but eventually law superseded the prescriptive legitimacy acquired over a long period of time. The completion of the task was left to Cornwallis who succeeded Hastings and eliminated every form of private agency performing public duties.

With Cornwallis as Governor-General, state took over itself the responsibility of keeping peace through appointment of daroga (Station House Officer) in each police thana (Police Station). All landholders and Zaminders maintaining private army or chowkidars were asked to discharge them forever. The rural militia of chowkidars and others were subjected to work under the supervision of daroga who was put under the immediate authority of the Magistrate. Modernist that he was, Cornwallis did not wait long before replacing all the Mahomedan judges by European Covenanted Servants as circuit judges. The system of codification of Hindu law also continued. Code of Procedure drawn up by Sir Elija Impey, after his appointment as Chief Judge of Sadder Division Adalat, i.e., the Supreme Court, was revised and enlarged by Sir George Barlow. Cornwallis entertained very poor opinion of the characters of the Indians and recorded 'I should by no means propose to admit the natives to any participation in framing Regulations'.[5] He replaced the Indians officials engaged in revenue administration whose efficiency was widely acknowledged by Company's Covenanted Servants. The anomaly of vesting the authority of Executive, Civil and Criminal justice on a single incumbent of Collector was rectified. A separate judicial department was created at the Central Secretariat and Revenue Officers were divested of their authority to decide civil suits. Furthermore, the actions of revenue officers themselves were subjected to review by the District Judge. A set of code was formulated defining the responsibilities and authorities of the civil officials and salaries assigned to each post.

Lord Wellesley was first to perceive that the change in the role of Company's Civil Servants implied a difference of education. He viewed Civil Service as 'an inexhaustible supply of useful knowledge, cultivated talents and disciplined morals'[6] which was to be attained through training of the Civil Servants. None of the three Acts of Parliament which were passed between 1773 and 1793 to reform the Company's administration of Indian territories was concerned in any way with the question of education and training of the Civil Servants in India. From 1790 onwards each writer was paid a monthly allowance of Rupees 30 for one year so that he could engage a 'munshi' for learning Persian. There was, however, no provision for ascertaining whether the money was actually spent for the purpose. In December 1798, Wellesley made the first step, by appointing John Gilchrist, a scholar in the country languages, who later became a Professor at the Fort William College, to give lessons to the junior Civil Servants in Persian and Hindustani on a regular basis at the Writers' Building at Calcutta. It was agreed that the money payable to the officials would be paid to Professor

Gilchrist directly. A notification was issued on 21 December 1798 requiring the junior Civil Servants of the Bengal establishment to pass an examination in native language in order to be eligible for certain posts. It was decided to hold an examination after a year to judge the merits of the scheme. Wellesley, however, was not satisfied with the arrangements of language training only and devised a scheme of full-fledged College for imparting training. He was encouraged by the reply of the Directors regarding Gilchrist's seminary and his idea of starting a College. In the minutes on the subject, Lord Wellesley set out that 'the civil servants of the English East India Company, therefore, can no longer be considered as the agents of a commercial concern. They are in fact the minister and officers of a powerful sovereign'.[7]

Fort William College

Wellesley was clear in his objectives and two sound maxims underlay his scheme of training. One was that the education of the Company's servants must be of mixed character combining studies of both East and West. The second was that of merging education with discipline. Wellesley himself represented a remarkable assimilation of strong academics and rich administrative experience. At Eton College, Berkshire, England Wellesley showed great proficiency in the classics while he won the Chancellor's prize for Latin verse at Christ Church. Wellesley figured out the requirement of Indian administration and utilised his rich academic background in designing the scheme of education. Thus the curricula were founded on general knowledge of those branches of literature and sciences which formed the basis of the education of persons destined to similar occupations in Europe. With this combined, the subjects purported to intimately acquaint candidates with history, language, customs and manners of the people of India. On top of these rested the professional element, imparting knowledge of Mahomedan and Hindu codes of law and religion, and the political and commercial interests and relations of Great Britain in Asia. Wellesley, with this scheme of education, intended to reorganise the departments concerned with important legislative and executive work in such a way as to place at their heads only men of ability, integrity and experience. An assertive man like him did not wait for the sanction of the Directors to start the College. Wellesley's draft regulation with formal approval of the Council became the Regulation IX of 1800, an unprecedented step indeed without any prior dispatch to the Directors. The College was inaugurated on 24 November 1800 to impart lessons in Arabic, Persian and Hindustani.

The Governor-General was the Patron and the Visitors of the College were the Members of the Supreme Council, Judges of the Sudder Dewani Adalat and the Nizamat Adalat, and the Governors. The Governor-General in Council was the trustee for the management of funds of the College, being required regularly to submit accounts to the Court of Directors. Though the ultimate controlling authority was thus the Supreme Government, the immediate governance of the College vested with Provost and a Vice-Provost. The Provost was a clergy-man of the established Church of England and was entrusted with the responsibility to instruct and confirm the junior Civil Servants in the principles of Christian language. Only Europeans were appointed Professor and Teachers. Professors were paid a fabulous salary of Rs 1,500 per month, and the salary for the Teachers was Rs 1,000 per month. Among the Professors were G H Barlow, N B Edmonstone, John Baillie, John Gilchrist, C Buchanan and Colebrook. William Carrey joined the College as Teacher but soon rose to eminence. At its opening in 1800, Colebrook was in charge of Sanskrit and Hindu law, Gilchrist was professor of Hindustani and Francis Gladwin of Persian with Indian assistants in all departments. Early in 1801, Lord Wellesley agreed to the appointment of Carey as Lecturer in Bengali and Sanskrit. Later Carey also taught Marathi and his work continued till 1831. Two public examinations, each year, were provided for, and to stimulate exertion in the students, prizes and rewards were announced on the result of the examination. Although the College was mainly meant for the Civil Servants of Bengal by order of the Governor-General, provision was made for admission of any Military Servant of the Company and Civil Servants of the other two Presidencies as well. All Civil Servants of the Bengal establishment of less than three years' standing were attached to the College for three years from the date of the regulation. Wellesley was in favour of a central institution at Fort William in order to secure uniformity in the standard of acquirement of all the Civil Servants of India. In his minutes on the scheme of the College, Wellesley suggested that instead of fixing up the ultimate destination of the student to a particular Presidency at the time of his first appointment in England, it would be more advantageous to determine in India under the authority of the Government on the spot considering the inclination and acquirements of the students themselves.

Fort William College at Calcutta remained the sole training institution till 1806 much to the displeasure of the Directors who never appreciated Wellesley's independent style of working. They smarted under a sense of wounded pride and Wellesley's prolonged correspondence with them yielded no result. They felt the need to retard the pace of their Governor-General who was marching very fast zealously overstepping his jurisdiction. Very soon their resentment grew into a form of personal animus. The Directors blinded to all reason and failed to see Wellesley's activity in proper perspective. The order of immediate abolition of the College was dispatched in January 1802. They contradicted Wellesley's plan of a central institution at Fort William serving the needs of all the Presidencies and directed the Government of Bombay and Madras to make their own arrangement. Madras reacted quickly and in 1803, the Government established a Collegiate Institution at Fort St George, providing for instruction to its Civil Servants in the languages of the province, besides Sanskrit, Hindustani and Persian. There was, however, no appointment of European Professors and the Civil Servants alone acted as examiners without any additional remuneration. Bombay Presidency showed no urgency for training of the Civilians. Subsequently the provincial Government was reminded by the Court of Directors in 1819 to submit a plan for the instruction of the Civil Servants of the province. Mountstuart Elphinstone as Governor of Bombay sent a proposal, intending to start a College. But by this time, they had lost the opportunity as in 1806 a Centralised Training College was fully established in Haileybury at Hertford, England. Directors, therefore, declined to make additional expenditure for the same purpose and thus Bombay Governor's plan was dropped.

Wellesley though lost the uneven battle, saved further embarrassment with sanction of the Directors being given to continue Fort William College for the Civilians of Bengal Presidency only. Though the name of the College stuck to the institution, it was reduced to a rudimentary arrangement for vernacular training. Residential arrangement was wound up and for some time Writers' Building at Calcutta accommodated the writers. Some Professors continued to serve the College till 1830, but on the recommendation of the Civil Finance Committee, all professorships were surrendered, leaving the College under the tutelage of a Secretary supported by a number of Munshies and Pundits. By that time, the requirement of training of writers had been addressed by foundation of East India College at Hertford in 1806. Directors learnt from the initiative of the Governor-General but never acknowledged it. Meanwhile a proposal, dated 29 January 1804, from a British official in China (The East India Company also accounted for a large part of the China trade until 1833) was received by the Court of Directors. The letter from Canton implored that Writers not be sent to China 'until they had successfully passed through a process of complete education and system of occupation under the directives of the honourable Court'.[8] This measure was considered essential to convert the young lads 'to be more capable servants of the Company and give them a chance to become more distinguished members of the society than they could be, when quitting Europe at the very early age they frequently do'.[9] This time Directors reacted with uncanny fervour and embraced the proposal. It was taken up by the Committee of Correspondence under the guidance of Charles Grant. In course of time, the Committee produced an influential report outlining the scheme of training. It proposed that the curriculum of the new College of the East India Company be designed to contain provisions for vocational training as well as a comprehensive course of classical learning. This mandate for classical learning was further elaborated in terms of class and civility. The report evinced a hope that with such learning the students will become 'good subjects',[10] 'enlightened patriots',[11] and 'good servants of the Company'.[12] Nonetheless, it strongly advocated the teaching of other subjects including oriental languages. Importance of Greek and Latin was not at all compromised, and retained supremacy. The suggestion that the Headmaster of the College himself would teach classics, in addition to 'the principles and duties of Religion and Morality',[13] established the fact. But for the student society named after the Governor-General, the foresight of Wellesley was all but recognised. It was only through the effort of disinterested historians that the role of the imaginative statesman was acknowledged. The sapling sowed by Wellesley was extirpated from Indian soil and planted at the favoured location of Hertford where it could grow under the watchful supervision of the Directors. The East India College was subsequently shifted to a new building at Haileybury in 1809.

East India College, Haileybury

Training College established at Hertford in 1806 was subsequently shifted to Haileybury in 1809 and started formulating regulations for admission into the College. Malthus who served as Professor at the College wrote in 1817, 'Every candidate for admission into the College is required to produce a testimonial from his school master and to pass an examination in Greek, Latin and Arithmetic before the Principal and Professors'.[14] Gradually the College transformed itself into a place of higher education, abandoning its school features and the standard of the entrance examination was also revised. Since 1838, it started testing the nominees on English and Greek language, Ancient History, Geography, Moral Philosophy as well as elements of Mathematics. This form of entrance examination continued till the closure of the College. However, the independent board of examination, consisting two men from Oxford and two from Cambridge, was put in charge of conducting the examination. 'The examination for Haileybury',[15] George Campbell, an eminent Haileybury Civilian described 'was not competitive but qualifying, and qualifying examinations seldom keep many out'.[16] Yet, as a lad of sixteen, Campbell went up with 'some trembling'[17] and was pleasantly surprised to find himself greatly distinguished and complimented by the examiners. The examination, Campbell continued 'not only threw out a few of the worst, but frightened a good many more'.[18] This trend discouraged the Directors to send up nominees who were likely to fail. The considerable lot sifted out of Haileybury, was absorbed in Company's cavalry.

The College started with a Principal and six Professors in the following subjects

1. Mathematics and Natural Philosophy
2. Classical and General Literature
3. History and Political Economy
4. General Policy and Laws of England
5. Arabic, Persian and Hindustani Literature
6. Hindu Literature and History of Asia

Curricula of training did not deviate much from what Wellesley initially conceived for Fort William College. Liberal studies formed the core and was supplemented by subjects on the general principle of Law and Government of India and oriental subjects. Arabic and Persian were taught as Asiatic language, so also the history, conventions and norms of different Indian races. Elementary instructions were given in different branches of natural science. Besides, the candidates were familiarised with general Policy, Laws, British Constitution and the commercial relations between England and India.

Haileybury lasted for 52 years, functioning under four Principals viz. Dr Henley, Batten, Le Bas and Melvill, and prospered most during the tenure of Batten. Handsome payment and liberal facilities offered by the Company could secure services of distinguished men like Sir James Mackintosh, Sir James Stephen and Malthus as Professors. Many of them were amply rewarded of their good work by nomination of their sons in Indian Civil Service. Company could justifiably boast of the Professors they could induce to join the College. It was not far from truth when Chairman during one of the half-yearly visits of the Court of Directors, told that such body of Professors could hardly be surpassed in any similar institution in Europe. Very few professors ever resigned, and when retirement became necessary due to advancing age or broken health, 'liberal pensions were always granted'.[19] Throughout its history, Haileybury was affected by the perpetual interference in its internal affairs by Directors and their refusal for years to entrust ultimate authority to the Principal. Until the time of Principal-ship of Melville, the Directors retained full power, acting as the Court of Appeal in all cases. Twice in the year, at the end of terms in June and December, Chairman of the Court of Directors accompanied by others visited the College. These days were celebrated in the College library or hall with participation of students and liberal distribution of prizes which was followed by dinner.

No Indian student ever crossed the threshold of the College. The name of Raja Ram Roy, the foster son of Raja Ram Mohan Roy was proposed by Sir John Hobhouse for appointment. This young man had accompanied his foster father to England and studied there acquiring all the requisite qualifications to secure writer-ship. The Court of Directors, however, turned down the proposal under the pretext that it would be inexpedient to accommodate an Indian youth in the Haileybury College. It was cleverly presented that the boy would be unhappy at Haileybury where chapel attendance was compulsory. Three Indians, however, had the fortune to be associated with the College. Gulam Hyder, an Indian from Patna, was the first to be appointed Persian writing Master while Mir Abdul Ali was made Maulavi of the College to help in teaching of Hindustani. Shortly afterwards a third Indian, Mirza Khaleel of Calcutta was added to the list.

Imparting academic rigour or achieving excellence was never considered to be the goal of the Haileybury College. Neither did it ever attain it. Richard Temple, who became Lieutenant-Governor of Bengal, felt 'All things considered, a man, who at the age of twenty or twenty-one years passed through the College successfully, in order to join Company's service, had enjoyed the benefit of comprehensive education'.[20] It rather fostered the *esprit de Corps* among the embryo Civilians staying together for two years. 'The friendship and association formed at college',[21] Temple continued, 'constituted one of the several bonds of comradeship among all the Civil Servants during their administrative career'.[22] Concurring the same observation, George Trevelyan wrote 'Haileybury formed a tie which the vicissitudes of official life could never break. In the swamps of Dacca, in the deserts of Rajputana...wherever the Haileybury men met they had at least one set of associations in common'.[23] Distance from London also helped the students to desist from the temptation of the bustling city. They had the liberty of breakfast in their room but dinner was compulsory at Lodge Hall in which the Professors also participated. College encouraged students to participate in cricket and other sports, debating society and literacy clubs.

Moral training formed an integral part of the daily routine, with morning and evening service, often attended by the Principal and Professors. The Collage had a debating society known as 'Wellesley Club' in which many students made their debut on the way to become prominent speakers afterwards. Later on it became 'Wellesley Whist Club' with its own special song in honour of its original proponent. Campbell assessed the effect of Halieybury life as 'altogether, a good many were weeded out from the bottom and the rest being caught young and kept apart, the best did not go off from the top, as they might under other circumstances. The young men... taught to believe themselves equally fortunate, took a pride in the service'.[24] With wonderfully effective training in India, Campbell continued, 'Almost all became zealous'.[25]

Open competition was introduced in 1855 for recruitment of the Civilians, replacing the practice of Directors' nomination. On acceptance of the recommendations of the Macaulay Commission that suggested the reform, an Act was passed in the Parliament in 1855 and the College was closed in the winter of 1857. Before closure, the Indian mutiny broke out. The Haileybury community, with unabated passion, followed progress of the Company army. They rejoiced the award of Victoria Cross to Ross Mangles, the son of the Chairman of the Court of the Directors. The young Civilian Ross was relatively a new entrant to the Service and earned the distinction which until then was unknown among Civilians. The whole community went utterly mad with excitement and delight when the news of the storming of Delhi reached Haileybury. A bonfire was lighted in 'Quod', which spread fast and raised alarm throughout the countryside. Fire-engines from Hertford and elsewhere were called to douse the fire, much less the excitement. The other civilian who was similarly awarded during Mutiny was Fraser Macdonnell. Sadly enough, the Mutiny snatched away 42 Civilians in all. Thirty three members of the Service were killed and nine others died from sickness and exposure.

The last Directors' day was observed on 7 December 1857. At the end of the luncheon in the College hall, Ross Mangles, M P, Chairman of the East India Company, the father of the Bengal Civilian, proposed the health of the Principal and Professors of Haileybury. Gloom descended with Principal Melvill's reply, 'I have also to express our earnest and unfeigned hope that the new system, whose operation sweeps this College away, may prove itself as good as the old'.[26] The Principal proudly remembered the bravery of the old students of the College for what they had done, amid the fearful outrages which darkened and devastated India during Mutiny. He made no attempt to conceal despair and observed, 'I feel this is a mighty and comprehensive wish, that the system of competition may prove itself equal to the system it displaces'.[27] On the following day, Haileybury community met for the last term dinner at the London Tavern. The event passed off as a mingled cheerful and melancholy affair. On closure, the resources so painfully marshalled at Haileybury by the Company, all mindlessly scattered away. The building started housing the new founded public school and the Professors joined other vocations. Monier Williams, the Professor of Sanskrit joined Oxford University as Regius Professor of the subject. Jeremie, the Professor of Classics joined Cambridge University as Regius Professor of Divinity. Edward Eastwick who taught Hindustani dabbled with politics and came to represent Falmouth in Parliament.

The Act of 1813 required the attendance of four terms at the College for every person before proceeding to India as 'writer'. In the twenties of the 19th century, a great shortage of men in Covenanted Service was complained of by the authorities in India with the rapid expansion of the Company's territory. Court of Directors and Board of Control agreed to approach the Parliament seeking dispensation of the provision to meet the exigency. Directors' proverbial influence in the Parliament worked wonder and the Parliament swiftly passed an Act in 1826, empowering the Directors to waive the condition and send writers directly without the need for undergoing requisite four terms at Haileybury. Directors reacted closely and prepared a scheme known as 'London Board of Examiners'[28] which would screen the prospective candidates. The plan for the examination consisted of two parts viz. the Classical and Mathematical test, and the Oriental test. The dispensation though granted initially for a period of three years was extended till April 1834 by a subsequent Act of Parliament. The beneficiaries were chiefly those who were withdrawn from Haileybury or sent down from it as their continuance proved injurious to the discipline of the Institution. Directors thus could send 34 Civilians of their choice to India obviating the need for Haileybury residence for four terms. Parliament never objected and only winked at it.

In its 52 years of existence, the College admitted 1975 students of which 1754 entered the Indian Civil Service and 80 joined the Company's Army. Though the doors of the East India College at Haileybury were closed in 1857, demand for a separate training College for Civilians was raised again in 1870s, especially after the establishment of Royal India Engineering College at England's Coopers' Hill in 1871. Most of the Indian Civilians approved of Lord Mayo's plan of an Indian College at one of the universities where the selected candidates might read the special subjects and have the advantage of the university system. Passionate as they were, majority of

Haileybury Civilians could never reconcile to the closure of the College. One of the eminent members, George Campbell who became Lieutenant-Governor of Bengal, did not hesitate to write 'I confess I am very much inclined to regret the abolition of Haileybury'.[29] Nothing moved forward, however, with Viceroy Mayo's sudden assassination. A couple of years later, Civil Service Commissioners while conducting enquiry directed by Lord Salisbury, considered the issue, but the idea was never accepted. Nonetheless the issue remained dormant most of the time and occasionally drew attention. Even in the 20th century, nearly half a century after the closure of Haileybury, Royal Commission enquired about relative advantage of a separate institution. By this time, Oxford and Cambridge had established special facilities for training of the ICS men and were drawing majority of the successful candidates. The British witnesses acknowledged the benefit the members of the service would derive, by way of getting to know each other much more intimately at the special institution. At the same time, it was pointed out that training at the special institution would deprive the probationers from getting the wide perspective nurtured at the great English universities. An Indian witness presented the idea of training the embryo Civilians in an Indian environment. The training institute of Imperial Cadet Corps at Dehra Dun, supplemented by necessary personnel, the witness believed, would be ideal for training the selected candidates of ICS. Arguments continued but the plan of special college for training Civilians did not advance beyond the stage of deliberation.

Chapter III

INDIA UNDER THE CROWN

Open Competition and the Service

Notwithstanding the noble declarations of Charter Act of 1833, no change was made in next two decades in the regulations for the selection of candidates. Company's Charter came up for revision in 1853 and on this occasion, John Bright, the Liberal member, could not hide his resentment. Bright reacted sharply in the House of Commons and pointed out that during 20 years that had elapsed since renewal of the Charter in 1833, not one of the natives had been appointed to any offices except such as they were eligible before the Statute. The statesman pronounced that 'the Ministerial scheme did little or nothing to promote those salutary reforms',[1] which were demanded of Britain to effect without delay. Sir Charles Wood, President of the Board of Control, on 29 July 1853 presented Government of India Bill to the House of Commons. Macaulay and Wood set out to introduce two major reforms in the Company's Civil Service. The first was to abolish the patronage that the Directors had so far retained in the appointment in the Service. The second was to introduce the principle of competitive examination in the system of appointment. The Bill came to the House of Lords, with significant amendments. Lord Granville, who introduced them, hoped that the amendment would improve 'The Indian Civil Service' to an even greater extent than Macaulay, Trevelyan and Wood had anticipated in the original measure. Granville's amendments allowed the Board of Control to open up the final examination to prospective candidates outside Haileybury. The changes proposed were:[2]

'All Powers, Rights, or Privileges of the Court of Directors of the said Company to nominate Persons to be admitted as Students' should cease; and that 'Subject to Such Regulations as may be made by the Board of Commissioners for the Affairs of India, any person being a natural born Subject of Her Majesty who may be desirous of being admitted into the said college at Haileybury, shall be admitted to be examined as a candidate for such admission.'

Reform exercise in the field of education and administrative affairs, undertaken in Great Britain during the middle of the 19th century, provided the appropriate background for such fundamental change. Those were the days when British ruling class retained all the privileges. Leading authorities in Britain were unable to reconcile to the idea of purity in public service without the practice of patronage. The Reform Act of 1832 and the growing liberal atmosphere were putting the conservative element into difficult position. Gladstone's decision to appoint a committee to enquire into the state of Home Civil Service was a natural outcome in the sequence of events. Responsibility fell on Northcote and Trevelyan to suggest the requirements of administrative reform. This committee found itself ill equipped to stave off the surging waves of liberal demands for administrative reform. Northcote-Trevelyan Committee recommended in November 1853 that political patronage be abolished, a Civil Service Commission be appointed in Britain and recruitment be made through open examination.

Gladstone himself at the same time was involved in Royal Commissions on the conditions of Oxford University and the state of Public Schools. Northcote sat both on the Oxford Commission as well as that on the reformation of Civil Service. This intermingling of university, public school and administrative reform led to the proposal of a permanent commission of examiners for all appointments to the Civil Service. The other proposal made was the grounding of the Civil Service upon a caste drawn from the reformed Public Schools and Universities, and judged by the curricula of these institutions. The Trevelyan-Northcote recommendations for the English Civil Service, however, ran into difficulty against the resistance of conservative element to give up the privilege. It soon became evident that very few of leading British politicians had their hearts in the matter. The outcry of the dispensers and expectants of public employment was hard and fierce, and the advocates of the new system were forced to admit that its hour had not yet come. 'I went to Brook's',[3] said Macaulay 'and found everybody open mouthed. I am sorry to say, against Trevelyan's plan about the Civil Service'.[4] 'The pear is not yet ripe',[5] Macaulay commented, at the same time feeling that Trevelyan would be 'much mortified'.[6] Politicians assembled in flock, wondering how Parliamentary support could be ensured without patronage. Only concession that the liberals could derive on the occasion was the appointment of Civil Service Commission in 1855. It was itself a great beginning though the adoption of competitive element into selection of personnel for Home Civil Service was delayed by nearly two decades more. The death of Lord Palmerston in 1865 finally removed the last obstacle to the adoption of liberalistic ideas in the process of selection of Civilians.

As for Indian Civil Service, the task was relatively easier as it was the Directors who heretofore had retained the privilege of nomination albeit without displeasing the political eminence. Subsequent to the Act of 1853, Wood in 1854 set up a Committee to advise on specific operations of the Act. The Committee was asked to enquire and recommend the age of qualifications of the candidates for Haileybury, the subjects to be used in the competitive entrance examination and the mode of training for Haileybury students. It was also asked whether the Board should admit outside candidates to the final examination for appointments to the Covenanted Service. With the help of Trevelyan, Wood was successful in inducing Macaulay to head the Commission. Besides Macaulay, the other members of the Commission were Lord Ashburton, Melvill (Principal of Haileybury College), Benjamin Jowett (afterwards Master of Balliol College, Oxford), and John George Shaw Lefevre. Commission examined the issue in great details and the recommendations of the Commission addressed three key issues. First, age of admission was fixed at 23 to allow men who had taken the first degree in Arts at Oxford or Cambridge. The second principle laid down that good general education would be the basis of competitive examination. This general education was considered to be the most useful to enlarge the ambit and strengthen the understanding of the candidates. The special education or technical study of India was thus not linked to the competition and left for the candidates to acquire subsequent to selection in open competition. Finally, ideal period for such probationary training was thought to be between one and two years during which the successful candidates would undertake both theoretical and practical training. Besides clearing examination on subjects like History of India and its legal system, the candidates ought to have attended both civil and criminal trials as preparation for their judicial work in India. The report provided for periodical examinations during this period to be concluded with 'final examination'. Though not commenting directly on the future of Haileybury, the report left it to the Board of Control 'to consider whether any plan can be devised by which such a training can be made compatible with residence at Haileybury'.[7]

Eventually gates of the College were closed in 1857 leaving the successful candidates to make their own arrangement for training and final examination. They could of course join the British universities and prosecute their studies. The entire report on the public service bore the handiwork of Lord Macaulay, the first Law member of the Viceroy's Council who was equally adept in educational and administrative reforms. Benjamin Jowett, the translator of Pluto's work was known for his forthright advocacy of transforming Indian

Civil Service to the model of Pluto's ideal of guardian. Other member Melvill, as Head of Haileybury College, had the hands on experience of training requirement of Indian Civilians. Lefevre, associated with both public service and politics, was the appropriate man to provide the necessary link between Government and bureaucracy. Macaulay's clarity of understanding and practicality of implementation allowed him to prevail over other members. He was so thorough with the Indian affair that he could finish such a delicate job in a week's time. 'I am to draw the Report',[8] he wrote on the 1 July 1854, confident of accomplishing, 'I must and will finish it in a week'.[9] He completed his rough draft on 7 July and wrote it out fair on the following day i.e. Saturday, 8 July 1854. As he read it to his brother-in-law on the Sunday, Trevelyan was 'much pleased'.[10] It was rather expected as Macaulay had skilfully framed his plan as to bring out all the strong points of the competitive system, and avoid its perils. He provided simple but effective machinery for admitting into the service men of energy and ability, whose faculties were keen and whose acquirements were sound. The realistic scheme was designed to exclude those candidates who rested their hopes of success upon means of half-digested heterogeneous learning. The plan entailed that the young men thus selected would be trained in Indian affairs before sailing out for India to carry out the sacred imperial trust. Macaulay prescribed a complete list of subjects of examination, with the proportion of marks that would be allowed to each. The Government adopted this list in its entirety and high compliment was paid to all the recommendations of the Committee. One passage in the report that deserved mention, testified the confidence with which Macaulay anticipated the nicety of honour and uprightness of character. He conceived that young civilians of the future would be inferior to no class of public servants in the world. Henry Beveridge, a Civilian selected through competition, appearing before the Public Service Committee, declared, 'I have no wish to speak ill of the competition-system. It was an immense improve on the old rule of patronage, and is a fine instance of England's stately march, and of the manner in which her concessions broaden slowly down from precedent to precedent'.[11]

The first examination under this new system took place in 1855, and was held under the direction of Commission for the affairs of India. So were also the examinations of 1856 and 1857. The provision for special training of the selected candidates and further examinations, rules of which were framed in 1855, could not be put into practice before 1858. The condition of probation and further training was waived to meet the urgent need of civilians in India. Successful competitors of first three years thus went out to India without having passed any further examination. In 1858, a partial return was made to the scheme as originally designed. A short period of probation was prescribed to be followed by an examination on a limited range of subjects. In the next year, the term of probation was extended to one year, the range of final examination being considerably expanded so as to include at least one oriental language and theory and practice of law. An allowance of £ 100 was made to each selected candidate to assist him in prosecution of these studies.

A still more important change took place in 1864. Acting on the proposal of the Government of India, Secretary of State decided that the examination hitherto being held at Presidency towns should be abolished, and the preliminary training of the young Civilians, even in the vernacular languages, should be completed in England. It was understood that the same degree of proficiency in the languages which had previously been required in the examination held at Calcutta, Madras and Bombay should henceforth be exhibited at the final examination in England. A probationary period of two years was allowed to the candidates to prepare for this final examination and an additional allowance of £ 200 was granted to cover the expenses of the second year.

Scheme of competitive examination started in the year 1855 when East India Company was in possession of India. The policy of full and equal status of Indians for admission to the Civil Service of their country was proclaimed by Queen Victoria in 1858. Queen declared her will 'so far as may be, our subjects, of whatever race or creed be freely and impartially admitted to office in our service, the duties of which they may be qualified by their education, ability, and integrity duly to discharge'.[12] Number of appointment offered for Civil Service went up substantially. Against offer of 73 appointments during the period 1855-1858, the number climbed up to 282 for the subsequent four years' period and thereafter stayed at a level of 40-50 each year till 1876. Initially no fee was charged from the candidates for competing in the examination. A fee of £ 5 was charged from the candidates from the competition of 1871. The Civil Service Commission in its Annual Report of 1872 observed, 'Both in this year and the previous year the attendance of candidates was somewhat smaller than those which preceded, partly, no doubt because the vacancies were fewer, and partly also owing to the fact that in 1871 and 1872 a fee of £ 5 was required from each candidate. The diminution, however, was not so much in the class of effective competitors as in the number, previously considerable, of those who presented themselves without sufficient preparation to warrant any hope of success'.[13]

Interestingly, India was many years ahead of England in the matter of Civil Service, where competition was not introduced till 1873. When the idea of a competitive examination for Home Civil Service was discussed, it was remarked about the privilege of ministers that, 'it was one thing to have required the Directors of East India Company to abandon patronage in India, it was quite another thing to expect Ministers to surrender it in their own office at home'.[14] The Civil Service Commission which was established in 1855 had its powers further extended by certain provisions of the Superannuation Act of 1859. Its role for Home Civil Service during the first decade and a half of its existence was restricted to administer a system of limited and permissive competition. No real progress was made towards the goal of open competition in Home Civil Service until after Gladstone became the Prime Minister in 1868. His Chancellor of Exchequer, Robert Lowe, was an enthusiastic Civil Service reformer, and at the end of 1869, he appealed to Gladstone, 'As I have so often tried in vain, will you bring the question of the Civil Service before the Cabinet today? Something must be decided. We cannot keep matter in this discreditable state of abeyance'.[15] Gladstone encountered opposition when he raised the matter, but devised a compromise whereby all the branches of the service were thrown open to competition where the minister concerned agreed. The resulting order in Council of 4 June 1870 introduced open competition into all the major departments except the Home Office, which relented by 1873, followed by the Foreign Office and the Education Office. It was not till 1894 that the Treasury with complete accuracy could say that open competition for the higher division was 'now the rule'. The form that the 'competing literary examinations' eventually took, owed to the scheme that Macaulay had drawn up for recruitment to the Indian Civil Service than the plans that Jowett had outlined in a letter appended to the Trevelyan-Northcote Report. Macaulay's theory that the best preparation for an administrative career was 'a liberal education' than a relevant professional training not only dominated the examination, but still has a considerable influence in the present day arrangements for administrative class recruitment.

Other imperial powers of Dutch and French were behind the English in their scheme of competitive examination in Colonial Service. While entry to Dutch Colonial Service in East Indies of Java and Malay was made through competition in 1864, the French were as late as 1896 in introducing the scheme. The small size of appointment for Dutch Indies and the emphasis on special education for competition were largely responsible for making the Colonial Service a rather unattractive one. The French scheme, though depended on competition for selection, allowed concurrent entry through army and navy into Civil Service. French experience of the military personnel as administrator was quite satisfactory, though sometimes they were found to be strict disciplinarians.

In India, after 1876, military officers ceased to be employed as civil officers in Oudh, the Central Provinces, and the non-regulation tracts of Bengal and North Western provinces. Although the Charter Act of 1793 had reserved for the Civil Service, all offices below that of Member of Council, it was found in practice to be impossible to maintain such a monopoly. Other provinces gradually implemented the regulation as Sind, Punjab and Assam in 1885, 1903, 1907 respectively. The practice of employing military men in civil offices was introduced by Lord Cornwallis and the 'military civilians' were an important part of the executives as well as diplomatic staff. With the expansion of English power, vast tracts were annexed one after the other. The Civil Service could not spare enough men for both their Government and pacification. Sometimes the administration was entirely in the hands of 'military civilians', as for instance in Arakan, where they were most successful in introducing settled Government in 1826.

The provinces in which military officers were employed were known as Non-regulation, while Civilians were exclusively employed in the regulation provinces. The latter were the older provinces governed by the laws made under Charter Acts, which were called regulations until 1834, when the modern designation of the Act was adopted. Appointment of staff corps for civil posts continued in Burma and the North-West Frontier Province. When Government of India proposed that the practice should be abandoned, Government of Burma opposed it in 1906. Provincial Government contended that officers of diverse qualifications were required to serve the varied nature of work. Military officers neither lacked intellectual qualifications nor were wanting in qualities equally essential to the administration, such as resource, force of character, knowledge and sympathy with the people. It was further contended that limited recruitment of military officers for civil posts had provided Burma with many officers of exceptional capacity and merit, a practice that could not be substituted by sole employment of Civilians. Government of India, sensing the extraordinary situation of the province concurred with the view. The issue was raised again in 1915 when the Royal Commission suggested that the system of recruiting military officers to fill civil vacancies be gradually abolished. Government paid little heed and Burma thus continued with a composite Commission formed of happy combination of Civil Servants and 'Military Civilians'. Though staff corps lost many posts in civil administration, the introduction of police reform starting from early 1860s opened up alternative opportunities for them. The demand of the Police Service perhaps suited their disposition and both the service and the military personnel benefitted from the arrangement

Age of Candidates

Competitive examination started in the year 1855 with maximum age of 23 and minimum age of 18. This along with one or two years' of special training made the maximum age of going to India to 24 or 25, which was advance of a year or two over the age at which they had been in the habit of going out from Haileybury. As the candidates went out to India directly after the competitive examination during 1858, the new system did not produce any change. When in 1859, probation of one year was established, it was felt that the age of departure to India was very high and maximum age for the competition was reduced to 22. The same motive induced Lord Lawrence to say in 1864 that men came out to India were very old. The result was that when in 1865, the probation period was extended to two years, the maximum age for candidates at competitive examination was further reduced to 21. In all cases, the decisions had been strongly resented by Indians. It was in 1859 that Dadabhai Naoroji commenced his campaign of agitation against the inherent injustice in the system of recruitment in Indian Civil Service. The reduction of age debarred the very first Indian candidate, Rustomji Hirjibhai Wadia, then a student in England, from competing in the examination. Dadabhai submitted a protest to Lord Stanley, Secretary of State for India, urging that the change ought to have been notified beforehand. Not stopping at this stage, Dadabhai asked Sir Erskine Perry to take up the issue in Parliament. Before the member could raise the issue in Parliament, American Civil War broke out engrossing the tiny island's attention. The issue of Indian Civil Service was pushed to the background. Nevertheless, Dadabhai, through his continued correspondence, was able to secure an assurance from the Secretary of State, stating 'No further changes in the Civil Service regulations would at any time be made, without due publicity being given to them at the earliest possible period'.[16]

Open competition could not totally eliminate controversy about the recruitment. Question arose for testifying the ability of the new recruits. Civilians recruited through this scheme came to be known as competition-wallah, a distinct entity from Haileybury Civilians. Complaint about the competitive system became so loud and persistent that Lord Salisbury, Secretary of India, desired to review the system. His objective was to determine the nature of possible changes so as to improve its efficacy. One chief objection to the system was that the age made it difficult for the young man to complete his university education before taking the examination. Neither did it allow prospective candidates to postpone their university study till completion of the examination. The effect was a marked fall-off of the university candidates competing for the service. This trend was visible since 1865 simultaneously with an increase of candidates specially prepared under 'Crammers'. In 1874, the percentage of successful candidates prepared under 'Crammers' rose to 84% with the average time spent for preparation being nearly 16 months. There was also objection that the successful candidates were encouraged to spend their time at London for the final examination. The candidates were left to themselves to stay in London where they scarcely develop the *esprit de Corps* that prevailed at Haileybury.

Salisbury at this time received a number of communications, the first of which came from H G Liddell, Dean of Christ Church, Oxford. He proposed a reduction of maximum age to 18 or 19 in order to give the candidate an opportunity to attend university and obtain a degree. The university, Liddell declared, was willing to allow candidates to take the moderation examinations required by the university at the end of the first year which would permit them to concentrate on Indian subjects in their second year of residence. It would also be possible for a candidate to obtain a degree in the humanities, jurisprudence or modern history. Liddel further stated that the university would be willing to create professorships to meet the training requirement of the Civilians. University was prepared to expand its curriculum to include instruction in Sanskrit, Persian and any other modern Indian language that a candidate might be required to know, as well as political economy. Cambridge, however, was less inclined than Oxford to sacrifice its academic curriculum to attract the young Civilians for which Jowett was at least partly responsible. Another indication of Oxford's enthusiasm for bringing the candidates to the University was demonstrated by Monier Williams, Boden Professor of Sanskrit. Monier believed that Oxford should do everything within its power to recruit as many candidates as possible to spend probationary training at the University. He recommended that Oxford should establish an Indian Institute, and all the selected candidates, once matriculated, should be required to attend lectures offered by these institutions. George Phear, Vice-Chancellor of Cambridge, indicated to Salisbury that he believed that residence at the University during the probationary period would be beneficial to the candidates. If the candidates were brought under its auspices, the University would provide them with the virtues of moral discipline which were said to be lacking in the young men being sent to India. Phear hoped that the Government of India might see it fit to promote the universities as a more suitable place of residence. He also wanted to change the periodical examination schedule so that they would not conflict with the university curriculum. As an alternative, it was proposed, that the university examinations be accepted in place of the periodical examinations. Benjamin Jowett, Master of Balliol College, Oxford who served in the Macaulay Commission opined, 'If the selected candidates could be brought to Oxford or Cambridge, the service would greatly gain popularity and in prestige. It would be much more attractive both to young men and their parents'.[17] Salisbury, therefore, advised the Civil Service Commissioners to enquire into the prevailing system.

On 16 March 1875, the Civil Service Commission presented its report which was, however, inconclusive owing to lack of authoritative information about the working of the system in India. They were not willing to recommend any departure from the existing age limit, narrowing down the number of subjects or system of examination. They, however, agreed to the proposals of the universities and recommended that those candidates who resided at a university be paid a stipend. Before making a final decision on the manner of training men for the Indian Civil Service, the Commission decided to contact senior Civil Servants from the different Presidencies at Calcutta, Bombay and Madras. Their opinions were called for on issues varying from the method of selecting candidates to the system of training, the question of age, the number of subjects a candidate would be allowed to offer and the allocation of marks to each subject. A large number of Indian officials responded to the query. Of the 96 officers of Indian Civil Service of all ranks who gave their opinion, 33 were in favour of increasing the age while 27 favoured a reduction. Remaining 36 officials were agreeable to retain the prevailing regulation. Thus the point of opinion was greatly fractured on the issue of age.

When the question of age came before the Council of India in England, Sir Henry Maine strongly inclined towards early specialisation of studies, and advocated reduction in age. Most of his colleagues accepted this standpoint. Finally, Lord Salisbury, Secretary of State, in February 1876, announced his decision to lower the maximum age to 19. This reduction was to reverse the recommendation of Macaulay's report that the candidates ought to have completed a general education before competing for the examination. Before the new policy came into effect, a series of correspondence exchanged between Lord Salisbury and the Civil Service Commissioner dealing with specific details of the examination. Commission recommended that the standard of the examination be lowered, the list of subjects be modified and maximum marks allocated to each subject be revised to bring the examinations in line with the reduction in age. They also recommended that Arabic and Sanskrit be retained in the examination, with each receiving a maximum of 500 marks. Other than disagreeing that the marks allocated to Greek was very high and urging the Commission to increase the marks given to French and German, Salisbury concurred with the Commissioner's recommendations. He accepted that all candidates who resided at the universities would receive subsistence allowance of £ 150 a year from the Government.

First examination with upper age of 19 was conducted in June 1878 in which 134 candidates, all European, competed for 13 appointments. This was the second examination conducted in the year, the earlier having taken place in April 1878 with old age regulation of 21 year. Reduction of maximum age to 19 generated strong protest in India and afforded Surendranath an opportunity to enter into national politics. Surendranath with his newly formed Indian Association started the campaign against this decision to lower the age limit. He travelled whole of North India and held meetings at many places including Lahore, Amritsar, Kanpur, Aligarh and Agra. Political association on the line of Indian Association sprang up at many of these places. Surendranath came into contact with a number of eminent personalities of North India which included Sardar Dayal Singh Majeetha, Pandit Ayodhyanath and Babu Harish Chandra. Syed Ahmed Khan presided over the Civil Service meeting at Aligarh. With his zeal in forming public opinion, Surendranath could defy the intense summer heat of northern India. His extensive tour, however, generated more heat and helped countrymen in overcoming the inhibitions to start agitation against British racial supremacy. The gain achieved by the Empire through this reduction of age had been temporary but the psychological effect was more enduring.

As Surendranath was leading the nationwide agitation, Lalmohan Ghose was entrusted with the task of campaigning in England against the move. He was placed in charge of the Civil Service memorial to Parliament. Lalmohan like his elder brother Manomohan competed unsuccessfully for Indian Civil Service in 1870. He returned to India as Barrister and joined legal profession. He was barely 30 years old when he proceeded to England on this mission. The first public meeting he addressed was in Willis's Room and under the chairmanship of no less a man than John Bright. This inexperienced young man made a speech of which John Bright said, 'I will not spoil the effect of the magnificent oration we have heard by any feeble words of my own'.[18] And of John Bright, it was said that but for him British premier Gladstone would have been the greatest orator of England. Lalmohan's phenomenal success in the mission thus fully justified his selection. 'His marvellous gift of oratory was not known to us for he had never before taken to public life as a serious occupation',[19] Surendranath concluded, feeling happy over his selection. The cost of deputation to England was financed to a great extent by Maharani Swarnamoyee, known as 'Lady Bountiful'[20] of Cossimbazar. The agitation thus formed one of the earliest political activities since mutiny and generated interest among a large section of people both in India and England. Perhaps the most relevant observation on the age limit came from Monier Williams. With his varied experience in Halieybury and Oxford in educating the Civilians, he pointed out, '... And here it may be asked, why has the age of candidates for the Civil Service of India been so lowered that they are allowed to compete from 17½ to 19½, while the age for the Ceylon Civil Service is permitted to range from 21 to 24?'[21]

Though agitation for change of the upper limit of age was continuing in India and abroad, the campaign was not successful in achieving the desired result. Nearly a decade lapsed when the imperial authority finally advised the Government of India to review the issue. Lord Dufferin, the Governor-General constituted a Commission headed by Charles Umpherston Aitchison to examine the issues related to public service. The Commission submitted its report in December 1887. It took several years for authorities in India and England to come to the final decision. Maximum limit of age was restored to 23, as originally proposed in Macaulay report. Lord Cross, the Secretary, however, had to overrule his Council who objected to this move on the ground of delaying the departure of the successful candidates to India to a late age. The possibility of facilitating the admission of Indians into the service, imperilling its English character was also raised. Finally the agreed plan of reforms was notified in April 1892. First examination under the new age regulation took place in 1892. In this competition, eight Indian candidates competed with 61 British candidates for 32 appointments.

Reduction of age severely affected aspiration of Indian candidates. Starting from 1868, quite a few Indian students started reaching England for competing for the Service. Success of four Indian candidates in 1869 greatly encouraged them. During the ten years' period from 1869 to 1878, 61 Indian students competed in the examination. Lowering the maximum age to 19, however, blighted their hope. In the next four examinations, only six Indian candidates appeared with no success. Kharsedji Ratanji Bomanji from Bombay was in England for three years. When he left India the age limit was 21 which was subsequently cut down to 19 when he reached. This sudden decision deprived him from competing for the Covenanted Service. He studied under a famous coach William Baptist Scoones for one year and incurred a heavy expenditure of £ 350. Narrating his case before the Aitchison Commission, Bomanji regretted the miserable circumstance which ruined two valuable years of his career. He came back and had to be content with appointment in Statutory Service. Sorabji Pudumji Pestonji equally despaired of his aspiration to join the 'heaven-born service'. He belonged to the prominent Padumji family and matriculated from Poona High School in 1872. An undergraduate of Bombay University, Pestonji proceeded to England. He spent two years in England, studying under Scoones in London. He enrolled at the Middle Temple and kept seven terms. Reduction in age limit upset his plan and he returned home before being called to the Bar. He was one of the early probationers under the native Civil Service of Bombay and was confirmed in Statutory Service in March 1882. Sorabji Pudumji's father Khan Bahadur Pudumji Pestonji was Member of the Legislative Council of Bombay. Sorabji served as Assistant Collector at various places in Bombay Presidency and retired as Collector of Broach.

No less appalling was the misery of Ashutosh Gupta of Bengal. Ashutosh obtained high place in all the examinations of Calcutta University and succeeded in securing MA degree from Presidency College. As Gilchrist Scholar of 1877, he was about to proceed to England to study in an English university and compete for the Indian Civil Service Examination. Sudden decision to lower the age limit compelled him to drop his plan of England tour. He was appointed Lecturer of Mathematics for a short period in Krishnanagar College. Subsequently, he accepted the offer of professorship in St John's College, Agra. Ashutosh was very happy when Lieutenant-Governor of Bengal appointed him in Subordinate Executive Service. Lured by administrative work, he served as Deputy Magistrate and Deputy Collector at Malda. The onerous administrative work did not, however, extinguish his academic pursuit. In February 1882, Ashutosh came first in the selection test for Premchand Roychand Scholarship of Calcutta University. In the same year, he was nominated to Statutory Civil Service.

New age regulation required Indian students to reach England in their teens for competition. They gradually adjusted to this requirement and many Indian lads reached England to have their school education there. Fourteen examinations were conducted between 1878 and 1891 with maximum age of 19. Total number of Indian candidates competed in this period was 55 of whom 15 were successful. Acting on the recommendation of the Public Service Committee, Government raised the minimum and maximum age to 21 and 23 years respectively. The same continued till 1905 and was further revised to 22 and 24 years from the competitive examinations held since 1906. The upward revision greatly benefitted Indian candidates.

Subjects of Examination

Subjects for the competitive examination along with maximum marks were elaborated in the Macaulay report. English language and literature were chosen clubbed with History and the Constitution of England. Total marks allotted for English was 1,500. Latin and Greek were chosen as the ancient languages with severity of the examination desired as no less than those examinations by which the classical distinctions are awarded at Oxford and Cambridge. Each subject was given a weight of 750 marks. Three modern languages of the Continent were selected viz. French, Italian and German with 375 marks each. Mixed Mathematics was assigned 1,000 marks. Natural Science including Chemistry, Geology, Mineralogy, History and Zoology was given 500 marks. Moral Science was proposed to be included in the scheme of examination. As oriental language no vernacular was chosen, and Sanskrit and Arabic were selected as classical languages with allotment of 375 marks each. Total marks proposed for the examination was 6,875. The report did not expect a man of 22 years to have considerable proficiency in all the subjects. No subject was obligatory and candidates were allowed to pick up as many subjects as they wished. The stress was on the depth of knowledge of any particular subject and intended to discourage knowledge of wide surface with small depth. In all subjects other than English and Mathematics, candidates were not allowed any credit when securing less than 20% of the maximum marks assigned to the subject. In 1859, the marks for Mathematics were increased from 1,000 to 1,250 and that for Arabic and Sanskrit rose from 375 to 500 each. Thus the total marks went up from 6,875 to 7,375.

The scheme of subjects for the examination was subjected to number of changes. In 1864 marks for Sanskrit and Arabic were again lowered to 375 each. Indians considered this decision to be an outcome of selection of Satyendranath by virtue of his superior performance in these two subjects. Satyendranath obtained 381 and 347 marks in Sanskrit and Arabic respectively in his total score of 1,574 marks. In 1878, when the upper age limit was lowered to 19, material changes were introduced in the branches of knowledge admissible for examination. Boys from public school being the prospective candidates, the standard was relaxed for English language and literature. Literature and its history were generally excluded from language. Standard of Mathematics was lowered and was limited to Arithmetic, Algebra and Elementary Geometry. So also was Natural Science which contained Chemistry, Electricity with magnetism and the experimental laws of heat and light. Moral Science was substituted by two subjects, namely Logic and Political Economy.

The situation, however, changed when the maximum age was restored to 23 in 1892. Mathematics was split into two parts, the first came to be known as 'pure and applied' and the other as 'advanced', each carrying 900 marks. Natural Science subjects were divided into seven groups each carrying 600 marks each. These were Elementary Chemistry and Elementary Physics, Higher Chemistry, Higher Physics, Geology, Botany, Zoology and Animal Physiology. Candidates were allowed to attempt a maximum of three subjects from this group. The shift towards specialisation was observable in History subjects also. Earlier these were clubbed with language and literature. New regulation provided for separate History subjects distinct from language and literature. These were Greek History (400), Roman History (400), English History (500) and General Modern History (500). Moral Philosophy was bifurcated into Logic and Mental Philosophy (400) and Moral Philosophy (400) with introduction of a new subject Political Science (500). The number of subjects grew from about 12 in 1855, to 21 in 1892. More subjects were added during the next reform in the scheme of examination in 1906. The number went up to 32 and the next revision pushed it to 67 in the 1920s. But the unlimited choice of subjects was stopped in 1906. Candidates were allowed to choose subjects in a way so that the maximum did not exceed 6,000. The revision in 1921 reduced this to 1,800.

English composition remained the most popular subject with nearly everybody trying for it. At least two-thirds of the successful candidates offered ancient languages Latin and Greek, so also Political Economy. Among the continental languages, French was the most popular. From 1858 to 1878, each year an increasing number of candidates offered Mathematics and Natural Science. Sanskrit though popular to the British candidates till 1865, started to fall off and was chosen only by Indian Hindus. Presumably, this was due to the university men, for whom Sanskrit was favourite, started losing interest in the competition. Few British candidates offered Arabic till 1865 and rarely thereafter. Only the Mahomedan candidates from India offered this subject. Indian students from Parsee community were rather unfortunate as they could offer neither of the oriental languages. During the period 1858-1878, before the age was reduced to 19, 429 candidates of a total of 960 successful, offered Mathematics. Natural Science was offered by 355 candidates. 224 candidates offered Sanskrit, of whom only eight were Indian and remaining Europeans. At that point of time Sanskrit was taught in many British universities including Oxford, Edinburgh and Dublin Universities.

Competitive examination with its scheme of subjects put the Indian candidates in great disadvantage. Many of the subjects were not taught at Indian universities or other educational institutions. British successful candidates could usually offer nine or ten subjects. Indian candidates struggled to attempt even six or seven. No Indian could make out how disadvantageous was the scheme to Indians as did Surendranath, a successful candidate himself. Presiding over the annual session of Indian National Congress at Ahmedabad in 1902, he exposed the devious scheme with clinical analysis. 'Not only Greek and Latin are each valued at 750 marks where as Sanskrit and Arabic are allotted 500 marks each, but Roman and Greek History and Roman Law and Political Science were also made an appenage to European classical languages and literature',[22] Surendranath explained. This scheme allowed a British candidate to avail a good 2,300 marks where as an average Indian student struggled to attempt 500 on his side.

Satyendranath was perhaps the only successful Indian candidate who attempted both Arabic and Sanskrit. Persian rather than Arabic was more widely used in India as court language and both these languages were part of Haileybury curriculum. But Persian was not included in the competitive examination. Cursetjee Rustomji, a Parsee candidate who was selected in 1874, was called as witness by Aitchison Commission. Rustomji pointed out the omission of Persian to the Commission and desired its inclusion which was, however, never done. A successful Indian Romesh Chunder Dutt stood third in order of merit in the examination of 1869 in which other three Indian candidates were also selected. Johnstone Pierce de Lacy Henry headed the list that year. Romesh, however, secured more marks than Johnstone in all the subjects he offered. He did not attempt the continental subjects viz. Greek, French, German and Italian and was thus placed in uneven competition. Indian students performed exceedingly well in Mathematics. Anundoram Borooah, the first Civilian from Assam was successful in the examination of 1870. It was his second attempt and his failure on earlier occasion was due to his ailing health and late arrival in England. A score of 836 in Mathematics out of a maximum of 1,250 helped his selection. He ranked third in the subject among 332 candidates who competed that year. Pulicat Ratnavelu Chetti stood fifth in order of merit, again displaying mathematical proficiency of Indian students. Pulicat reached England in July 1873 from Madras and placed himself at once under an experienced tutor. His score of 929 in Mathematics was the highest among all candidates in 1874. Indian students continued to do well in Mathematics and were ahead of British candidates in English also. In 1885, the year when W C Bonnerjee presided over the first Indian National Congress, his cousin Debendranath sailed for England. He competed for Indian Civil Service and though unsuccessful, topped the list in English. Debendranath's son N B Bonarjee who was selected in 1924 wrote about his father, 'In 1885 my father proceeded to London to sit for the ICS Examination. This was a far more difficult to handle for young Indians though it was to be later, the age limit being fixed at 19. Young Englishmen took the examination straight from school, and if successful, spent the next two years at Oxford and Cambridge. Since the subjects were closely related to the ordinary curriculum of the public schools with its emphasis on Greek and Latin, the hardship for the Indian was present from the start. Although my father was not successful, one of his achievements was remarkable. He headed the list in English. For this reason, perhaps it was not altogether surprising that on his return with a small feather in his cap he tried his hand at journalism, a profession for which he retained his liking throughout his life'.[23] Aravind Acroyd Ghose, who received education at English public school since the age of seven was successful in the examination of 1890. He attempted ancient languages Greek and Latin and scored 457 marks in Greek and 554 in Latin, out of 600 and 800 respectively. He did not, however, attempt the oriental language Sanskrit. In the same year, Satis Chunder Mukherjee obtained 316 marks in Sanskrit and Md Yusuf scored 472 in Arabic out of 500 each, thereby securing the highest places in those subjects.

Jyotish Chandra Mirta reached England in 1884 to compete for the Service. On his failure, the famous coach Walter Wren, under whose supervision he prepared for the examination, wrote to his father that despite his hard labour and merit he had been unsuccessful for his decision to offer lot many subjects against the advice of the coach. None would also expect an Indian candidate to fail in Sanskrit. But this was indeed what happened to Golak Nath Chatterjee. Golak Nath was a convert to Christianity whose family settled in North India. Appearing before the Aitchison Commission, Golak Nath stated that his knowledge of French was better than Sanskrit and the inadequate knowledge was the reason for his failure in the examination. Chatterjee returned to country after doing BA in Mathematics at Cambridge and joined as faculty at Lahore College.

Michael Madhusudan Dutt, the rebel poet, was the first to figure out the deficiency of Indian students and suggested measures to equip them appropriately. Madhusudan was the fourth Indian Barrister and was a close friend of Manomohan Ghose. When Manomohan failed in 1865, Madhusudan wrote in a letter succinctly pointing out, 'Poor Menou has failed again; I am afraid he will not succeed, for the examination has been made more difficult and his ignorance of Greek and Latin will always tell against him. I hope his failure will not discourage our countrymen. The fault is, we ought to send to Europe, not grown up youth, but young lads of 12 or 14. A preliminary English education is absolutely necessary'.[24]

The new regulations coming into effect from August 1892 further increased the marks of Mathematics and Natural Science elevating the standard to a comparatively high scale. Under the old regulations which continued till August 1891, Mathematics was relatively an easy subject with the Indian candidates. Mathematics and the Science papers, especially those of 1892, were as stiff as the Cambridge or Dublin papers, and in some parts, even stiffer. Ashutosh Mukhopadhyay, the then Vice-Chancellor of Calcutta University, to whom the mathematical papers of 1892 were shown, viewed them far harder than the University's Premchand Roychand Scholarship papers. They were stiffer, even in parts, than the Cambridge Mathematical Tripos papers. Kiran Chandra De, a successful candidate that year scored 830 in Mathematics out of a maximum attainable 1,800 marks, securing the second position in order of merit in Mathematics. In the same examination, Hemnath De scored 730 in Mathematics but was not selected. In 1896, a Parsee student, Ardesar Kaikhoshru Cama, who was a Wrangler of Cambridge, surpassed the marks of Kiran Chandra De in Mathematic by scoring 1,055 marks.

The essay, 'Indian Civil Service Examination', authored by Atul Chandra Dutta, a successful candidate of 1887, contained valuable advice for the prospective native candidates. Prior to his success in open competition, Atul Chandra secured the Senior Mathematical Scholarship at Christ College, Cambridge. Atul Chandra prepared himself under the guidance of famous coach Walter Wren. 'Indian candidates generally stand or fall by Mathematics',[25] was Atul Chandra's observation. A really good Mathematician would have little difficulty in securing three-fourth of the maximum. Atul Chandra himself scored 799 out of maximum possible 1,000. But the most paying subjects in his assessment were French, German and Italian in which candidates were asked to translate passages from an ordinary English author into the continental language idiomatically correct. Though the standard was high, a candidate with an aptitude for learning language could expect to secure 450 or 500 marks with two or three years' hard work. Atul Chandra with his preparation had no difficulty in offering Latin, French and Germany. Logic and Political Economy appeared to him rather snare and delusion. He felt that the temptation to offer these subjects, though very strong to an Indian who is naturally fond of abstruse mental science, must be resisted. This was more so, Atul Chandra suggested, as in

Period of Age-Limits, 17–21, i.e., down to 1877.		Period of Age-Limits, 17–19, i.e., 1878–1891.	
Subjects.	Marks.	Subjects.	Marks.
1. English Composition	500	1. English Composition	300
2. History of England, including that of the Laws and Constitution.	500	2. History of England, including a period selected by the candidate.	300
3. English Language and Literature	500	3. English Literature, including books selected by the candidate.	300
4. Language, Literature, and History of Greece.	750	4. Greek	600
5. Language, Literature, and History of Rome ..	750	5. Latin	800
6. Language, Literature, and History of France ..	375	6. French	500
7. Language, Literature, and History of Germany.	375	7. German	500
8. Language, Literature, and History of Italy ..	375	8. Italian	400
9. Mathematics (pure and mixed)	1,250	9. Mathematics (pure and mixed)	1,000
10. Natural Science—that is (1) Chemistry, including Heat; (2) Electricity and Magnetism; (3) Geology and Mineralogy; (4) Zoology; (5) Botany. The total (1,000) marks may be obtained by adequate proficiency in any two or more of the five branches of Science included under this head.	1,000	10. Natural Science—that is, the Elements of any two of the following Sciences, viz., Chemistry, 500; Electricity and Magnetism, 300; Experimental Laws of Heat and Light, 300; Mechanical Philosophy, with outlines of Astronomy, 300.	800 or 600
11. Moral Science—that is, Logic, Mental and Moral Philosophy.	500	11. Logic	200
		12. Elements of Political Economy	200
12. Sanskrit Language and Literature	500	13. Sanskrit	500
13. Arabic Language and Literature	500	14. Arabic	500

Period of Age-Limits, 21–23, *i.e.*, 1892–1905.		Period of Age-Limits, 22–24, *i.e.*, 1906 to Date.	
1. English Composition	500	1. English Composition	500
2. English History	500	2. English History, either or both sections may be taken—	
		Section I., to A.D. 1485	400
		Section II., A.D. 1485 to 1848	400
3. English Law, viz., Law of Contract—Criminal Law—Law of Evidence and Law of the Constitution	500	3. English Law	500
4. English Language and Literature (including special period named by the Commissioners).	500	4. English Language and Literature	600
5. Greek Language and Literature	750	Greek, not less than two sub-divisions of which one must be Translation :—	
		5. Translation	400
		6. Prose Composition	200
		7. Verse Composition	200
		8. Literature, etc.	200
6. Greek History (Ancient, including Constitution)	400	9. Greek History (Ancient, including Constitution).	500
7. Latin Language and Literature	750	Latin, not less than two sub-divisions, of which one must be Translation :—	
		10. Translation	400
		11. Prose Composition	200
		12. Verse Composition	200
		13. Literature, etc.	300
8. Roman History (Ancient, including Constitution)	400	14. Roman History (Ancient, including Constitution)	500
9. Roman Law	500	15. Roman Law	500
10. French Language and Literature	500	16. French, History of the Language and Literature.	200
		17. French, Translation, Composition and Conversation.	400
11. German Language and Literature	500	18. German, History of the Language and Literature.	200
		19. German, Translation, Composition and Conversation.	400
		20. Italian, History of the Language and Literature.	200
		21. Italian, Translation, Composition and Conversation.	400
12. General Modern History (period to be selected by Candidates from list in the syllabus issued by the Commissioners, one period at least to include Indian History).	500	22. General Modern History	500
13. Mathematics (pure and applied)	900	23. Lower Mathematics	1,200
14. Advanced Mathematical subjects (pure and applied).	900	24. Higher Mathematics	1,200
15. Natural Science, *i.e.*, any number not exceeding three of the following subjects ;—		25. Natural Science, *i.e.*, any number not exceeding four of the following or three if both Lower and Higher Mathematics be also taken :—	
Elementary Chemistry and Elementary Physics 600		(1) Chemistry 600	2,400 or 1,800
(*N.B.*—This subject may not be taken up by those who offer either Higher Chemistry or Higher Physics)—		(2) Physics 600	
Higher Chemistry 600	1,800	(3) Geology 600	
Higher Physics 600		(4) Botany 600	
Geology 600		(5) Zoology 600	
Botany 600		(6) Animal Physiology 600	
Zoology 600		(7) Geography 600	
Animal Physiology 600			
16. Logic and Mental Philosophy (Ancient and Modern).	400	26. Logic and Physiology	600
17. Moral Philosophy (Ancient and Modern) ..	400	27. Moral and Metaphysical Philosophy	600
18. Political Economy and Economic History ..	500	28. Political Economy and Economic History ..	600
19. Political Science (including Analytical Jurisprudence, the Early History of Institutions and Theory of Legislation).	500	29. Political Science	500
20. Sanskrit Language and Literature	500	31. Sanskrit Language and Literature	600
21. Arabic Language and Literature..	500	32. Arabic Language and Literature	600
Candidates are at liberty to name any or all of these branches of knowledge. No subjects are obligatory.		Consistently with the limitations specified above Candidates are at liberty to name any of the foregoing subjects, provided that the maximum number of marks that can be obtained from the subjects chosen is limited to 6,000.	

India candidates could profitably attempt to learn Mathematics, English literature and Sanskrit or Arabic. This might be supplemented by study of French, Roman or perhaps Italian when the candidate reached England. The candidate with spare time for other studies might also study English History with advantage.

The existing rule of no obligatory subject and no restriction on number of subjects offered by a candidate was, however, not changed under the regulations of 1892. Arthur Berriedale Keith, a Scotsman from Oxford came out first in the examination of 1901 beating all past records as regards the number of marks obtained in that examination. Keith got 5,382 marks, an unprecedented high score and offered no less than fifteen subjects. At last in 1906, the rules were altered so as to prevent any candidate from offering more subjects than would command a total of 6,000 marks. The change was an improvement, for most of the candidates could offer subjects to the required total without any material departure from the ordinary course of their study. Philip Woodruff described the salutary effect of this change as 'cramming became less valuable'.[26] Otherwise, Woodruff continued 'in Victorian times a good crammer could undertake by six weeks' tuition to add five hundred marks to a young man's total'.[27] The alteration came as an outcome of the consultation that the Civil Service Commissioners and India Office started with the universities in 1904 about the evaluation system. Strachan Davidson, who succeeded Jowett as the Master of Balliol, concentrated his attention on three issues. Rather ignorant about Indian society, he was bent on ensuring that the examination should strengthen and not harm the Oxford Graduate Schools. Davidson advocated limiting the maximum number of marks which could be obtained in the competition, thus diminishing the need for a man to cram additional subjects. Other universities including Cambridge supported him on this issue. The other point on which the universities were unanimous was the upward revision of the maximum age of candidate from 23 to 24 years. Davidson's final wish to increase the allocation of marks for Philosophy met with the natural response of Cambridge's fury. Obtaining more marks for Latin and Greek verses was the campaign of Cambridge. Strachan Davidson sent out the Chancellor of the University, Lord Goschen, a former Cabinet Minister to lobby with the counsel that 'nothing will please Cambridge unless it injures Oxford'.[28] In the same vein he continued, 'Cambridge will doubtlessly consent to lose one eye provided Oxford can be deprived of both'.[29]

Chintaman Dwarkanath Desmukh before proceeding to England consulted Mahadeva Vishnu Bhide on the choice of subjects. Mahadeva, a successful candidate of 1906, strongly advised Chintaman to avoid Mathematics.

The subject was very chancy but Science was more reliable for a diligent student. Of the total of 6,000 marks in nine or ten subjects which one had to offer then, Lower and Higher Mathematics could make up 2,400 and so could four science subjects. English Composition and English Language and Literature made up 1,800 and Sanskrit Language and Literature 800. The other subjects to make up could be History, Political Science, Economics and English Law each for 500 marks. Chintaman offered History, Economics and English Law making up a total of 5,900. With a score of 3,520, he was at the top of the list in open competition of 1918. The next revision in subjects was effected in the year 1921. The total marks were reduced to 1,800. The syllabus, to the delight of the graduates of Oxford or Cambridge, was brought more or less in line with that of the great English universities. Viva voce test carrying maximum score of 300 marks became compulsory element of the examination. Subjects apart, the hand writing of the candidates also counted considerably for the selection. An Indian candidate from Malabar, Arathil Candeth Madhvan Nambiar passed in Historical Tripos from Cambridge University, carrying the first prize in English essay from among a large number of English competitors. Appearing in the open examination of 1913, he topped the list in Modern History and stood fifth in literature. The Indian lad, a Barrister as well, stood 87th in the list, missing the selection for deduction of 125 marks for bad writing. He was finally offered an appointment in the Indian Educational Service and posted at Madras. His was not a singular case and the same year 'Oxford Magazine' reported a few other instances. J B Taylor had only himself to thank for being second instead of being first. Another candidate lost no less than 14 places and would have got the offer of a place in the Home Service instead of being without a billet.

Civil Service Commissioners carried on the responsibility of conducting the examination since 1857, but the examiners were all drawn from university faculty. Edward Ryan acted as Civil Service Commissioner for a long time. He had the experience of India serving as the Chief Justice and was associated with Macaulay and Trevelyan in the work for spread of European education in the country. Monier Williams, who was both a student and professor at Haileybury College and afterwards joined Oxford as Boden Professor, was the examiner of Sanskrit for a long time. Colonel J W J Ouseley who was professor of Persian and Arabic at Fort William College, Calcutta and later joined Haileybury College, conducted the Arabic examination. W Seaton Kerr, a retired Civilian who served as Vice-Chancellor of Calcutta University acted as the examiner of Bengali. Perhaps the only Indian associated with the examination process during this period was Dadabhai Naoroji. He was the examiner of Marathi and Gujarati in the final examination for selected candidates of Bombay Presidency.

Training and Final Examination

Competitive examination was designed to test the general education of the candidates, totally unrelated to the special knowledge of Indian affairs. Macaulay Commission recommended that the successful candidate would acquire this knowledge during probation and would be subjected to periodic assessment. It was desired that the candidate should make himself well acquainted with the history and geography of India, its different races and social customs. Knowledge about principle of jurisprudence was thought to be essential as the Civilians were employed in the administration of justice. Political Economy was another subject which the probationer ought to have prepared himself for discharge of duties in India. He ought to have clear understanding of mode of keeping and checking accounts, different systems of taxations and its effect on national prosperity, regulation of exchange rates and public debt. Finally, a candidate ought to have knowledge of vernacular language of the Presidency to which he was allotted. In the area of jurisprudence, it was recommended that the candidates should see the actual working of the machinery through which justice is administered. They were required to attend both civil and criminal trials and take notes of evidence and discussions. It was also desired that the candidates attend the sittings of judicial committee of Privy Council when important appeals from India were placed under consideration of the tribunal.

Training of successful candidates under the new scheme started from the year 1859 with probation of one year. An important change took place in the year 1864. Acting on the proposal of Government of India, the Secretary of State decided that the examination hitherto held at Presidency towns should be abolished, and the preliminary training of the young Civilians, even in the vernacular languages should be completed in England. It was understood that the same degree of proficiency in the languages which had previously been required in the examination held at Calcutta, Madras and Bombay, should henceforth be exhibited at the final examination in England. A probationary period of two years was allowed to the candidates to prepare for this final examination and an additional allowance of £ 200 was granted to cover the expenses of the second year.

Following the enquiry by Civil Service Commissioners, Lord Salisbury made university residence compulsory for the successful candidates to avail of the allowance. The institutes approved by the Secretary of State were the universities of Oxford, Cambridge, Dublin, Glasgow, Edinburgh, St Andrews Aberdeen, Victoria, Manchester, University College of London and King's College, London. This arrangement did not, however, please either Oxford or Cambridge who expected exclusive privilege for training the Civilians. Monier Williams conceived the idea of 'Indian Institute' at Oxford with facilities for oriental studies, which he hoped, would attract the successful candidates. In 1883, the memorial stone of Indian Institute at Oxford was laid in presence of the Prince of Wales. On this occasion, Shyamji Krishanvarma and Bhabendrabala, daughter of Gyanendra Mohan Tagore, Barrister were the two honoured natives of India who were present. Many Indians subscribed to the fund required for the extension of the Institute. Monier Williams received £ 200 from Bhagat Singhal, £ 200 from the Thakore of Gondal, £ 100 from Maharaja of Travancore, and Rs 1,000 from Maharani Swarnamoyee. With facilities for appropriate training, Oxford, Cambridge and University College of London attracted a big chunk of the successful candidates. Oxford was way ahead of others with 498 candidates spending their probation during the period 1895-1915. Cambridge and University College of London trained 278 and 216 candidates respectively. Few Irish men stayed with Dublin, the number totalling up to 62. Four Scotch universities could not attract a single candidate for probation. They had no teachers in the languages and other subjects, and did not receive any subsidy from the India Council either. The universities, seeking their role in the Empire, were obsessed with the programme of training ICS men.

Cambridge joined the race as a slow starter trying to catch up its predecessor with bountiful scholarships and flexible regulations. But Oxford with Indian Institute remained a distinct first, not at all prepared to lose its position. It lined up a host of facilities including constitution of a delegacy for the purpose of superintending the instruction of selected ICS candidates which appropriately reflected the priority accorded. Nearly every college under the university admitted selected candidates without entrance examination and besides waiving off the normal college tuition fees, offered scholarships. Oxford offered four Boden scholarships of £ 50 a year each for proficiency in Sanskrit, supplemented by two additional scholarships of the value of £ 50 offered by Christ Church College. The ancient university, on many fronts, reconciled to its role and sacrificed its tradition. The condition of passing ordinary examination was waived and with such favourable environment being created, selected candidates were drawn in large number. Cambridge was never to miss the imperial glory and did not trail behind in creating facilities for training the probationers. All its colleges, with partial remission of tuition fees and offer of scholarships, tried to attract the selected candidates. The favourite of Indian students, Cambridge indeed abounded with offer of scholarships but the medal, founded by the late Maharaja of Bhavnagar,

Final Examination of 1891 when the Period of Probation was 2 Years.		Final Examination of 1913 when the Period of Probation was one Year.	
Subjects (a).	Marks.	Subjects.	Marks.
		Compulsory—	
1. *Classical languages of India—		1. The principal Vernacular language of the Province to which the Candidate is assigned.	400
Sanskrit	500		
Arabic	400	2. Indian History ...	400
Persian	400	3. Indian Penal Code ...	400
2. †Vernacular languages of India (excepting Hindustani when taken up by Madras Candidates, and Gujrati) each.	400	4. Code of Criminal Procedure ...	200
		5. The Indian Evidence Act ...	200
3. The History and Geography of India.	350	*Optional*—(Not more than one of following subjects)—	
4. ‡Law	1,250	1. §Sanskrit	400
5. Political Economy	350	2. §Arabic	400
		3. Persian	400
		4. Hindustani (for Candidates assigned to the Province of Burma only).	400
		5. Hindu and Muhammadan Law	450

(a) In addition to the above, candidates were permitted to take up any one of the following branches of Natural Science, viz., Agricultural Chemistry, Botany, Geology and Zoology, for which 350 marks were allowed.

* One or more of these subjects could be taken.

† One of the languages prescribed for the candidates' Presidency or Province.

‡ The course of reading in law included—

(1) General Jurisprudence—
- Blackstone's Commentaries.
- Austin's Jurisprudence.
- The Institutes of Justinian.
- Maine's Ancient Law.
- Mackenzie's Studies in Roman Law.
- Bentham's Theory of Legislation.

(2) Law of Evidence—
- The Indian Evidence Act.
- Pitt Taylor's Treatise on the Law of Evidence.

(3) Law of India—
- The Code of Civil Procedure.
- The Indian Penal Code.
- The Code of Criminal Procedure.
- The Indian Law of Contracts.
- The Intestate and Testamentary Succession Act.
- Hindu Law.
- Muhammadan Law.

Simultaneously the candidates attended courts and supplied the following detailed reports, with an analysis and notes on each case:—

1st Periodical Examination	..	Seven reports of police court cases of a stipendiary magistrate, embracing cases in which the magistrate exercised final jurisdiction and cases which he committed for trial.
		Four civil cases of a county court in which the parties were represented by counsel.
		One separate report of the whole business, of whatever kind, transacted in a police court during one day.
2nd Periodical Examination	..	Five reports of civil actions in the superior courts of London in which the defendant was represented by counsel.
		Five reports of cases decided in the Central Criminal Court in which the prisoner was represented by counsel.
3rd Periodical Examination	..	Three reports of civil cases of importance tried before special juries in the Superior Courts of London.
		Three reports of criminal cases of importance tried before juries in the Central Criminal Court and selected for some special quality such as the gravity of the offence, the nature of the evidence produced, the number of the prisoners, &c.
Final Examination ..	..	One report of the investigation before a London police magistrate of a grave criminal charge ending in committal.
		One report of the whole business, of whatever kind, transacted in a London police court in one day.
		Two reports of important civil cases tried by a special jury in London.
		One report of a case heard in the Judicial Committee of the Privy Council on appeal from India.

§ These subjects cannot be offered by any candidate who has offered them at the Open Competition.

stood out in the lot. The honour, reserved for a Cambridge Tripos succeeding in the open competition, expressed the admiration that the Indian prince nurtured for the 'heaven-born', acknowledging at the same time Cambridge as the home of Indian students. The medal was given to the probationer who headed the final list arranged by the combined results of the exhibition for selection and the final examination for ICS. A couple of other English universities were manifestly interested in attracting selected candidates, perhaps seeking their role in the imperial administration. They also made arrangements, albeit at much smaller scale, and altered regulations, favouring the probationers in their preparation of the final examination. Trinity College, Dublin, was actuated more than any other consideration, by its desire to maintain ethnic identity. In order to allure Irishmen, the College allowed residence for the selected candidates on the same terms as other students and waived the requirement of passing terms in Arts while pursuing their special studies.

The final examination was not merely a qualifying test. It did have a wider implication for the successful candidates. The order in which the selected candidates stood in the final examination determined their service seniority. The poor performance of the candidates in final examination, therefore, raised many eyebrows. Between 1859, when the system of probation was introduced and 1905, a total number of 65 candidates were denied appointment as they could not pass the final examination. Till 1862, selected candidates who failed in their final examination were allowed a second trial by the Secretary of State, provided they were not beyond 24 years of age. But the generous application of relaxation marked the sagging diligence on part of the probationers. In 1862, a total of 24 candidates out of 85 failed in the final examination. Candidates fared very poor, especially, in the examination of jurisprudence and Indian Law which chiefly constituted the sphere of their official work in India. Authorities reacted and in the regulations of 1863, it was announced that candidates rejected at the final examination, would in no case be allowed to present themselves for re-examination. Poor result in the final examination of 1870, in which 10 candidates failed, prompted many to question the prevailing system of training through which 'the future judicial administrators of India' acquire their legal knowledge. In half-jest, a British paper concluded that 'it is no surprise that we hear news of so much injustice in that country'. The training curriculum was designed to equip the Civilian to the requirement of Indian working. It naturally suited Indian candidates and the European candidates struggled hard to familiarise themselves with Indian History and vernaculars.

Successful Indian candidates worked diligently, allowing no indulgence or relaxation. This was manifestly established as no Indian candidate had ever failed in the final examination. Most of them actually clawed up the ladder and quite a few reached the top of the list. Surendranath who was successful in the open competition of 1869, lost one year of his two years' probation period in legal battle. He was initially removed from the list allegedly due to over age and his selection was restored through a Court order in February 1870. The same order allowed him a dispensation of one year to take the final examination. Surendranath, however, worked hard and passed the final examination with his other two friends Romesh Chunder and Behari Lal. Their native successors many a time came on top beating all the British candidates. Mancherji Pestanji Kharegat, Mohsin Tyabji, Kiran Chandra De and Yusuf Ali all came first in the final examination glorifying the country through their achievements. Most remarkable performance of the Indian candidates was the final examination of 1895 when they monopolised the top of the list. Yusuf Ali headed the list followed by Dadachanji who ranked third. Tek Chand, Jyotsnanath Ghosal and Albion Rajkumar Banerjee captured the fourth, fifth and sixth places respectively. The year 1884 heralded the crowning glory for the Indians. Arthur Goodeve Chuckerbutty headed the list of successful candidates in the open competition while Mancherji Pestonji Kharegat, a selected candidate of 1882, achieved the same honours in the final examination. The trend improved in twentieth century and Indian candidates exalted in greater number. During the first fifteen years of 20th Century, Indian candidates headed the final examination in no less than six occasions. The solitary case of an Indian candidate losing the appointment for failure in final examination was that of Arabinda Ghose. Divinity ordained a greater role for Arabinda as he evaded the riding test conducted during the probation and was denied appointment.

Medical Examination

Health of Indian Civilian had been a major concern of the imperial authority, more so, for the stifling heat and the numerous tropical diseases. Medical examination was an integral part of the selection process which was usually conducted just after the notification of the result by the doctors nominated by the Commissioners. A further test was done at the time of final examination. Till 1914, in the first sixty years of open competition, a total of 36 candidates had the misfortune of rejection on medical ground. Interestingly 10 candidates, who passed the initial medical test, were rejected at the stage of final examination. But for ICS and IMS, the Medical Board of the India Office carried on the test of recruits in all Imperial Services. The Medical Board consisted of a President and a Member, both of whom had Indian experience. The Member was changed every third year and the President had to retire at the age of 65. The Board examined especially those who were joining the Public Works, the Ecclesiastical, the Railways and other departments as to their fitness for entering into the service. It carried on the test with a set standard and was, by and large, successful in avoiding controversy. The same set of doctors inspected the Indian Civil Service officers when they were in England on sick leave. The medical test of selected candidates of ICS was fundamentally different. It was undertaken by private medical practitioner, engaged by the Civil Service Commissioners and did not have a set standard. A series of correspondence on this issue took place in the year 1883. Civil Service Commissioners, however, could not be persuaded to handover the responsibility to the Medical Board at the India Office. They clung on to the job citing that the role of Medical Board was inconsistent with provisions of an Act. The doctors engaged were, however, all reputed with considerable practice. But as the test had no set standard, rejection sometimes produced grievances in the minds of the candidates.

Malcolm Peter Gasper, a Calcutta Armenian, studied at Doveton College of the city. He passed the Indian Civil Service competition in 1869 along with four successful Indian candidates. He ranked 45th in the test in which a total of 53 candidates were selected. Malcolm along with the Bengali youths Romesh, Behari Lal and Surendranath was allotted to the province of Lower Bengal. He continued his training and passed the final examination displaying fair knowledge of the native vernaculars viz. Hindustani and Bengali. Following the final examination, he had to undergo further medical examination. In June 1871, when Gasper was rejected, the Armenian contended that the complaint was the same notwithstanding which and in spite of which, he was passed by the same medical examination in the year 1869.

By the time the results were declared, Malcolm had married and had a child. He had borrowed money from his friends to meet the expenditure during the training period and was all set to start a Civilian's life. He narrated his misfortune saying that, 'I have spent two of the most valuable years of my life in undergoing a mere technical training, the result of which that now I am comparatively unfit for any other profession'.[30] Following the medical rejection, Malcolm consulted six of the most eminent medical professionals in London, including one late President of the Royal College of Surgeons. All the medical men, surgeons or physicians of the London Hospitals, certified that they did not find any valid reasons for disallowing him to proceed to India in the Civil Service. The doctors opined that he was as likely to continue in good health as the majority of those who would proceed to India in that service. Malcolm then appealed to the Civil Services Commissioners to reconsider their decision. Doctors' opinion, however, did not influence the Commissioners who refused to change the decision. The Secretary of State for India also refused to intervene in the matter. Finally, Malcolm approached the Court of Queen's Bench, seeking a mandamus to oblige the Civil Service Commissioners to grant him another medical examination. Nothing favourable happened but Malcolm, though dejected, did not give up. He enrolled at the Bar and returned to India as a Barrister. Soon he established a lucrative practice at Calcutta High Court. Besides legal profession, he had keen interest in sports and emerged as winner of more than one trophy on the Calcutta Race Course, including the Viceroy's Cup in 1886.

In 1879, again an Indian candidate was rejected after completion of probation. The unfortunate young man was a Parsee student Gustasp Ardeseer, son of A Cursetji Wadia, a merchant settled at Richmond. The most tragic case of rejection was, however, of Jotindra Nath Ray who passed the open competition twice. Kedar Nath Roy, a Statutory Civilian sent his two sons Jnanendra Nath and Jotindra Nath to England in the year 1892 to compete for the ICS. Jnanendra Nath successfully passed the examination in 1897 and so did Jotindra Nath in 1998. But the misfortune started soon after. During medical examination, Dr Ord, the appointed medical officer unconditionally rejected Jotindra Nath on the ground that they had detected a certain sign of irregularity in one of his lungs as an indication of some malady coming on.

Jotindra Nath then demanded a Medical Board, and the request was granted. His own physician, Sir Richard Douglas Powell, Physician Extraordinary to Her Majesty the Queen, wrote a letter to the President of the Board giving a detailed history of the case which he pronounced to be a marvellous one, and pointing that as Jotindra Nath was about to return to his native country he was fit for service.

A medical board consisting of Dr Ord, Dr Clayton and Sir Samuel Wilkes, President of the Royal College of Physicians of London examined the case. Dr Clayton gave his opinion that the candidate was perfectly sound. The other two doctors were perhaps influenced by Dr Powell's view and modified their opinion. They admitted that the irregularity was the sign of a disease that had passed away and not of one that was to come. Indeed, they held that Jotindra Nath would be fit for service in India in twelve months, just the time that all selected candidates had to pass on probation in England. Such a clear pronouncement on part of four of the most distinguished medical professionals in England ought to have settled the question. But the Commissioners stuck to their decision turning down the appeal.

Jotindra Nath followed doctors' advice and sojourned for two months and half at Cannes in France. After his return to London in December 1898, he presented himself before Sir Samuel Wilkes, who after re-examining, found him quite well. He recommended his case for the consideration of the Commissioners. The Commissioners declined to re-open the case on the grounds of having taken another candidate in his place contending that 'it was their invariable practice to treat a decision arrived at in this as irrevocable'.[31] Maharaja Jotindra Mohan Tagore Bahadur wrote to Sir Comer Pethran urging him to take up the case. Pethran met the young man but could do little.

Misfortune could not dampen the spirit of Jotindra Nath. He competed again in the following year and came out with flying colours. But misfortune never left him. He caught a chill before the day appointed for his medical examination by Dr Ordand and very naturally asked the Commissioners to excuse him for a week by which time he hoped to get rid of this cold. But the prayer though supported by a medical certificate, was not granted.

The Medical Board was called in but in such a hurry that Jotindra Nath was deprived of the opportunity of producing independent medical opinion for consideration of the Board. His own doctor Sir Richard Douglas Powell was away from London, while Sir Samuel Wilkes had retired from practice. Jotindra Nath respectfully submitted to be examined by the old Board that had examined him in September 1898, and had reported that there was every reason that he would be quite fit for the Indian Civil Service within the next twelve months. The new Board before whom he had to appear was necessarily at disadvantage in as much as they had no personal knowledge of his condition in September 1898. The opinion of Sir William Broadbent should have allowed Jotindra Nath three months' time to ascertain his fitness or recoup his health. But the new Board rejected him as before and the Commissioners accepted their opinion as final.

Kedar Nath, the father of Jotindra Nath, memorialised the Secretary of State for India on the subject and prayed for the appointment of his son in the Civil Service or in some other department. On the earlier occasion, Lord George Hamilton showed considerable sympathy with the unfortunate position of the young Indian. Lord Curzon also recommended for consideration of the case, which reached late, only after Hamilton upheld the decision of Civil Service Commissioners. Indian press entirely sympathised with the misfortune of the young lad. Anglo-Indian paper *The Englishman* considered the case 'to be a rather hard one'[32] and desired that 'this is one of those cases, which occasionally, crop up, in which the Secretary of State might profitably exercise his discretion'.[33] There was a demand that like riding, the benefits of a second Medical Examination in India be extended to the successful candidates. It was proposed that a candidate's fitness for active work be tested by experience in India. Requesting Grand Old Man of India, Dadabhai Naoroji, to take up the issue, *The Behar Herald* desired that 'before he can be successful in his mission for simultaneous examination in India and England, it is essential that he should press for a second medical examination in India'.[34]

Lord Curzon felt the injustice done and had genuine sympathy for Jotindra Nath. In July 1900, the Bengal Government, being advised by the Viceroy, appointed Jotindra Nath as Deputy Magistrate in the fifth grade. The young man was posted to Bankura where his father was the District Judge. In the next decade, Royal Commission on Public Service recommended that medical examination of candidates for appointment in England be made more stringent. It prescribed two examinations, one at the commencement of the period of probation and one after its completion. At the same time Commission desired for closer co-ordination between the Medical Board of India Office and the practitioners employed by the Civil Service Commissioners. A rejected candidate, Commission felt, should possess the right of appeal.

Riding Test

In 1882, riding was introduced as part of probationary training and the successful candidates were tested of their 'ability to ride'[35] in the final examination. The test used to take place shortly after the result of open competition had been declared and again at the time of final examination. A military officer acting for the Commissioners conducted the test which included saddling and bridling, mounting and dismounting, trotting, trotting without stirrups, trotting without reins or stirrups, cantering, jumping the bar at moderate height and jumping a moderate hedge hurdle. Within a decade, riding test became widely known in India through the incident of Arabinda.

Surgeon K D Ghose studied medicine in England in 1869 before settling in India. He travelled back to England in 1879 with his family of wife, daughter and three sons whom he wanted to compete for ICS. Parents and the daughter soon returned to India leaving the three sons studying in England. Eldest Binoy Bhusan attempted for ICS unsuccessfully. Second son Manmohan was too deeply in love with literary pursuits to be distracted by worldly charm of ICS. Thus it fell on Arabinda to fulfil his father's dream. With his knowledge of Greek and Latin, Arvind Acroyd Ghose successfully passed the examination in 1890. Though he won prizes for Greek and Latin iambics in the university examination, he did not seem to have cared to keep up his high rank in ICS. Oscar Browning of King's College, Cambridge, his examiner rated mental calibre of Arabinda as very high. Walter Wren, the acclaimed tutor pronounced him a genius. Oscar was so impressed by Arabinda's knowledge that he remarked, 'I suppose you know, you passed an extraordinary high examination. I have examined papers at thirteen examinations and I have never during that time, came across such excellent papers as yours'.[36]

In the first periodic examination, held in March 1891, Arabinda stood 23rd of 46 ICS candidates which was enough to keep him a probationer in good standing, but it was, however, a sharp drop from his entering rank. Six months later, in the second periodic examination, a dramatic improvement in Sanskrit brought his over-all position to nineteenth. Meanwhile, Arabinda was doing well in his classical studies at Cambridge. In 1891, he was named joint winner for the best composition in Greek iambics. At the same time, he carried off singly the prize for Latin hexameters, and was awarded £ 40 worth of books for his performance in college examinations. In the final examination, he did badly, falling to 37th place out of 44. Even in Sanskrit he finished in the lower half of his class, and in Bengali he did even worse. Still he passed, and at this point that was all that mattered. His father had already arranged with his friend Henry Cotton to get Arabinda, posted in the desirable district of Arrah (Bihar), and was impatiently looking forward to his third son's return. Just a few months before embarking on the journey back home, Arabinda realised that he had 'a disgust for [the] administrative life'.[37] So far he had never questioned his father's choice of career for him and could not risk disappointing him. He was, as he later said, 'too young to understand', [38] what the ICS was all about.

The result of final examination was announced with footnote: 'Those candidates opposite whose names the letter P occurs have passed the examination in riding in a satisfactory manner. Mr Arabinda Acroyd Ghose had not passed this Examination at the time of going to press.'[39] Arabinda failed to qualify the medical examination on the first occasion due to minor problems. He was given a year's grace to improve and when he was reexamined, his health was judged acceptable. Thus riding test remained the last obstacle for Arabinda to overcome. But for few riding lessons at Cambridge, he never learnt anything of it. He failed his first two trials, once by falling off the horse and not presenting himself on the next occasion. After the final examination he and all other poor horsemen were given a last trial. He again failed to appear, but two days later sent a medical certificate by way of an explanation. In turn, Arabinda received two letters in August 1892 from the Civil Service Commissioners asking him as to when he would wish to be examined. Arabinda preferred to remain silent. In October, the Commissioners again wrote to Arabinda asking him to fix a date to take his riding examination. Arabinda agreed to go on 26 October 1892, but did not turn up. An official then asked him to meet the riding instructor to make another appointment. He did not bother to see the man. Arabinda was called to the office to explain and after deliberation it was decided to afford him one more chance. Arabinda had to meet the riding instructor on the platform of Charing Cross Station, London at 2:15 pm on 15 November 1892. The two would go to Woolwich, where Arabinda would be examined. Arabinda went neither to Charing Cross nor to Woolwich. Two days later, he was told that he had been rejected from the service.

At the behest of the family friend James Cotton, Arabinda reluctantly agreed to write to the Civil Service Commissioners for allowing one more opportunity. But his letter, stiff and formal, read as though it had been dictated by Cotton. Arabinda committed that if given another chance, it would be 'the object of [his] life to remember it in the faithful performance of my duties in the Civil Service of India'[40]— a phrase that must have stuck in his craw. Cotton readily sent the letter to the Secretary of State, attaching one of his own and one from G W Prothero, Arabinda's tutor. The file moved from one office to another as no one was willing to reconsider. Finally, on the recommendation of George W E Russell, the Parliamentary Under Secretary for India, the case went before the Secretary of State, Kimberley. He knew nothing about Arabinda but had clear view of the importance of riding. Informed the previous June about the poor horsemanship of some ICS recruits, he had directed that 'no candidate ought to be allowed to go out to India who cannot ride'.[41] After leafing through Arabinda's file, Kimberley declined to intervene, as the precedent of interfering with the Commissioners' discretion would result nothing but confusion. The case was thus closed and in December 1892, Under Secretary Russell informed Arabinda of the decision of his rejection in the ICS. Arabinda was, however, not denied the allowance of £ 150 on the ground that on earlier occasions, candidates, who failed on medical ground, were paid the same.

Arabinda's rejection from the ICS remained a controversy for many years. Nearly half a century later in the twilight of his life, he wrote that he managed 'by certain manoeuvres',[42] to 'get himself disqualified for riding without himself rejecting the service, which his family would not have allowed him to do'.[43] This is consistent with his behaviour in October and November 1892, in particular, his failure to go to Charing Cross Station, London. On the particular day, he explained on another occasion, he was 'wandering in the streets of London to pass the time'.[44] Though associated with Indian Majlis, Arabinda's conduct was rather moderate at that point of time. Indian students were excited that summer as Dadabhai Naoroji, on liberal ticket, was contesting for the House of Commons. Arabinda was unmoved when Naoroji defeated his rival in the election that brought Gladstone back to power. More to his taste was a meeting held a short while later, when he, his brothers, and some of their friends established a secret society called Lotus and Dagger. Each member 'vowed to work for the liberation of India',[45] but the group had no second meeting. The rejection from ICS appeared a calamity to his brother Manmohan. But Arabinda had nothing to despair, as he later wrote, 'greatly relieved and overjoyed by his release from the ICS'.[46] Long before this, when he was implicated in the Alipore Bomb Case in 1909, the newspaper reporters enquired about his rejection. Arabinda replied candidly that he failed in the final for the Civil Service because of his inability to ride. 'If I was not actually glad, I was certainly not disappointed',[47] Arabinda continued, 'because the Civil Service was barred to me. I have never been fond of constraint of any sort and I was really not sorry to forego the service'.[48]

Shortly after the incident of Arabinda, the provisions of riding test were altered. Candidates satisfying the Commissioners with their ability to ride and perform journey on horseback were given certificates. Those who failed to obtain riding test certificate, but attained certificate of minimum proficiency, were allowed to proceed to India. They would, however, receive no increment in their pay till they pass the riding test arranged by the Government. Beginning with the final examination held in 1893 for the successful candidates who passed the open competition in 1891, maximum possible marks of 200 were allocated for riding test. Riding thus became more like other subjects of the final examination in which candidates were tested, the marks obtained in it contributing to the total. The open competition used to take place in August each year and the results were usually notified in October. The riding test started with a preliminary examination in December, followed by an intermediate examination during Easter to test progress of the candidates. The final examination usually took place at the same time as in other subjects. The Riding Establishment office, Royal Artillery Barracks, Woolwich was the venue for the test. The examination used to last for an hour and the height of the hurdle used to be 3 feet at the final examination. Before undergoing the test, each candidate was required to pay a fee of six shillings to the Quarter Master – Sergeant. In first three decades since riding test was institutionalised, only two candidates were denied appointment for poor horsemanship. Besides Arabinda, the other hapless candidate was a European. H W Masterton succeeded in the open competition of 1911 and was assigned the province of East Bengal and Assam. He continued probationary training and but for riding test, passed the final examination. Masterton was, however, rejected for failing to show minimum proficiency in riding.

Birendra Chandra Sen, a successful candidate of 1891 established Indian skill in riding by scoring maximum possible marks of 200. But for Hussein Ahmed Ali, all the eight candidates who succeeded in open competition during the years from 1893 to 1895 maintained the trend by securing full marks in riding test. Hussein missed the final test due to an injury. But the shocking news came within a decade. *The Times* reported on 11 January 1902: 'Accident at Cambridge – Mr Byramji Navroji Cama, an Indian Student at St John's College, Cambridge, who was sixth Wrangler last June, died yesterday at Addenbrooke's Hospital from fracture of the skull, caused a by a fall from his horse on Thursday. He was riding in preparation for the Indian Civil Service Examination, when his horse bolted, and he was thrown off. His brother was with him at the time of the accident.'

Noarojee Pestonjee Cama, the father of the young Parsee Wrangler, received a telegram from one of his twin sons, Camaji. Nothing could be more sudden than this piece of news as the father received a letter in the previous week stating that his sons were receiving their training in riding at Woolwich. The brothers returned from Woolwich to Cambridge during the Christmas vacation. While Byramji was practising riding, he met with this fatal accident. The twin brothers received their education in Bombay at Proprietary High School and passed their matriculation examination in 1892, when they were only fourteen years old. They joined the Elphinstone College, where they had a most creditable career, passing the several intermediate examinations with conspicuous success. Byramji passed his BA Examination in 1896, but Camaji, the twin brother unfortunately became ill and was, therefore, not able to sit for the examination. He, however, made up for lost time by appearing for his BA and MA degrees at the same time, which he was allowed by the University on the recommendation of the professors, and succeeded in the double test in first class. In the MA examination, both the brothers obtained the maximum marks, and the examiners had some difficulty in determining which of them should be considered best. They ultimately declared in favour of Camaji who carried away the much prized Chancellor's Gold Medal. Byramji was appointed a Fellow of the College soon after he graduated, while Camaji occupied that position later in 1898. After becoming Masters of Arts, the twin brothers went to England in September 1898 to pursue their studies for Indian Civil Service. Camaji went to England as a Government of India Scholar, while Byramji undertook his studies at his own expenses. During the time they studied in England for the Civil Service Examination they continued to attend College at Cambridge, where they eventually competed for Mathematical Tripos and came out successful as sixth and seventh Wranglers. In September 1901, the twin brothers passed the Civil Service Examination.

On the death of Byramji Navroji Cama, Dr A W Ward, Vice Chancellor of the Cambridge University, wrote to the Master of St John's College: 'As having the honour to hold at present the office of Vice-Chancellor in this University, I venture to ask you to accept an expression of sincere sympathy with your college in the loss which it has undergone by the premature death, in circumstance of peculiar sadness of Mr Byramji Navroji Cama. The unusual ability and sustained power of application shown by him throughout a highly successful undergraduate career ending in a degree of much distinction would in any case have ensured him a regretful remembrance in this University, but we also mourn in him a fellow-subject whom a generous ambition had determined to denote this ability and power to the services of the Empire of his native land.'[49] 'I shall be grateful if you will communicate the substance of this letter, with a message of deep sympathy, to Mr Camaji Navroji Cama of your College',[50] he continued and 'request him to transmit it to his family at home'.[51]

Notwithstanding the expansion of Railways and motorable roads coupled with proliferation of motor cars, the gentle beast retained its utility, albeit dwindling, very fast. Riding test thus continued unaltered. None noticed the changing circumstance more closely than the examiners themselves. Kumara Padmanabha Sivasankara Menon headed the list of successful candidates in the examination of 1921. Padmanabha, popularly known as K P S Menon later became independent India's first Foreign Secretary, serving from 1948 to 1952. Captain Barry conducted their riding test at Woolwich. Clearing all the trainees of the test the examiner remarked 'when you go to India, I advise you to get motor cycles'.[52] Young Menon on joining his service met Chief Secretary to the Government of Madras, who told him

'If I had my way, I would prohibit every ICS officer from owning a car or a wife in the first ten years of his service'.[53] By the very first year, Menon had both. He did not regret either but, in addition, had a horse. His possession proved very useful when first time as an Indian, more so as a Hindu, he was appointed as political agent in Baluchistan. Local Zhob sardars and maliks were unprepared to accept the 'down country Hindu' and went in a deputation to the Chief Commissioner of Baluchistan protesting against his appointment. Menon's facile movement on horseback and his felicity with local vernacular Poshtu like any British sahib disarmed Zhob opposition. His teen-aged daughter with her skill in horse riding endeared him to the local community. Innumerable villages, inaccessible except on foot or on horseback dotted British India. Improvement in communication and transport was removing the problem of accessibility. Yet, there was a difference between a Collector riding to the village and the other reaching it by a car or a jeep. The old time officer reached the village by riding and talked to the villagers. He familiarised himself with their grievances and quite often spent the night under a tent in a mango grove. This established a bond between the officers and villagers, of which the best officers in British days used to be proud.

The useful company of the beast for many Civilians was not purely gentle. They could hardly overcome the fear of something unpredictably vicious about horse flesh. Gopal Das Khosla, who joined service in the year 1920, was presented a pony by his grandfather. Child Gopal Das loved cantering on it around the vast ground though he could scarcely learn to control it. One day the pony ran away with the master on its back, galloping through bushes and brambles. The pony suddenly turned towards the stable and threw the child into the depth of a thorny bush. Gopal Das was carried back home, badly bruised by the fall and pricked all over his back and legs. In after years, he had to take lessons in riding and jumping a five barred gate without reins and stirrups. Gopal Das passed a fairly stiff riding test on the back of a non-cooperative mount from the Woolwich cavalry stables to qualify for the Indian Civil Service. He subsequently owned a whaler which carried him around the countrywide on official tours. Nothing could, however, erase the memory of feeling himself flying through the air and falling into a thorny embrace. The most succinct observation was perhaps made by Jawaharlal Nehru, the first Prime Minister of independent India who himself was a good horseman. In conversation with Menon, he opined that one 'must know that it is always the first few moments which count with a horse; then the horse will decide who is to be the master — it or the rider'.[54] With his experience of journey on horseback all the way from

Srinagar to Chungking in China spread over 123 days, Menon was indeed the right person to appreciate the premier's humour. His ponies, however, miserably failed in the mountain trail. Menon shifted himself to the borrowed yak, mounting which, he felt as safe as Shiva on his sacred bull. The yak proceeded with singular unconcern, placing its feet with the deliberation with which a chess player would move his queen. His ponies followed the yak, slipping and falling and rising and slipping again. Independent India carried on the colonial legacy and riding test continued. Many people felt uneasy and pressed for discontinuing the practice. This time Jawaharlal's daughter as Prime Minister stayed the move. Indira Gandhi felt that the skill of riding did instil a feeling of self-confidence and fearlessness, the qualities essential in men holding the positions of responsibility. A man, who could control a horse, she felt, would also know how to control mob.

CRAMMERS

An article written by G T Chesney in 'The Edinburgh Review' in 1874 criticising the growing influence of crammers in the ICS drew public attention. Chesney was the founder of Royal Indian Engineering College at Cooper's Hill, Egham, Surrey and joined Indian career thereafter. The author charged that a top candidate from either Oxford or Cambridge with specialisation on a particular field, such as Mathematics, had no chance to pass the competitive examination because it favoured those with a smattering of knowledge in a multitude of subjects. The successful competitor, therefore, must resort to the crammers to acquire superficial knowledge of a variety of subjects. Once he had completed the examination, he would retain nothing in the way of substantial knowledge. The author described the method of cramming as totally out of touch with the English educational system.

In an article in *The Edinburgh Review* in 1876, Dr Bardwell, an acting physician for the Indian Civil Service posted at Bombay, stated that 'one or two of the smaller Colleges, indeed attempted to establish special courses to meet the wants of intending candidates, but the system did not take root in uncongenial soil, and to have a fair chance of success a man must leave his University or College in whatever part of the kingdom it may be and betake himself to the crammers who have made it their special function to new candidates for this particular examination'.[55] Almost all the successful candidates in the previous year, he continued, were prepared for their examinations by crammers.

A crammer was usually a former teacher or university instructor who hired himself out as a tutor to those preparing for Indian Civil Service Examinations. They usually resided in London and those wishing to prepare for the examination generally found lodging in London while studying under their direction. The time involved was usually one to two years, depending on how much preparation the student needed. The crammer was familiar with the examination, the subjects on which the candidate would be questioned, the type of questions asked, and the textbooks used. The tutoring programme was designed to aid the candidates in passing the examination.

Defending their role, Walter Wren who had been most successful in sending out selected candidates from his institute, addressed a letter to the Editor of *The Times* in April 1875: 'This charge is exactly the converse of true so far as I and the gentlemen who help me are concerned. Scores of pupils, and the printed report of the Civil Service Commissioners, can prove that I have used all the influence I possess with my pupils to make them take up the fewest subjects so as to get the highest scores in each.'[56] 'Few and good' and 'quality, not quantity', he continued 'are phrases constantly in my mouth. Pupils of ours have passed on two subjects, pupils too numerous to mention on three. We do exactly what we are said not to do. We continue what has been commended at Public Schools and Universities. Those who would be Wranglers if they went to Cambridge score highly in Mathematics. Those who would be first class classics at Oxford or Cambridge they would be lectured by First-classes in classics and Mathematics. So they are in my house. But we do what the College Lecturers and University Professors and private tutors do combined - and we charge much less for doing it. We work hard, and live by success. We have no endowment to fall back on if idle or incompetent. Our pupils, too, during Term time scorn delights and live laborious days. Do not, Sir, I pray call us 'crammers' and condemn us unheard, because we try to do well what we are paid to do'.[57]

The raging controversy on crammers was one of the objects which Lord Salisbury advised Civil Service Commissioners to enquire. Lowering the maximum age to 19 was intended to capture the best boys directly from Public Schools, eliminating the need for them to go to crammers. Influence of crammers, however, continued or rather increased. Results of first four examinations conducted under new regulation demonstrated that 'Mr Walter Wren, M A, is a successful tutor of candidates for the Indian Civil Service Examination. During the years 1867-78, he passed under the old regulations, 184 candidates out of 452 vacancies, and under the new regulation he has passed 50 out of 99'.[58] From 1892, the maximum age was increased to 23 and university men again started competing, in many cases, with the aid of coaching institutes. This trend was clearly visible from the results of the examination of 1893, summarised as 'Out of the 56 vacancies offered for competition in the Indian Civil Service Examination this year, so many as 37 fell to the lot of the private coaching establishments and the efforts to advance university men at the expense of the candidates brought up by 'coaches', have not been attended with desired result'.[59] The trend did not alter in subsequent years also as in 1895 it was reported that 25 of the 36 successful candidates have been engineered through the coach Walter Wren.

Brajendra Nath De, who did an MA from Canning College, Lucknow before proceeding to England and passed the examination of 1873, felt, 'I probably made a mistake in deciding to attend lecture in University College, as I would very likely have stood much higher in the list of selected candidates, if I had gone to Mr Wren'.[60] Many Indian students, however, availed the guidance of 'coaches' in their preparation for the competition. Edward Blunt, himself a successful candidate concurred the observation of Brajendra Nath. Questioning the scheme of allowing candidates to offer as many subjects as he chose, he stated 'The results were unfortunate. Some cut short a university career to take an intensive course of instruction from some crammers... And Even men who had taken a first class degree',[61] he continued 'often went to a crammer for a six weeks' course, wedged in between their final Schools and the ICS Examination, lest they should be handicapped in the general race of marks'.[62]

Life and work of Walter Wren merit more than passing recognition. A country lad, tall, strong and of great promise Wren entered the Christ's College, Cambridge, in the 1850s where misfortune struck him in the shape of a spiral infection. This disease, which was accompanied by the cruellest sufferings, caused him to go down and miss terms one after the other, so that it was not eight years before he took his degree. Wren did not allow the sufferings to overweigh him and trampling on his infirmities he resolved to become a coach for the various competitive examinations especially for Indian Civil Service. He carried on the work for nearly 40 years, at first, and for many years, alone and then in partnership with the Rev Edmund Gurney. During this long period, nearly half the Indian Civil Service had been furnished from Wren's house in Powis-Square and The Colonies, The Empire, The Army, were all full of his pupils. He secured with liberal payment, the service of best men that Oxford and Cambridge could produce men who besides scholastic excellence had the flair of teaching. He sent up his men for examination notoriously best prepared in those subjects that do not admit of cramming, such as languages and Mathematics. Wren's whole secret was to teach well and only to teach those lads who would work hard, and at the same time, those who refused to work, he sent them away. 'Madame' he wrote a lady who complained that his son did not go to the Church, 'my business is to fit your boy for the Indian Civil Service, not for the Kingdom of Heaven'.[63] Nurturing political ambition, Wren stood for Wallingford as a Liberal candidate. He was returned to the Parliament and sat in the House for a few days. He was then unseated, through the mistaken zeal of an agent, for bribery of which he knew nothing. His partner Taylor, late Fellow of Caius, who married his daughter, carried on the coaching after Wren passed away in 1898. In a letter to Lord Salisbury, Wren revealed the secret of his enviable success: 'Our sole fault is that by superior industry, energy and ability, we have beaten rivals less endowed with these qualities. So long as our knowledge and skill in teaching is equal to that of our graduates and we have enough influence for good over our pupils to secure more industry, more docility and less indulgence, and less extravagance, so long will our pupils beat all other competition.'[64]

William Baptiste Scoones, another coach though conducting at a much smaller scale than his illustrious contemporary, attracted his candidates with great charm of manner. A very diminutive man in appearance, Scoones was most resourceful in his methods. Absolutely bilingual in English and French, he taught for nearly 35 years at Garrick Chambers, next door to the Garrick Club, London. Less reputable for Indian Civil Service, Scoones specialised in the Home Civil Service. Scoones enjoyed a near monopoly of successful candidates for the Foreign Office, Diplomatic and Counsellor Services. Evan Maconochie who was trained at the Scoones remembered his guide for 'mastery of his business, his robust common-sense, his shrewd estimate of our capacities and his merry eye'.[65] Through long experience and innate shrewdness, Scoones was known to have acquired the ability of judging every question which was likely to be asked by the examiners. The year 1887 was the golden year for Scoones for Indian Civil Service as five of his candidates passed out. Maconochie was one of them.

The idea of conducting Civil Service classes interested others also. One of them, Dr Leitner, the Professor of Lahore Oriental College intended to return to England in 1877 to establish an 'Indian Institute' to prepare the sons of native gentlemen for Civil Service and University Examinations. 'The object of the institute',[66] he described, 'will be not only to give the highest possible training to its students, but also to preserve them in the un-tampered exercise of their religion and caste usages, whilst shielding them against the temptations which abound in London'.[67] His notice continued: 'The students will be brought into friendly relations with that class of English Society, the intercourse with which is likely to improve

WREN'S, 3, 4, and 5, Powis-square, Bayswater, W.
CANDIDATES PREPARED for all COMPETITIVE EXAMINATIONS, especially for WOOLWICH, SANDHURST, and all MILITARY EXAMINATIONS, INDIA and HOME CIVIL SERVICES, EASTERN CADETSHIPS, &c.

LIST of SUCCESSFUL CANDIDATES issued September 22, 1899.
Those marked thus (*) were prepared at Wren's.
TOTAL, 39.

	Marks.
C. Norwood, H.	4,366
W. F. Nicholson, H.I.C.	3,668
R. V. Vernon, H.	3,578
C. Clementi, H.C.	3,440
F. H. Williamson, H. ..	3,429
J. Y. Bell, H.I.	3,389
A. F. Fremantle, H.I. ..	3,091
A. Flint, H.I.C.	3,068
P. W. Monle, H.I. ..	2,980
H. L. Allanson, H.I.C. ..	2,963
*A. W. J. Talbot, H.I. ..	2,950
R. C. S. Keith, H.I. ..	2,932
J. P. Brander, H.I. ..	2,923
Galletti di Cadilhac, I. ..	2,921
J. A. Ross, H.I.C. ..	2,917
R. E. Stubbs, H.I.C. ..	2,892
J. Toplis, H.I.	2,854
W. Tahourdin, H.I.C. ..	2,852
236, H.	2,849
C. Blathwayt, H.I.C. ..	2,840
*270, H.	2,816
*J. L. Maffey, H.I.C. ..	2,750
*R. W. Davies, H.I.C. ..	2,748
*J. T. Griffith, H.I.C. ..	2,747
*H. A. Smith, H.I.C. ..	2,720
*J. C. Molony, H.I.C. ..	2,703
*D. T. Chadwick, H.I.C...	2,693
*E. H. Berthoud, H.I.C...	2,677
*F. M. Levi, H.I.C. ..	2,662
*A. Marr, H.I.C.	2,630
*W. W. Smart, H.I.C. ..	2,628
*G. E. Lambourn, H.I.C.	2,615
*C. M. Collett, H.I.C. ..	2,598
*W. S. Morrison, H.I.C. ..	2,553
V. M. Ferrers, H.I.C. ..	2,532
*R. J. Paterson, H.C. ..	2,531
*W. S. Milne, H.I.C. ..	2,512
248, H...	2,505
J. E. Hance, H.I... ..	2,477
De Montmorency, H.I.C.	2,470
*246, H...	2,469
*243, H.C.	2,468
*W. A. Doig, H.I.C.	2,463
*E. B. Howell, H.I. ..	2,458
P. P. Graves, H.I.C. ..	2,446
*H. Perrott, H.I.C. ..	2,420
C. E. D. Peters, I. ..	2,389
J. E. D. Hotson, H.I. ..	2,377
*A. J. Lainé, H.I.C. ..	2,364
J. N. Roy, H.I.C.	2,362
J. N. Pal, I...	2,360
*268, [illegible]	2,352
*C. W. Dunn, H.I.C. ..	2,335
*240, H.C.	2,327
D. J. Boyd, I.C.	2,309
*C. Henderson, H.I.C. ..	2,302
R. R. Garlick, H.I.C. ..	2,300
*R. F. L. Whitty, H.I.C. ..	2,297
*H. H. Burkitt, H.I. ..	2,285
E. R. Neave, I.	2,247
J. H. H. Bill, I.	2,214
*C. P. Browne, H. I. ..	2,204
R. N. Aiyar, H.I.C. ..	2,189
*S. Watt, H.I.C.	2,164
*235, H.C.	2,162
G. A. Thomas, I.	2,157
D. Ritchie, H.I.C... ..	2,141
E. Waterfield, H.I.C. ..	2,138
*244, H...	2,117
*W. Alder, H.I.C.	2,115
228, H...	2,114
M. C. M'Alpin, H.I.C. ..	2,109
260, H...	2,098
Balak-Ram, H.I.C. ..	2,095
*F. Robertson, H.I.C. ..	2,094
*H. A. Lomas, H.I.C. ..	2,088
*147, H.I.	2,078
B. Richardson, H.I.C ..	2,074
267, H.	2,072
B. J. Dutton, H.I.C. ..	2,062
*127, I.	2,039
E. B. Denham, H.I.C. ..	2,032
232, H.	2,026

The following stand next in order of merit :—98, I., 2,019 ; 224, I.C., 2,017 ; *83, H.I.C., 2,008 ; 223, H.I.C., 2,006 ; *160, H.I.C., 1,998.

NEXT TERM BEGINS on Saturday, September 30.

Applications for prospectuses and information should be addressed to T. M. Taylor, M.A. (Fellow of Caius College, Cambridge), 3, Powis-square, W.

CIVIL SERVICE CLASSES.

AGHOR NATH CHATTOPADHAYA, D. Sc., Hope Prizeman and Baxter Physical Science Scholar of the University of Edinburgh, and late Principal of H. H. the Nizam's College, Hyderabad, intends to open in Calcutta from January next classes for preparing youths for the examination of candidates for admission to Her Majesty's Civil Service of India, held annually in London.

Dr. Chattopadhaya is glad to be able to announce that he has secured a competent staff of Tutors (most of whom have been educated in Europe), and begs to assure parents and guardians that every effort will be made to make the classes successful.

It is also in contemplation to open an English School in connection with the classes, where Sound General Education will be imparted on the most approved scientific principles, which will combine thoroughness with ease and rapidity of progress. For further particulars, apply stating date of birth and course of studies hitherto pursued, to

AGHOR NATH CHATTOPADHAYA, D. Sc.
9, *North Road, Entally, Calcutta.*

their tone and interest in India. Sons of English gentlemen of standing will also be permitted to enter this Institute as students.'[68] Leitner was sensitive to the religious restrictions of Indians while planning, '...special arrangements are being made with an owner of one of the Canal Boat Companies to allow an arrangement of Brahmin Cooks, provided with Ganges water, to exist on board their steamers, so that the Hindu students may be able to leave India and to return to it without incurring the suspicions and penalties of his caste-fellows'.[69] The Institute, however, did never come up.

At the time when controversy on crammers was raging London, far away in India, a coaching institute was quietly opened. Dr Aghor Nath Chattopadhaya was the Principal of Nizam's College, Hyderabad and when deported from there, came to settle in Calcutta. With a competent staff of tutors, most of whom had been educated in Europe, Aghor Nath started a coaching institute for preparing youth to compete for Indian Civil Service. Aghor Nath, a Gilchrist Scholar himself, competed for Indian Civil Service and though unsuccessful secured the highest marks in Sanskrit. He then entered Edinburgh University for studying Chemistry and secured the first place in B Sc Examination, being awarded the Baxter Prize in Physical Science. Subsequently, he obtained Hope Prize also by coming first in the examination of Chemistry. Durga Mohan Das, uncle of Desbandhu Chittaranjan Das invited Bipin Chandra Pal, who afterwards became an extremist Congress leader, to take charge of his two sons, Satish Ranjan and Jyotish Ranjan whom he wanted to send to England to compete for the Indian Civil Service. Durga Mohan wanted to prepare them for it by withdrawing from their school and placing them under a whole-time tutor. Bipin Chandra, who was in Bangalore at that time returned to Calcutta in December 1882 for his new assignment. He was, however, soon relieved of this responsibility as Satish Ranjan and Jyotish Ranjan went to the new Civil Service Classes opened by Aghor Nath. Hyderabad called Aghor Nath back in March 1885 where he resumed the duties as Principal of Nizam's College. His return gave ample satisfaction to his old pupils marked by cordial reception, but the Civil Service College at Calcutta died rather prematurely. Subsequently, another attempt to conduct Civil Service class in Calcutta was made by Devendranath Das. Coming out first in the FA Examination from Presidency College, Calcutta in 1874, Devendranath secured the Gwalior Medal and a scholarship of Rs 40 a month. His father sent him to England in 1876 where he competed for Civil Service in 1878. It was his misfortune that only 13 candidates were selected that year and he ranked seventeenth. Heartbroken Devendranath joined Clare College, Cambridge, intending to study Mathematics. In the first two years, he did pretty well and carried off number of prizes. Just before the final examination, fever and swollen mouth troubled him so much that he missed first class and Wrangler-ship. Devendranath came back home for a brief stay of five months and thereafter returned to England. He started teaching Indian languages to English youths who intended to go to India. He was pioneer in this work and taught Hindustani, Persian, Bengali and Sanskrit. His competence in teaching was readily acknowledged as he joined the famous Wren's institution for training the Civil Service aspirants. Alongside he taught at Birkbeck Institution and City of London, College also. Unfortunately his health failed with repeated infection of bronchitis and doctors advised him to leave England. He returned to India in 1891 and was engaged by Ananda Mohun Bose as Professor in City College, Calcutta. Very soon Devendranath started Civil Service classes in his residence for the intending candidates. Though with labour and expertise he succeeded in starting classes but he could keep it alive for no time due to poor patronage. Subsequently, he founded Century School in Calcutta in the year 1893. With two years of painstaking effort and success achieved at the Entrance Examination, the institute was raised to the dignity of a College. Shortly thereafter plague phobia struck Calcutta cutting short his initiative to run the College. Civil Service class also was wound up rather premature.

Statutory Civil Service

Lord Lytton assumed the office of the Governor-General in April 1876, at a time when Lord Salisbury's decision to reduce the maximum age for Civil Service had caused strong resentment in India. Lytton had strong conviction that competitive examination for Civil Service should be held in England in a manner so as to retain the British monopoly of the Covenanted Service. Statute of 1870 attracted his attention and formed the core of his plan of meeting the native aspiration in official employment. This Statute empowered the authorities in India to appoint any native of India of proved merit and ability to any office, place or employment in the Civil Service of Her Majesty in India. Though the Act was passed in 1870, it did not make tangible progress before 1876. Duke of Argyll, as Secretary of State, asked the Government of India in April 1872 whether any rules and regulations had been framed for appointment of Indians as envisaged in the Act. The letter could not wake up the Government and in October 1872 the Secretary had to send a reminder. Government of India finally responded to this letter by submitting a set of rules for sanction of the Secretary of State. Detecting inconsistencies in the rule with the wide scope of the Act, the law officers advised the Secretary of State to disallow it and no further progress took place till 1876. Lytton with the intention of bringing the Act into operation to a limited extent resumed correspondence with the local Government of Bombay, Madras and Bengal. Government of Bombay fell in line with the proposal of an Indian officer, and appointed Gopal Hari Rao to a reserved judicial post. Sir Richard Temple, the Lieutenant-Governor of Bengal recommended appointment of Indians in two particular offices which were not accepted by Lord Salisbury. Strong opposition, however, came from the Government of Madras. Not only had the Government declined to make any appointment of the nature suggested by the Government of India, it even sent up representation opposing the policy underlying the Act of 1870.

Sir Ashley Eden who succeeded Temple in Bengal was equally convinced of the need for British monopoly of the Covenanted Service. He, however, propounded that some offices now reserved for the Covenanted Civilians might, without any danger to the safety of state, be taken out of the reserved list. These posts may be opened out to Un-covenanted Service, thus widening the scope of employment of the educated Indians. Eden maintained that Indians were not fit for responsible executive posts and their employment may be limited to judicial department only. Eden's note appealed to the political ideals of Lytton. Soon Lytton devised the plan of reduction in the number of admissions to the Covenanted Civil Service. The Conservative Viceroy planned establishment of a close Native Civil Service comprising the posts removed from the existing list of posts reserved for Covenanted Civilians. Lytton, dismissing the practicability of competitive system in India, decided that appointment to this Native Civil Services would be made through nomination. The new service though equal to Covenanted Service in status and position, would be paid at a lower rate.

Lytton, while sending the proposal to the Secretary of State, highlighted the advantage of the scheme on three grounds. He wrote, 'it is designed to give them (Indians) our aim and object in life which are not wanting; to render the administration less burdensome, and to impinge as little as possible, consistently with these objects, the interest and expectations of the covenanted civil service'.[70] At the same time, Lytton proposed that it would be expedient to exclude Indians from the competitive examinations for the Covenanted Civil Service.

Salisbury was happy to note that the scheme for appointment of Indians in the Native Civil Service had been prepared on the principles laid down in 1872 by Duke of Argyll. He did not, however, agree to Lytton's proposal of debarring the Indians from competitive examination. Such changes required the sanction of the Parliament, in which Salisbury saw no prospect of success. Cranbrook, who succeeded Salisbury, wrote to Lytton broadly agreeing with the proposal. He desired to give Indians 20 per cent posts in place of 18 per cent proposed by the Government of India. Cranbrook also opined that the maximum age of appointment be enhanced to 22. Some more correspondences were exchanged between the Governor-General and the Secretary of State. The issue was debated in the Governor-General Council and the circular was finally notified on 1 November 1879, announcing creation of Statutory Civil Service. The scheme permitted the Government to nominate natives to places in the Civil Service, one-sixth of the number of recruit appointed in England plus two additional posts for three years. For the year 1879, the number was assessed as eight which were distributed among different provinces. Madras, Bengal, North Western Provinces and Oudh got two places each while one place each was allotted to Bombay and Punjab. Each Government was advised to recommend three candidates not exceeding the age of 25 for each appointment. It was agreed that the age limit might be relaxed on the ground of merit and ability. Every selection was subject to the approval of the Governor-General in Council and required the selected candidates to spend at least two years of probation. The selected candidates for the first year were Nand Krisha Bose and S S Ghosal form Bengal, Kunwar Bharat Singh and Muhammed Abbas from the North Western Provinces and Oudh, and Gurdayal Singh from Punjab.

Statutory Civil Service held its position between the Covenanted Civil Service and the Un-covenanted Service. Statutory Civilians were automatically promoted by the local Government to any judicial office, but chief executive posts viz. district and divisional posts were generally kept out of their reach. From the beginning, though discharging the same responsibility, they were given inferior status and position. Their emoluments were only two-third of the Covenanted Civilians. In 1886, the authorities started questioning the utility of the system and its continuation. Pending enquiry by an expert body of Commissioners, fresh appointment to the service was suspended. Statutory Civil Service had not fulfilled its purpose, observed the Public Service Commission, headed by Aitchison. Government accepted its recommendation and further appointment to the service was finally terminated. Commission observed that in no case except in Bengal a person had been appointed Statutory Civilian on the ground of intellectual qualification alone. In Lower Provinces of Bengal, the system adopted in 1879 and for four succeeding years, only one nomination was made where family respectability ruled over other considerations. Madras Mahajana Sabha was not prepared to accept the practice of arbitrary nomination with total disregard to knowledge and efficiency. They presented a memorandum to the Government of India on the nomination of T Varada Rao to the Statutory Civil Service. Madras Government, following a resolution in January 1885, conducted selection test for appointment to the service. Fifteen candidates presented themselves for preliminary examination and nine were declared to have been qualified for admission to the final competition. Three candidates passed the final test and were recommended to the Government for appointment. The list was in alphabetic order and the Madras Mahajana Sabha contended that Varada Rao had been appointed though not being at the top of the list. The Sabha in due course received the reply from the Chief Secretary to the Government of Madras that the procedure of the local Government in the matter was entirely within the discretion left to the Governor in Council. Varada Rao was the son of T Rama Rao, a Member of the Legislative Council, Madras. Varada Rao obtained his BA degree from the Madras University in Mathematics and Natural Philosophy in 1881, followed by BL degree in the first class in 1883. Central Province toed the same line while nominating Shankar Madhav Rao Chitnavas, as Statutory Civilian. Shankar Madhav was the son of Ray Saheb Madhab Rao Gangadhar of Nagpore, one of the leading functionaries of Poona Sarvajanik Samaj.

Since 1884 Bengal Presidency followed a system of restricted competition among a limited number of candidates, and the results were submitted by the local Government for nominations. Other provinces did not follow the competitive system and rarely a candidate was selected on the basis of intellectual qualifications alone. Aitchison Commission observed that in Madras Presidency one candidate was selected for intellectual qualifications combined with social position and general qualities. Commission was aggrieved to discover that no domicile European or Eurasian had ever received a nomination or appointment under the scheme. Commission recorded that out of 48 Statutory Civilians, 27 were Hindus, 15 were Mahomedans and 2 members each from Parsee, Sikh and Burman communities. As the system could not please either the ruler or the ruled, its discontinuance caused no murmur. Henry Beveridge, a Civilian himself, in his testimonial before the Commission appropriately pointed out the deficient scheme as 'so long then as we have two sets of men working side by side and doing precisely the same work, but on different rules of pay and promotion, there will not cease to be heart-burnings and discontent, as well as needless expense to the state'.[71]

The privilege of appointment through nomination induced many wealthy and notable Indians to join the service. Rameswar Singh of Darbhanga Maharaja family was appointed by Lord Lytton to the Statutory Civil Service. He served as Assistant Magistrate of Durbhanga, Chapra and Bhagalpur. Service perhaps did not go well with his disposition and he resigned in 1885. Rameswar was appointed a Member of Bengal Legislative Council in 1888. On the death of his elder brother Lakshmeshwar Singh, he became Maharaja in 1899. Subsequently, he was elected by the non-official members of Bengal Legislative Council as their representative to Governor General's Legislative Council. Two more members of native aristocracy followed the trail. Kunwar Shiam Singh was the second son of Raja Pertab Singh of Tajpur in Bijnor District. In January 1881, Kunwar was appointed probationer in the Statutory Civil Service by North Western Province. He served as Probationary Assistant Magistrate, Bareilly and thereafter at Hamirpur. Kunwar's temperament was manifestly incompatible with the service requirement and he availed leave for 10 months from 21 March 1884. Finally, Kunwar resigned in November 1885. Nasir-ud-din Ahmad Khan Mirza Raza belonged to the Nawab family of Loharu. A Statutory Civilian of the same province, he resigned in December 1887. Moung Ba One of Burma went to England and joined Middle Temple in 1876. He temporarily suspended his studies and returned to country. Government appointed him to Statutory Civil Service where he served as Translator and Extra Assistant Commissioner. He distinguished himself in passing departmental examination with credit. Service apparently did not fulfil his aspiration. He resigned from service in April 1883 and went back to England. Resuming legal studies, he was subsequently called to the Bar in 1884.

If one Raja left the service, another was dismissed. Raja Chit Pal Singh was the Talukdar of Chitpalgarh of Pratapgarh district of North Western Province. A member of an influential family in Oudh, with a liberal education, Chit Pal served as Assistant Commissioner for nine years till 1886 when he was appointed to Statutory Civil Service without any examination. His noble birth elevated him to this position. Chit Pal served as Deputy Commissioner of Unnao, and then as Joint Magistrate of Ghazipur. In the course of Police Court enquiry into a charge of theft which he himself had brought against his Secretary, it transpired that the Raja was in habit, among other things, of having his judgments written out by his Secretary. As this came to the notice of the Government, a probe was ordered. A commission with two Civilians from North Western Province, Gilbraith and Rustomjee conducted enquiry into the charges. Commission found the charge fully proved against the Raja. Government, in the face of such a finding, could no longer retain him in service. After 17 years of service, Chit Pal was removed. His exit was, however, made to appear somewhat graceful by the Secretary of State granting Raja a compassionate allowance of twelve hundred rupees a year.

In the same year Sardar Gurdayal Singh Man, another Statutory Civilian, acting as Divisional Judge, Sialkot was also dismissed from service. Son of Sardar Bir Singh, a first cousin on the mother's side of His Highness the Raja of Jhind, Gurdayal joined Statutory Service in 1880. He completed the requisite two years of probation in 1882 and was the first native in the province to have been confirmed in the appointment as a member of the Covenanted Civil Service under the new rule. He was suspended under the order of the Lieutenant-Governor of Punjab, pending an inquiry into certain charges of bribery and corruption. Government of India appointed a Commission to hold a formal enquiry. G A Tweedie, Sessions Judge, Saharanpur and D C Johnstone, Divisional and Sessions Judge, Lahore constituted the Commission, continuing for three months from May 1898, generated a lot of public interest. Court house used to be fairly crowded during the conduct of enquiry, several leading Sikh gentlemen of Lahore, Amritsar and Ferozepur being present. *The Tribune* covered the entire proceeding of the enquiry. Gurdayal was charged of accepting bribery from appellants on number of occasions for reversing or modifying the decree of the lower courts. Commission held Gurdayal guilty of the charges and Government of India dismissed him from service on 8 August 1898. Interestingly, *The Tribune* unhesitatingly approved the decision, pledging support to every attempt to purge corruption of the public service.

Notwithstanding these unfortunate occurrences, Statutory Civil Service produced quite a few efficient Civilians also. Pundit Jwala Prasad Sankadhar was one such able Statutory Civilian. He was the first Statutory Civilian in North Western Provinces to be confirmed as District Magistrate. A total of 11 Statutory Civilians was appointed in that Province between 1879 and 1888. Pundit Jwala Prasad with 15 years' service received the honour. While congratulating Jwala Prasad on his promotion, native press did not forget to thank Sir Antony MacDonnell, Lieutenant-Governor for being the first to do justice to a deserving class of public servants. The Pundit was the most promising student of his day in Canning College at Lucknow. He became a member of the Theosophical Society of nearly 20 years' studies. His attainments, as well as family influences, introduced him to Government patronage in which he acquainted himself creditably. Pundit was a great Sanskrit scholar with broad and liberal views. He showed the courage of conviction by marrying a Bengali lady who was none else other than a granddaughter of Maharshi Debendranath Tagore. Official responsibilities could not, however, diminish his concern for the community and he followed social advancements with unfeigned interest. As Collector of Etah, Jwala Prasad accepted the invitation to preside over the 19th Social Conference. The Conference was held on 31 December 1905, at Benares at the same venue where the annual Congress met. Jwala Prasad addressed the delegates, marked by gathering of Hindu ladies in large number. Expressing their special gratification at the cordial interest taken by His Royal Highness in the welfare and progress of Indian women, the assembly offered the heartiest and most loyal welcome to the Prince and Princes of Wales to India. It acknowledged the initiative of the Government in the advance of female education. The conference devoted attention on social issues, stressing on the need for promotion of 'Temperance and Social Purity' and raising the marriageable age of boys and girls.

Kunwar Bharat Singh was another native to prove his competence in Statutory Civil Service. In 1888, Sir Auckland Colvin, Lieutenant-Governor of North Western Province appointed him to officiate as Collector and Magistrate of Bijnor. The appointment caused universal satisfaction to the native community of the province. Public meetings were held at various places to express sense of gratitude to Sir Auckland Colvin for his recognition of native merit and to congratulate Kunwar Bharat Singh on his new appointment. The sentiment was natural as Kunwar was the first native gentleman placed in independent charge of a district in the province. The unfortunate riot at Najirabad during the Muharram in 1888 afforded *The Pioneer* to denounce Kunwar. Inept handling of the incident was highlighted. Anglo-Indian newspapers happily reported that Kunwar was in-charge of the district administration at the time of occurrence of the riot. But the paper had to admit it's premature reporting as the truth soon came out that Acting Magistrate, Macpherson, was also present at the same time. *The Pioneer* changed the stance and finally lauded the conduct of Kunwar Bharat Singh during the crisis.

Punjab Government under Alfred C Lyall did not hesitate to acknowledge native ability. Sardar Gurdayal Singh was selected for District Judge of Multan in 1888. In the same year, native press reciprocated the gesture by congratulating Punjab Government in general and Lyall in particular on the appointment of Sarder Hyat Khan, CSI, as Divisional Judge of Ferozepur. This was a golden moment for the province as a native of India was appointed Divisional Judge in Punjab for the first time.

In Madras Presidency, it was Cuddalore Ramchandra Iyer who distinguished himself with competence and ability. He was to the delight of countrymen, appointed as District and Sessions Judge of Salem. Though natives had been admitted to the Bench of the High Court along with the members of English associates, district judicial administration remained a European recluse. Entrusting 'the judicial administration of the district to a native was considered to be too serious an experiment to be made without apprehension',[72] but the Governor risked that. Local paper was full of praise for Governor Lord Connemara, the Irishman 'for the excellent example he had set to the heads of other local Governments'.[73] District Collector Willock toed the example and rose above the racial bias. He acknowledged the ability of Ramachandras and sent Assistant Collector Partridge to Salem to undergo training under the native Civilian. Another competent Statutory Civilian that Madras Presidency had was Perungavur Rajagopala Chariyar MA, BL. He was appointed as Collector of Kurnool and served as Registrar of the Co-operative Credit Societies for the Presidency. Perungavur reorganised almost the entire administration of the native state of Travancore. Native State of Cochin was also benefited by his service as Diwan.

Bombay Government recognised the competence of Dayaram Gidmul, elevating him to the office of the Judicial Commissioner in Sind and Judge of the Sind Sudder Court. A descendant of Sind Zaminder family, Dayaram obtained the degrees of BA and LLB and was appointed to Statutory Service in 1884. He served as First Grade Assistant and Sessions Judge, Ahmedabad from January 1885. Subsequently, Dayaram was transferred to Shikarpur in the year 1891. Defying the traits of his lineage, Dayaram maintained simple life and was known for his frugal habits. He spent the Government pay which he received, after meeting his simple wants, towards the relief of distressed people. Subsequent to Morley Minto reform, his name was once considered for selection as Indian Member in the Executive Council of Bombay Government. Notwithstanding the strong rumour, he was finally denied the honour and the scale tilted in favour of Justice Chandravarkar.

Yet another exemplary reference was Barada Charan Mitra, MA of Statutory Civil Service of Bengal who besides his administrative ability possessed a thorough mastery of versification. Barada Charan joined Statutory Civil Service not through nomination but after being testified by a competitive examination conducted by Bengal Presidency in 1885. Engrossing official responsibility could not dispossess Barada Charan of characteristic calm which allowed him to nurture his literary pursuit in penning down his feelings. His anthology 'Abasar' (leisure) contained a poem expressing the emotion on passing of Herbart Paul's resolution in Parliament for simultaneous examination of the Indian Civil Service in England and India.

Concluding stanza of the poem which was published in 1895, a couple of years after the Parliament voted for the resolution, appropriately captured the prevailing sentiment.[74]

And when relaxed the godly spell,
With heat divine their hearts did swell,
They said, with will which none could quell,
In accents deep and low,
"By Mother's oath and Wodin's name,
We'll wipe this blot of blackest shame,
We'll wear the golden crown of fame"
The echoes faded slow.

Such a spirited soul could hardly desist himself from protesting when in 1888, Aitchison Commission recommended absorbing the Statutory Civil Service into proposed Provincial Service. He submitted a memorandum to Her Majesty's Secretary of State denouncing the downright injustice of depriving of the rights and privileges already conceded to Statutory Civilians. Barada Charan pointed out that the Statutory Service was created by Statute 33 Vic., Cap. 3 Sec 6 and the rules contained in the Statute, expressly provided that Natives of India would be employed in Her Majesty's Covenanted Civil Service. But Barada Charan's passionate letter could hardly break the insular pride of the Secretary of State. Recommendation of the Commission was accepted without any alteration.

Barada Charan and his compatriots formed an enviable company, greatly aiding to refine his literary taste. Surja Kumar Agasti and Ashutosh Gupta were ahead of Barada in the selection test for the appointment. Both Surja Kumar and Ashutosh initially joined the education department and proved their academic excellence by securing Premchand Roychand Scholarship of Calcutta University. In Statutory Service, they distinguished themselves with their ability. Equally competent was another Premchand Roychand Scholar Nanda Krishna Bose who served as Mathematics Lecturer at Patna College before joining the Statutory Service in Lower Bengal.

Bengal Presidency had the distinction of appointing two Barristers to the Statutory Service. Maulavi Ahsanouddin Ahmed was the son of Nawab Amir Ali Khan Bahadur. Educated at the Madrasa and Doveton College, Calcutta, Ahsanouddin proceeded to England in 1877 and entered Balliol College, Oxford. At the same time, he enrolled at the Inner Temple and was called to the Bar. After his return to India, Ahsanouddin was appointed to the Statutory Service in the year 1881. Sayad Nur-ul-Huda hailed from a Zaminder family of Patna. He received his education in England, and obtained the degrees of BA and LLB. As a Middle Temple Barrister, he returned to India and started acting as a Munsif in 1886. His conduct in

Subordinate Judicial Service was eminently satisfactory to the High Court. In the following year, Ahsanouddin was appointed to the Statutory Service without being required to undergo any period of probation. North Western Province also appointed a Barrister to its Statutory Service. Sayad Habibullah belonged to a landed family. His uncle Sayad Farid-ud-din was the Subordinate Judge at Agra Court. Habibullah spent four years in England, studying law at Middle Temple. Returning home as a Barrister, Habibullah started practising law at Allahabad Court. Waiving the condition of probationary period in his case, Habibullah was directly appointed to the Statutory Service.

A Cambridge graduate joined the Statutory Service of Bombay. Kumar Harbhamjee was the brother of Thakur Sahib of Morvi in Kathiawar. Having completed preliminary education at the Rajkumar College, Rajkot he proceeded to England and joined Trinity College. Kumar enrolled himself at Lincoln's Inn and was called to the Bar. Initially, he was appointed probationer in the year 1884. After a brief period of service, he was transferred to the Foreign Department of Government of India. Kumar served in Berar and subsequently became Dewan of Bharatpur state. In Central Province, he served as Deputy Commissioner of Akola and Buldana.

Kunwar Maharaj Singh was perhaps the most fortunate Statutory Civilian. Kunwar, son of Raja Sur Harnam Singh, KCIE, appeared in the open competition in 1901 in England without any success. He studied at Balliol College, Oxford and returned to India in 1904 and lost no time in getting appointed as Deputy Collector of Provincial Service of United Province. He was a scion of the royal family of Kapurthala and if the fate had not ordained otherwise, he would have ascended the *Gadi* himself. Being the Life Secretary of the Oudh Taluqdars' Association which came to be known as British Indian Association of Lucknow, he judiciously divided his time between Simla, Lahore and Lucknow. His wife, Rani Lady Harnam Singh, like himself, was a Christian, and belonged to an eminent family. Her father was a Bengalee who had been among the earliest Indian coverts to Christianity and a pioneer of English education in Punjab. Kunwar was next appointed Assistant Registrar of Co-operative Credit Societies and on the formation of the Education Secretariat, was transferred as Assistant Secretary in the Department of Education. When Sharp, the Joint Secretary proceeded on leave in 1914, Kunwar was promoted to act as Joint Secretary to the Government of India. Kunwar returned to provincial cadre in 1917 and was appointed to officiate in a listed post of Magistrate and Collector, created ad-hoc for him with the sanction of the Secretary of State. In 1919, he was confirmed in that post. The prevailing regulation thus placed him senior to three ICS officers of 1901 batch and all the officers of 1902, 1903 and 1904 batches. Ironically even the 1904 batch ICS officers had arrived in

India before 1 December 1904, the date Kunwar was appointed in PCS. Affected ICS officers submitted a memorandum demanding financial compensation. Government of India, advised by the Civil Service Commissioners, upheld the provincial decision and the Civilians' demand for compensation was regretted

Simultaneous Examination

As early as in 1860, an honest effort was made by John Bright, Henry Fawcett and Lord Stanley for implementing the pledges of Queen's proclamation. A committee was formed with members Sir J Willinley, Mangles, Arbuthnot, Macnaughten and Sir Erksire Perry. The committee favoured holding simultaneously two examinations, one in England and one in India. The report of the committee was, however, not acted upon and was not even made public until 1876.

In 1868, a deputation from East India Association met the Secretary of State, Sir Stafford Northcote. The members of the deputation were colonel Sykes, MP, R N Fowler, Captain Powlett, Captain Herby Barber, S P Law, Hodgson Pratt and Dadabhai Naoroji. Two plans were suggested, the one proposal that appointments should be assigned for competition in India, the other that scholarship should be given to enable natives to proceed to England to pursue their education. The first was manifestly the most convenient for the native themselves; but it was urged in favour of the second since it would secure a more enterprising class than the first. Henry Fawcett moved a resolution in the House of Commons urging that examinations be held simultaneously in London, Calcutta, Bombay and Madras. On the assurance of the Secretary of State of due consideration, Fawcett withdrew the resolution.

Indian National Congress from its origin in 1885 focused public attention on the issues related to Civil Service. 'Full justice will never be done to the people of this country',[75] Congress resolution at Allahabad in 1888 continued, 'until the open competitive examination for the Civil Service of India is held simultaneously in England and India',[76] It was Manomohan Ghose, who proposed the resolution after a short deliberation and the same was unanimously carried. In the following year, Congress assembled at Bombay and was addressed by Charles Bradlaugh, popularly known as 'Indian member' in the Parliament. The Congress on this occasion reiterated the 'National conviction'[77] that no real justice would be done to India so long as the examination for the recruitment of Civil Servants was held exclusively in England. This resolution was repeatedat the annual session in 1891 also.

By one of the resolutions adopted at the Bombay Congress in 1889, it was decided to send a deputation to England to place the views of the Congress and press upon the attention of the British public. The members of the deputation were A O Hume, Pherozeshah Mehta, Manomohan Ghose, W C Bonnerjee, Sharifuddin, Eardley Norton, R N Mudholkar and Surendranath Banerjea. The deputation addressed meetings in various towns of England, Wales and Scotland. Though its achievement was not immediately felt, it successfully influenced the British public opinion. It could even persuade Gladstone to lend his full weight for the introduction of the selective principle in Lord Cross' Bill pending before the House.

The question of simultaneous examination came before the Aitchison Commission also. European members of the Commission viewed it as a move organised by the Hindus to monopolise the public service. Mahomedan and other communities, the members opined, would be further marginalised. 'On a full consideration before it',[78] the Commission came to the conclusion that 'it is inexpedient to hold an examination in India for the Covenanted Civil Service simultaneously with the examination in London'.[79] The two Mahomedan members of the Commission fully supported the view of the European members who were in majority. Three of the Hindu members, however, dissociated themselves from this conclusion. But in view of other recommendations of the Commission, especially the upward revision of age, they did not press for acceptance of their view. On the same issue, British policy on Ceylon Civil Service was a good experiment. Simultaneous examination was introduced in London and Colombo as early as in 1870. Identical papers were set for both the centres and examinations were conducted. Ceylonese candidates, however, could not derive desired benefit of the scheme. Ponnanbalam Arunachalam who succeeded in the open competition in 1878 set the trend but had hardly any follower. As a policy, however, the scheme held great implication for the imperial power and the deviation was soon rectified. No sooner had it been operated for a decade, the facility was withdrawn. From 1880, the competition was held in London only. Sir James Longham, who was Governor of Ceylon at that time, justified the change by explaining to the Secretary of State that it was 'impossible for any young man without leaving the Island to shake himself so free of local ties and local feelings of caste prejudices and insular narrowness as to acquire any independence of thought'.[80] The statement sounded very familiar to the Indian nationalists who were absolutely disarmed before they could cite Ceylonese example to buttress their demand for simultaneous examination.

In the Parliamentary Election of 1892, Dadabhai Naoroji was elected from Central Finsbury Constituency. Dadabhai could successfully induce fellow member Herbert Paul to bring a motion in the House of Commons. Reminding the recommendation of the Committee of 1860 and the resolution brought by Henry Fawcett in 1868, Paul urged that simultaneous examination be held in England and India without further delay. The resolution faced strong opposition from the Under Secretary of State, George Russell and General Sir George Chesney. But Dadabhai through his presence in the House could secure the support of a sizeable number of members to propound the cause that Paul had intended through his resolution. William Wedderburn, Schwann, Caine, and other friends, with knowledge of India worked hard to obtain, by impressing upon the Parliament, a sense of its justice and finally ensuring the passage of the resolution. India was finally placed in a position to legitimately hope to have earned a much delayed justice.

The resolution, before coming into operation, had, however, other oppositions to overcome. Treasury bench strongly opposed it and the acceptance of the resolution, therefore, surprised many, none more than the Secretary of State himself. With them aligned the official elements both in the Council of Secretary of State and Indian Government. The Earl of Kimberley, the Secretary of State wrote to Viceroy Lord Lansdowne in June 1893, '...you will see in the newspaper that we were beaten in the House of Commons on a motion by Mr Paul (a very clever young member) in favour of establishing simultaneous examination of Civil Service in India and at Home. Every effort was made to prevent our supporters from voting for the motion and many abstained in consequence, otherwise we should have been much more heavily beaten as there is a strong feeling on the subject in our party. We could not, of course, expect much support from our opponents as party animosity runs high at the present time'.[81] Kimberley was surrounded by an array of old Indian officials known for their pernicious training. John Strachey emerged as the leader of the official group, proclaiming the imminent evil of increasing number of natives snatching away the Indian prize and a matching reduction in European supremacy.

Strachey on this occasion worked hard and could influence the whole Council with his ingenious idea. P S Lumsden, A Arbuthnot, John Pelie and Alfred Lyall were all unanimous in vehemently criticising the resolution, differing only in the shade and intensity. Paul's resolution was made to traverse the labyrinth of the Council, from where it could finally come out albeit losing much of the sting. Kimberley happily watched the development and was much relieved of the anxiety as he wrote while sending the resolution, 'I need scarcely add that in asking to be furnished with the opinion of your Government, it is not my desire to fetter any way their (Government of India's) discretion as to the observations they think fit to make on the resolution'.[82]

Lord Lansdowne, on receipt of the dispatch, referred the resolution to the different local governments. Three proposals were considered, the first two being a scheme of all-India examination and a separate examination for each province respectively. The third option was to supplement the result of provincial examination by suitable nomination. All the Governments except Madras opposed the resolution, citing prevailing circumstances in India and various other grounds. Government of Bombay invented a novel cause while opposing the resolution. They felt similar solicitude for the interests of the candidates from other colonies as well as from Scotland and Ireland. It was presented that if Indian candidates were favoured with examination in their own country, the colonial, Scotch and Irish candidates might complain. The unanimous objection from local governments relaxed the burden on Lord Lansdowne. Government of India, therefore, replied to the Secretary of State that competitive examination was wholly unsuited to the conditions of India. It was further stated that the demand had been sponsored by the Hindus, who through competition, expected to monopolise the public service. The Mahomedan community would be bitterly deprived. Indian Civil Service was still an attractive prize which could induce Professor Morris of the Melbourne University putting forth an appeal in 1901 for the establishment of an Imperial Service. Morris fervently desired the opening up of the Indian Civil Service to competitors from Australia by means of simultaneous examination. Indian press welcomed the idea observing that 'simultaneous examination in India must of necessity follow'.[83]

At the time when this correspondence was going on, the native papers generated lot of excitement sympathising with Indian demand. They fought a battle with Anglo-Indian papers, *The Pioneer* and *Indian Daily News*, charging them for instigating the Mahomedan sentiment to oppose the resolution. Meetings were held in muffasil towns and cities passing resolutions for simultaneous examination. A largely attended meeting held in Pachyappa's Hall, Madras with Rajah of Venkatachari as president recorded thanks for Dadabhai and Paul. All sections of resident community of Calcutta met at Town Hall in support of the resolution. Reaction of the Mahomedan community was rather fractured. The Mahomedan Union of Calcutta, in its annual meeting, expressed perfect sympathy with the proposal of simultaneous examination. However, at Bangalore (now renamed as Bengaluru) Mahomedan community held a meeting to protest against the

Dear Rajah Sahib,—I have duly received your letter of the 2nd instant, forwarding me copy of the Resolutions adopted at the public meeting in Pachaiyappa's Hall at Madras in connection with the Civil Service Simultaneous Examinations. It has given the British Committee much pleasure to learn that so successful a meeting has been held, and they desire to convey to you personally their appreciation of the services rendered by you to the Indian public by taking the chair on this important occasion.

Believe me,
Yours truly,
(Sd.) WEDDERBURN.

resolution. Demanding more extensive employment of natives in the public service and holding simultaneous examinations, Congress in its 9th annual session appointed a committee comprising W C Bonnerjee, Surendranath Banerjea, Pherozeshah Mehta, and Rao Ananda Charlu. The intention was to prepare a petition for presentation to the House of Commons, making a reference to the disappointment felt on the report of the Public Service Commission and subsequent modification in the scheme of examination.

Parliament beyond passing the resolution did not take much interest in its implementation. Sporadic interest was shown by individual members like Sir B Samuelson, Seymourkey, Paul, J Kelly and Dadabhai Naoroji. They wanted to know whether dispatch had been sent by the Secretary of State to Government of India. Chairman of the Committee on Public Petitions in reply to the question of Herbert Paul informed the House that 44 petitions, containing 20,232 signatures, had been presented in favour of holding simultaneous examinations. Petition received against the resolution was only one signed by the Chairman of a public meeting and 17 other signatories.

When the reply from Government of India was received, H H Fowler, the Secretary of State, informed the House that Government of India had observed insuperable objection to the establishment of competitive system. In April 1894, the Secretary of State confirmed that after examination in detail, Her Majesty's Government had arrived at the conclusion that there were indeed insurmountable objections to the resolutions of the House of Commons. Indian Council and the Government of India finally became successful in killing the initiative of members of 'Indian Committee'.

The argument and conclusions of the Government could not go unchallenged by the Indians. Presiding over the annual session of Indian National Congress at Poona in 1895, Surendranath quoted the results of the competitive examination held in London in 1894 and 1895. By contradicting the argument that competitive system would put Mahomedan, Sikh and other classes at disadvantage, he said, 'the only successful Indian candidate at the open competitive examination for 1895 was a *Mohamedan* gentleman; among the successful candidates for 1894 was a Sikh person and last but not the least, the candidate who heads the list of passed probationers at the Final Examination for this year is a *Mohamedan*'.[84] But all these agitations fell to the deaf year of the colonial masters. It was not till the lapse of another three decades that the first examination in India was held at Allahabad in 1922. Dadabhai, the man who toiled most for the cause, had breathed his last by that time.

Chapter IV

BRITISH YOUTHS AND THE INDIAN PRIZE

British India-Executive Domination

At the time of transfer of control of India from Company to the Crown, British territory consisted of three old Presidencies of Bengal, Bombay and Madras and a North-Western province carved out in 1836. Along with this territory, there existed Indian states, big and small, numbering upwards of 550. A new post of Secretary of State for India was created by the Government of India Act of 1858, and the Governor-General assumed the ceremonial title of Viceroy, a representative of the Crown. Secretary of State inherited generally all the powers and duties which were formerly vested in the Board of Control, the Directors and the secret committees in respect of the government resources in India. Secretary had a Council of 15 members and all orders and communications with India had to be laid before them. Besides this, Secretary transacted for Government of India all their business in England. The Governor-General in Council had to obey Secretary's order and required his sanction for introduction of any legislative measure or any change in taxation. Furthermore, Secretary was the constitutional adviser to Crown on all matters relating to India.

The Council of Governor-General had its fourth executive member through the Act of 1833. The earlier three members were servants of the Company, two of whom were Civilians, whilst the third could be a Civil or Military officer. In due course, he came to be known as Military Member. The Law Member appointed by Her Majesty was either a Barrister or a member of the faculty of Advocates in Scotland of not less than five years' standing. In 1861, a fifth member was added to the Executive Council to provide expert financial advice. At that time, the experience of mutiny was rather fresh and the Secretary of State in Council was empowered to appoint the Commander-in-Chief of Her Majesty's forces in India to be an extraordinary member of the Council. His rank and precedence at the Council, as an appropriate match of the prevailing circumstance, were fixed next to the

Governor-General. As British India progressed under the Crown, a sixth member was added in 1874 for public works, which was converted in 1904 into a Member for Commerce and Industry. Justifiably enough, public works under imperial rule was initially constituted as part of Military Board. It was a relic of the early days of British rule when the Government was fighting for existence. As a natural corollary, army infrastructure was the priority item and construction of buildings, roads or other works for which means could be found, nearly all belonged to the army. A specialised group of engineers was formed with professional ability but they were all drawn from Military. Some of them, however, won distinction in construction works of purely civil nature. On the abolition of the Military Board, Lord Dalhousie formally constituted a Public Works Department for each of the provincial governments. The department had two branches, one Civil and the other Military. The recognition of the civil element in the Public Works became essential to induct civil engineers from England. In course of time, was established The Royal Indian Civil Engineering College at Coopers' Hill, Bedfordshire, UK.

The constitution of the Executive Governments in Madras and Bombay was not altered by the Act of 1861, and they retained some signs of their former dignity and partial independence. The local Commander-in-Chief and two members of the Civil Service constituted the Council. The Governor and the members of Council were appointed by the Crown, the Governor usually being an English statesman sent from England. Council members were, however, chosen from Civilians of the Presidency. The Council was authorised, on certain matters, to correspond directly with the Secretary of State, a privilege not possessed by the Governments of other provinces. Government administration in other provinces of India varied in constitution. Bengal and North Western Provinces, and the Punjab were administered by the Lieutenant-Governors. They were chosen from officers in the service of the Crown who had served in India for at least ten years and were appointed by the Governor-General with the approval of the Crown. They were, by and large, members of the Covenanted Civil Service with rare exceptions. The Lieutenant-Governors had no Councils for executive business, but the Governor-General in Council was delegated the authority to establish in each province a Council for legislative purposes only. This power was exercised in Bengal and North-Western provinces in 1862 and 1886 respectively creating their Legislative Councils similar to those in Madras and Bombay. In these provinces, Lieutenant-Governor was at the helm of the administration in place of Governor.

By an Act of 1854, the Governor-General in Council was empowered with the consent of the Directors and Board of Control to take under his immediate management any part of the territories in possession of the Company. On the dissolution of Board, the power was transferred to the Secretary of State. Successive Governor-Generals made ample use of the clause and created Central Province in 1861 and Lower Burma in 1862 in the annexed territory. These provinces were placed under the Chief Commissioners who were delegated administrative authority. Upper Burma was annexed to Lower Burma in 1886 and the post of the Chief Commissioner was elevated to Lieutenant-Governor placing him in-charge of united Burma. Assam was under the Chief Commissioner since 1874 with brief hiatus for the period from 1905 to 1912 when it was added to Lord Curzon's dream province of Eastern Bengal. Order was changed as the scheme could not sustain the popular agitation and the new-born province met with a premature end. The scheme was modified to create the province of Bihar and Orissa with an administrative head of Lieutenant-Governor. The other administrative reform of Lord Curzon in North-Western Frontier Province, however, faced no difficulty and functioned efficiently, without any alteration, under the Chief Commissioner since 1901. Delhi, the new imperial capital was put under the Chief Commissioner in 1911. As regards the post, dignity and the amount of salary and patronage, the Chief Commissioners had little ground to grouse. In every aspect, these posts matched with their high sounding counterparts of the Lieutenant-Governors. Executive Council of the Presidencies, designed in the model of cabinet, assisted the Governors. Such Executive Council did not exist for Lieutenant-Governors and Chief Commissioners who exercised absolute authority. Chief Commissioners were usually assisted by two other Commissioners, one each for judicial and financial responsibilities.

District Administration- Executive and Judicial Responsibility

District emerged as the unit of the Company's administration in India. Initially the Collector was placed in charge of it and performed all the duties of Revenue Collector, Judge and Magistrate. Court of Directors of the Company, for the sake of simplicity and economy, preferred this arrangement of combining all the activities in a single functionary. District Officer was thus entrusted with diverse responsibilities. On the one hand, District Officer assessed the revenue and arranged its collection. On the other, he tried the civil and revenue cases and was responsible for maintaining peace in the district. This rudimentary arrangement worked for some years, more as an experiment. The inherent flaw of this arrangement did not escape the attention of Lord Cornwallis. He was not at all happy over the fact that an officer, who had been responsible for assessing the revenue, was also to hear complaints against the same assessment. Cornwallis felt that it was general human nature that the District Officer would like to justify in his judicial capacity what he might have done as a Revenue Officer. In order to remove the anomaly, a new regulation was adopted in 1793 by the Governor-General in Council. It was decided that the Collectors would no longer try revenue cases. Revenue and judicial functions were thus separated and placed in different hands. In each district, two important officers were placed, one being responsible for the collection of revenue and being known as Collector. The other was responsible for general administration and judicial duties and came to be known as Judge–Magistrate. The Collector's functions were limited to collection of revenue only while the Judge-Magistrate was entrusted with the performance of all other duties within the territory. Besides functioning as the Civil Judge, he maintained peace, supervised police work, apprehended suspects and tried them as Magistrate. The responsibilities entrusted to the Judge-Magistrate were indeed heavy for a single functionary.

This arrangement worked for over three decades. Eventually in 1829, the Governor-General in Council decided to create new administrative units each consisting of four or five districts. These units were placed under the charge of new functionaries known as Commissioners of Revenue and Circuit. They were to go out in circuit to different districts as Sessions Judges. They were also to supervise the activities of the District Officers, both Collector and Judge-Magistrates. Nonetheless, the district remained the basic unit of administration upon which this new higher unit was placed. In course of time, the Divisional Commissioners became the fifth wheel in the coach of local administration. This arrangement worked for a short while and in 1831 there was a further change in the duties of the District Officers. In that year, civil and judicial duties were separated from the other functions of the Judge-Magistrate. The civil duties of Judge-Magistrate were now taken out of his hands and made over to Civil Judge while the rest of his functions were entrusted to the Collector. At the head of a district thus operated two functionaries. One was known as the Collector who discharged all functions of the chief executive officer of the district including the collection of revenue, administration of local criminal justice and maintenance of peace in that district. The other was known as the Civil Judge who performed duties related to administration of civil justice. In addition, the administration of higher criminal justice, which was earlier entrusted to the Commissioner of Revenue circuit, was assigned to Civil Judge. The District Judge thus became both a Civil and Sessions Judge.

Weakling Legislature and Reforms in the Councils

Executives dominated the British Indian administration with all authorities concentrated and incipient legislature being too weak to counterbalance. A separate Legislative Council was for the first time created in 1853 under the Company's rule for the Supreme Government. Even in this arrangement, Executive Council remained its nucleus, whose Law Member became a full member, with the right to attend all meetings. Few legislative councillors were added to the Executive Council for the purposes of legislation. It consisted of the Chief Justice of the Supreme Court of Calcutta, one of its puisne Judge, a senior Civilian nominated by either Governor or Lieutenant-Governor, and two other civil servants. This initial experiment did not work satisfactorily, chiefly because of the constitution of the Legislative Council. The two judges were entirely independent of the government and proved unexpectedly obstructive. Other legislative councillors were for the most part men who had been passed over the post of Executive Councillors in their own provinces. Having had no hope of further promotion, their conduct was rather unrestrained. They had views of their own, and did not hesitate to express them, often causing embarrassment to the government. These Councillors utilised their knowledge of bureaucratic function and in their attempt to interfere with executive business, started calling for papers and asking questions.

The official legislature of Governor-General was abolished by the Council Act of 1861. The process of making laws and regulations was amended by empowering Governor-General to nominate six to twelve additional members. These additional members, half of whom were to be non-official, were to assist the Executive Council in formulation of law. The powers of this Council were, however, restricted to legislation and the members were not entitled to sit or vote at any meeting of the Council. They could neither ask questions nor move resolutions, nor did they have any power to deal with finance. It was to this Council that Indians were first nominated. Governor-General retained supreme authority and any law or regulation made by the Councils, for its validation, required his assent. Governor-General had the choice of withdrawing his assent from the same, or reserving the regulation for the approval of Her Majesty, who possessed the power of disallowance of such laws. Furthermore, Governor-General had the authority, in cases of urgent necessity, to make ordinances having force of law, for a period not exceeding six months.

In 1892, the central legislature was further changed both in its composition and nature of representation. Its membership was increased with nominated member numbering not less than ten but not exceeding sixteen. Number of official members was limited to six. Of the non-official members, five were to be nominated by the non-official members of the four provincial legislatures of Bengal, Madras, Bombay and the North Western Provinces and Oudh, and a fifth by Calcutta Chamber of Commerce. Thus the principle of representation was introduced, and indirectly the principle of election. The legislature had greater scope than its predecessor with 'financial statement' being explained in Council every year. A printed copy was given to each Member who had the liberty to offer any observation. Financial Member, however, retained the right of reply and the discussion was closed by the President. The question asked and the answer given to it was entered in the Proceedings of the Council.

All these changes amounted to tinkering with the legislatures. Changes more fundamental in nature came long after through the Indian Councils Act of 1909 in which were embodied the Morley-Minto reforms. It created a legislative body with some of the attributes, though elementary in nature, of a parliamentary institution. The number of members in the central legislature was increased to sixty, including eight ex-officio members. Of these, twenty seven were elected, the remainder being nominated. The non-official members of the two Presidencies of Madras and Bombay together with five provinces of Bengal, United Province, Punjab, East Bengal and Assam and Burma were to send up eleven additional members. Six members, scattered over the geographic spread, were to represent landholders. Mahomedan community formed separate electorate being allocated five members to choose. Importance of business community was acknowledged and Chamber of Commerce both at Calcutta and Bombay had one member each. The re-formed Council was now enabled to move resolutions on any item of budget, and to vote upon them. It was also allowed to move and vote upon resolutions relating to matters of general public importance. The right of interpellation was extended by allowing the member who put the original question to ask a supplementary question.

The supreme authority of Governor-General, of course, was not touched and he remained the ex-officio president of the imperial legislature. Almost on the identical line, the legislative activity in the Governments of Fort St George and Bombay advanced since 1861. The Presidencies had history of legislation as old as 1807. The same was taken away by the Charter Act of 1833. Restoring the legislative authority, the India Act of 1861 empowered the Governor to nominate not less than four but not exceeding eight additional members. These members, with non-official majority, along with the advocate general of the presidency expanded the council when it met for legislative purposes. Validation of every law, however, required assent of the Governor and the Governor-General remained the supreme authority to decide the admissibility of such laws and regulations. The same Act empowered him to establish Councils for making laws and regulations in the Bengal Presidency, which Robert Napier profitably exercised in the year 1862. Successive Governor-Generals marched ahead with other provisions of the Act. New provinces, headed by the Lieutenant-Governors, were created for the North Western Province in 1886, for Burma and the Punjab in 1897 and for the Central Provinces in 1913.

The Act of 1892 was formulated with the experience of three decades of council functioning. Purported to catch up with changing time, it attempted to modify the Constitution of the Council and its functioning. The number of nominated members was fixed at not less than eight, and not more than 20 in the case of Madras and Bombay. In Bengal and North Western Provinces, the maximum number was fixed at 20 and 15 respectively. Alongside increasing the size of legislature, it introduced a modicum of representative legislature. The Chambers of Commerce, the landlords and the universities were all given representation in the Council who mingled with the members nominated by district and municipal boards. There was no question of altering the position of the Governor or Lieutenant-Governor who retained the president-ship of the legislature.

The Indian community, impatient with the ambling pace, aspired more. Some changes, basic in nature, came through the liberal reform of 1909. It increased the size of the legislature with commensurate increment in non-official membership. In Madras, Bombay, Bengal, the United Provinces and Eastern Bengal, the maximum number was 50, whilst in Punjab and Burma it was 30. The immediate increase in the number of elected members in all the legislatures was from 39 to 135. Though the reform afforded a small majority of non-official members, it failed far short of the expectation, more so of the majority community. Constituencies were chiefly formed of municipalities and district boards who gave their votes in groups. The special constituencies, such as Chamber of Commerce and universities, continued. The grievance of the majority community was the crucial decision to extend privilege to Mahomedans. The minority community was allowed separate electorates, and empowered to send their own representatives. In effect, the functions and privileges of the provincial legislatures were the same as those of Indian legislatures.

Reforms notwithstanding, the concentration of authority in supreme government marked the administration of British India. The first time a departure was made from this tendency of centralisation was during the Viceroyalty of Lord Mayo. The provincial governments gradually became more independent with declining interference of imperial authority. This change was chiefly the outcome of the measures of financial decentralisation initiated in 1870. Successive Governor-Generals recognised the fact that the provincial governments necessarily possess far more intimate knowledge of the local requirements and conditions than any to which the distant authorities of the central government can pretend. The branches of the public business which concerned the whole of India, and which obviously could be efficiently managed by the central authority, remained outside the scope of this general trend of decentralisation. Supreme Government retained the military defence of India, and the conduct of Indian relations with foreign powers as well as with the Native States of India. Judicial administration featured in the prerogative of both the governments. Provincial Governments with the local court and authorities was entrusted with administering the law. Government of India could hardly ignore the importance being responsible by great measure for the excellence or lack of it.

Development in Judicial Administration

Company's rule in India introduced a judicial system which lacked harmony. The underlying reason was the Parliament's concern to regulate the Company officials and the Government's initiative in modernising the legal administration. The outcome was the complex system, much beyond common men's intelligence. The lack of uniformity arose on various scores, the different authorities under which the Courts originated and functioned being the chief contributor. To this contributed the diverse range of laws and regulations which formed the legal provision.

No less important was the great variety of people, their background and training of those who were appointed as judge to administer the judicial system. The Supreme Court, established by an Act of Parliament in Calcutta, in 1774, was intended to check the avarice of the Company officials. While attempting to protect natives from oppression of the Europeans, it gave the English community the benefit of their own laws. Sadar Dewani Adalat came up from the initiative of Warren Hastings, the Governor-General. It was the highest Court for civil and revenue cases and soon spread to every part of the country. The Supreme Courts thus differed from other Courts, deriving its authority from the Crown. Other courts being established by the Company, under the terms of various charters, introduced duplicate jurisdiction. The jurisdiction of the Supreme Court was strictly limited. The Calcutta Court, for instance, had jurisdiction extended over all persons living in Calcutta proper and over all British subjects and descendents of British subjects who were resident in the Bengal Presidency or in the North-Western Provinces. Indians in general, of course, had the liberty to bind themselves by written contract to accept its jurisdiction where the cost of action exceeded Rs 500. Jurisdiction of Supreme Courts of Madras and Bombay, which were established in 1801 and 1823 respectively, closely matched the provisions.

The courts thus established, purely English institutions no doubt, could not afford to discard the native laws altogether. Hindu and Mahomedan laws were followed in the areas of inheritance and succession, and also in cases of contracts where a Hindu or Mahomedan was involved. Alongside the native element resided the various provisions of pure English laws. English Common and Statute Laws as they existed in 1726 formed the core, supplemented by English Statutes which had been expressly applied to India. Added to it were all the laws and regulations made by Governor-General Council in accordance with the Charter Act of 1833. The other element was the English Civil Law for ecclesiastical and admiralty jurisdiction. The two Presidencies had more or less identical system but other parts of India had varied practices. North-Western Provinces closely resembled the Bengal system. In Sind, judicial control was exercised by the Commissioner, whilst Collectors presided over both civil and criminal administration of justice, in addition to their magisterial power. All other provinces at that time were non-regulation where judicial authority was vested in the Deputy Commissioner with the right of appeal to the Commissioner. Privy Council sitting on top actually did very little supervision. Appeals to it were possible, under certain limitations, from decisions both of the Supreme Courts and the Sadar Adalats. In reality, however, few appeals were made and it was not only in 1833 that a Judicial Committee of the Council, including members with overseas experience, was constituted as a Court of Appeal.

The Indian High Court Act of 1861 terminated this parallel jurisdiction by establishing High Courts. The diverse legal system of the British India, however, could hardly be simplified. Consisting of a Chief Justice and not more than fifteen puisne judges, of whom one-third, including the Chief Justice, was to be Barristers, these High Courts replaced both Supreme Courts and Sadar Adalats. One third of the judgeship was reserved for

Civilians and the remainder could be chosen either from within or without these classes. In 1911, another High Court Act was passed, authorising the Governor-General in Council to establish High Court in any part of India as and when need arose. The maximum number of judges was raised from fifteen to twenty with the provision of temporary additional judgeship for a period not more than two years. The judges ought to have been either Barristers of England or Ireland, or advocates of Scotland of not less than five years' standing. Pleader of an Indian High Court of not less than ten years' standing also qualified for judgeship. So also did the Indian Civilians of not less than ten years in service. High Courts came up at Calcutta, Madras and Bombay in 1862 and at Allahabad in 1866 with jurisdiction over the North-Western Provinces. The other developments that took place between 1861 and 1868 were that Punjab received a Chief Court and the Central Provinces, Oudh and Sind received Judicial Commissioners. As Burma was annexed, a Judicial Commissionership was constituted in Upper Burma in 1890 and a Chief Court was set up in 1900 in Lower Burma. North-Western Frontier Province was carved out with a Judicial Commissioner in 1901. On the creation of Bihar and Orissa in 1912, a High Court was established at Patna. In 1919, the Chief Court of Punjab was raised to the status of a High Court. In 1922, the two judicial authorities in Burma were amalgamated to form a new High Court at Rangoon (Yangon). In 1923, Oudh was given a Chief Court, and in 1935, the Central Provinces were also given a High Court.

High Court, Chief Court or the Judicial Commissioner remained the apex legal authority for both criminal and civil cases. Only in revenue matters, in case of conflict, the rulings of Board of Revenue were given precedence. Administration of criminal justice was organised in a three tiered structure. At the top of it existed the High Court, Chief Court or Judicial Commissioner, as the case may be. At the lowest level operated the magisterial staff of the district, grouped into three grades. Sessions Judge, whose jurisdiction usually coexisted with the district, functioned as the intermediary. They had the power to try all criminal cases committed to them by the Magistrates within their jurisdiction. Civil work of High Court was almost of appellate nature as three classes of Civil Courts viz. the District Judge, the Subordinate Judge and the Munsif were subordinate to it. The post of District Judge was usually combined with that of a Sessions Judge. Besides appellate role, High Courts, Chief Courts and Judicial Commissioners had administrative control over all Courts under them. These apex authorities in India had power to call for proceedings, to order the transfer of suits and to make rules of procedure. Privy Council in England functioned as for other parts of British Empire, as the highest appellate Court for India. An appeal from the decision of High Courts, both in respect of its original and appellate jurisdiction, lied with it. In civil cases, the money value of the suit ought to have been not less than Rs 10,000 and for criminal cases an appeal could only be made on a substantial question of law.

Settlement of revenue cases was the chief work of the Civil Courts in British India, manifested in the development of Board of Revenue. The Regulating Act of 1773 made all servants of the Company amenable to the jurisdiction of Supreme Court. The Board of Revenue had actually been established a year prior to it. With Councillors as its Members and the Governor, Warren Hastings, as its President, it was in general charge of land revenue matters. It set its footmark on the legal history of India with the land settlement carried out in 1773. Spectacular was its growth in the next decade, first becoming a distinct body and eventually receiving judicial authority, as the Appellate Court for revenue cases. Governor-General in Council, for a very brief period, acted as the second appellate authority. In course of time, the Commissioner of Revenue and Circuit was interposed as an appellate Court between Collector and Board. In the process of becoming the final Revenue Court of Appeal, the Board was positioned both as an administrative as well as judicial body. Besides having under its charge, settlement, land records and the land revenue, it functioned as Court of wards.

Codification of Law and Procedure

The task of engrafting the European element in the administration of an Asiatic country marked with varied and complex socio-economic condition was simplified through the process of codification. Most remarkable manifestation in this attempt to bring uniformity in the widely differing areas of British India had been the Indian Penal Code. The codification came out of long years' of deliberation and examination. It was in the first instance drafted by the Indian Law Commission appointed under the Charter Act of 1833 of which Macaulay was the President. The Commission ceased to exist in 1853 and the code did not become law till 1860. The Penal Code, supplemented by the Code of Criminal Procedure, introduced uniformity in the administration of criminal justice in British India. The success of codification of legal procedure generally spurred its expansion into practically every branch of administration in the form of manuals which contained the law on the subject as well as rules and regulation. Land acquisition, police, jails, registration, stamps and excise all were gradually brought under codification. The process had been immensely helpful in systematising the administration and to a certain extent in making it uniform for different areas. This was the necessity for a small set of superior staff organised under a carefully regulated supervision and appeal.

Post and Pay of ICS

Members of the Indian Civil Service worked in three different departments viz. Judicial, Executive and Political. The Statute of 1861 with Schedule of Judicial and Executive Offices annexed to it, defined the appointments which were reserved for the members of the Covenanted Civil Service. Except for the departments of Military, Marine and Public Works, there was hardly any office beyond the reach of ICS man. From the Viceroy's Executive Council downwards, it spread into every nook and cranny of the Government and the administration, the Judiciary as well as the Executive. Philip Woodruff summed up as, 'The Viceroy himself, perhaps the Commander-in-Chief, probably the Governors of Madras and Bombay who were increasingly often politicians for whom it was not convenient to make provision elsewhere - possibly the Finance Member of the Council, a High Court Judge or so in Presidency towns - these were the exceptions. The rest of the administration was in the hands of the cadre'.[1] Members of the Service found their way into Customs and Postal departments. Director General of Post and Telegraph and Post Master General in the provinces were appointed from the Service. Revenue collection and expenditure management were in exclusive control of ICS. On the one hand, ICS men served as Collector and Assistant Collector of Customs, thus contributing to revenue collection. On the other, their compatriots maintained watch on expenditure as Comptroller and Auditor-General of India and Accountant-General in the provinces. Even the post of North-Western Salt Commissioner and Opium Commissioner, Benares were manned by ICS people. Recruitment for Indian Police through open competition started in the year 1893. But well into 20th century, many superior posts in police department were occupied by the Covenanted Civilians. Government of India had the post of Director, Criminal Intelligence reserved for ICS. In each province, police department was headed by the Inspector General. Aitchison Commission in 1888 reported that the Inspector General of Bengal and North Western Province were Covenanted Civilians. In other provinces, however, military men occupied the posts. Chairman of Port Commissioners at Madras and Calcutta were also the Collector of Customs and these posts were reserved for Civilians. The multifarious expertise of Civilians was amply recognised as the province of Berar reserved the post of Director, Agriculture for Civilian. Similar was the case of Registrar, Cooperative Credit

Societies in Bombay. Among other posts, Civilians served as Chairman in the Municipal Corporation of Calcutta and Bombay. Stuart Hogg and Henry Harrison distinguished themselves as Chairman of Calcutta Municipal Commission simultaneously holding the post of Commissioner of Calcutta Police. When Harrison availed furlough to England in 1892, Henry Cotton succeeded him as Chairman of the Municipality and the Commissioner of Police. The Commissionership of Police, which at a later date was separated from the Municipal Commissionership, appeared to Cotton 'a comparatively easy post, as the principal burden of the duties was borne by a very efficient Deputy'.[2] Calcutta Improvement Trust, which was formed in 1911, was also headed by Covenanted Civilian.

Woodruff's expression was rather conservative as ICS men were not very uncommon among the Governors of the two Presidencies, viz. Bombay and Madras. Her Majesty for once reposed faith in a Civilian to rule the Indian Empire. A Haileybury Civilian, John Lawrence, belonging to a renowned East Indian family had the Indian experience during the upsurge of 1857. He retired from the post of Chief Commissioner of Punjab in 1858. Lawrence was sent to India in 1864 following the untimely death of Lord Elgin. The remarks of Hovell Thurlow turned out to be prophetic as he observed, that 'The first Civilian Viceroy inherited his office by an accident and whether the experience will merit repetition must depend on the measure of its success'.[3] A Civilian Viceroy was regarded with envy by many members of the 'Heaven-born Service' because they thought to have been superseded by him. The Civilians were so hopelessly distanced, that they never co-operated and directed their initiative to thwart him. Nonetheless, he retained the trust of the Crown and served India for full five years. Lawrence laboured hard against these oppositions, but the disadvantages discouraged the Empire to repeat the experiment of appointing a Civilian as Viceroy.

In judicial department, ICS members served as District and Sessions Judges, and a few, according to seniority and ability, acted as Judges and Registrar in the High Courts. Law provided that one third of the High Court judges should be Civil Servants and one third Barrister, leaving the freedom to choose the remaining from outside. The posts of Judicial Commissioners in Sind and Assam were appointed from the Service. The objective was to unite the training and legal knowledge of the Barrister with the intimate knowledge of local customs and habits possessed by the Civilians.

Executive officers served in the Secretariat of the different provincial governments or of the Government of India, but the great majority remained in the districts. Government of India had four Secretaries, one each for military, foreign, home and finance departments. The Secretaries of the provinces differed in strength, but all were numerically small. Bombay had a Chief Secretary and three other Secretaries. Madras had a Chief Secretary and two Secretaries. Bengal and North-Western Province had only one Secretary each who dealt with all the remaining departments. The Secretaries were selected exclusively from Civil Service and each had a junior Civilian as his Deputy Secretary. The burden of administrative work in the districts was borne by the district officer. He acted both as district Magistrate and Collector. The former role entailed the responsibility for maintenance of law and order with both jails and police working under him. As Collector, he was responsible for collection of land revenue and supervised the work of the different executive departments of the civil government in his district. Below the district magistrate worked the joint magistrate and deputy collector, the second in command and at the bottom Assistant Magistrate which usually was the Civilians' first assignment. In non-regulation provinces, the district officer was known as 'Deputy Commissioner' and no separate post of Judge existed; he was Magistrate, Collector and Judge in one. In between the Deputy Commissioner and the provincial government, was placed the Commissioner in charge of an area of six or seven districts being clubbed together. The position of the Collector of the district was unique where he was at once in close contact with the lowest village servant, the village accountant, on the one hand and had access to the highest authorities in the government (the Governor and members of Government) on the other. The extensive touring which the Collector and his assistants did almost as 'slaves' of a tour programme enabled them to keep in close contact with the rural people. This enabled the Collectors to act as the mouth-piece of rural people in matters affecting their welfare, just as they were representatives of the government in the eyes of village people. The district officer was often called 'backbone'[4] of the administration, but the people of the district gave him another name, 'hamara collector sahib'.[5] The origin of the title, however, remained largely un-understood. No one cared to probe whether it came up due to Indian demand or British imposition. But the title perfectly captured the relationship and was good enough honour for many Civilians.

The Foreign and Political departments were divided into two sides. The evolution of the department matched the spread of the Empire with perfect accuracy. Its creation was as old as the beginning of Indian Empire of the Company. During the premiership of Robert Clive and his successors, the relations of the East India Company with the 'native' rulers were conducted through a department called the Secret Department. The department was reorganised by Warren Hastings and renamed as 'The Political Department'. Subsequently, with the addition of the North-West Frontier, Baluchistan and the Sheikhdom of the Persian Gulf, which were administered from India, the department came to be called the Foreign and Political Department. It was constituted of ICS men, who were generally recruited between the third and fifth year of their service as well as from army officers. Viceroy himself retained the charge of the department and its administration was never delegated to any member of his Council. The foreign side dealt with external and political affairs with the Indian states. For these duties, a separate body of European officers was organised and trained of whom most were drawn from the staff corps of the Army, and some from the Civil Service. For all the larger native states, and for Asiatic countries beyond Indian limits, the political business was under the direct management of the Governor-General in Council. 'Foreign Secretary' used to transact this business and the post was regarded as the choicest post in the Indian Secretariat. The foreign department was divided into three sections – F, N and X. 'F' dealt with the North-West Frontier, Afghanistan and Nepal; 'N' attributed to the North-East; and 'X' looked after the rest of the world. Members of the Foreign Department thus served in foreign countries or near the frontier. Two of its members had the rank of His Britanic Majesty's Minister at the Courts of Kabul and Kathmandu. Others held consular posts at Kashgar, Bushire in Muscat or stationed at Aden. Kashgar held its strategic importance for keeping watch on the Russian advance and Aden perhaps possessed the importance for trade expansion. Resident of Bushier, the principal sea-port of Persia, carried through naval operations and energetic diplomacy, and ensured protection of Sultan of Mascot. Sultan was an ally and in some respects dependant of the British Government and his territory lay in the shore of the Gulf. This very necessity was the reason behind drafting military personnel in diplomatic service.

Another part, indeed the bulk of the political work was in a strict sense internal, relating to Native States inside India, which were under the British paramountcy though not under the direct administration of the Indian Government. Seven states had immediate political relations with Indian government. These states, bigger in size and greater in importance, were Hyderabad, Mysore, Baroda, Kashmir, Gwalior, Bhutan and Sikkim. The first five states had its own resident and the remaining two shared a political officer. The great bulk of smaller native states were grouped in ten agencies. Two were linked to the British administration of Baluchistan and the North-West Frontier Province respectively. The other eight agencies operated as Central India, Deccan, Eastern, Gujarat, Madras, Punjab, Rajputana and

Western India. These agencies were under an officer entitled 'Agent to the Governor-General' who in some cases was assisted by residents and political agents. An idea of the great variety of work done by the political department may be obtained from the description given by Lord Curzon at the time of his departure from India in 1905 where he said, 'The public at large hardly realises what are the political called upon to do. At one moment he may be grinding in the foreign office, at another he may be required to stiffen the administration of a backward native state, at a third he may be presiding over a jirga (assembly) of unruly tribesmen on the frontier, at a fourth he may be demarcating a boundary amid the wilds of Tibet or the sands of Seistan. There is no more varied or responsible service in the world than the political department of the government of India'. [6] Michael O' Dwyer, who served as Resident at Hyderabad, found the work as Acting-Agent to the Governor-General in Central India 'much more varied and interesting than in Hyderabad'.[7] At Hyderabad, he had only to conduct the political relation with a single great state. The political assignment in Central India, required him to 'deal with one hundred and fourteen states, several of which were, from one cause or another, temporarily under British administration and therefore under the direct control of the Agent to the Governor-General'. [8]

Scholar administrators had the opportunity of satisfying their academic inclination by heading the universities. No less than four Civilians had the honour of becoming the Vice-Chancellor of the Calcutta University. The list included W S Seton-Karr, H J Reynolds and W W Hunter known for his work of 'The Imperial Gazetteer of India'. Similar was the case with Bombay and Punjab University. Civilians Alexander Kinloch Forbes, Raymond West, James Braithwaite Penile and John Jardine occupied the chair of the Vice-Chancellor of Bombay University. Punjab University had the opportunity of growing under the tutelage of eminent civilians J B Lyall, Thomas Gordon Walker and Lewis Tupper. The situation was no different at Madras University. An array of civilians starting from Walter Elliot became the Vice-Chancellor. He was succeeded by William Ambrose Morehead, William Holloway and Lewis Charles Innes. Alexander John Arbuthnot had the distinction of occupying the post of Vice-Chancellor of both Madras and Calcutta University.

Besides the lure of great and varied responsibility of the posts, Civilians were rewarded by liberal pay and leave. A Civilian joined with a monthly salary of Rs 400, rising to Rs 700 after five years' service. At the end of ten years' service, he could expect a salary of Rs 900 and at the end of twenty-five years' of service necessary for pension, he would probably be drawing Rs 2,000. If he continued for some more years, he could confidently hope to get Rs 2,500 or 3,000 as Commissioner or Judge. A considerable number of highly paid appointments were also open to Civilians such as Lieutenant-Governor with Rs 8,000 a month. After twenty-five years' of service, the Civilian could retire any day with a pension of £ 1,000 a year. The wholesome pay did not escape the notice of the parliamentarian John Bright who taught Economics at Cambridge University. Through his speech, the Parliament came to know in 1859 that the ICS were 'more grossly overpaid than anyone except Bishops'[9] and received salaries fifty to one hundred per cent higher than those in Ceylon.

Leave rules were equally liberal entitling the Civilians a month's leave on full pay every year. He was entitled to two years' furlough after a service of eight years and thereafter a year's furlough out of every five years. Furlough allowance was £ 500 a year, and towards the end of his service £ 1,000 a year. Should this civilian fall ill, he could obtain sick leave on lower allowance. First furlough after a service of eight years was the most charming period for young Civilians. Many of them by that time were happy with Anglo-Indian wives. But those who remained bachelor till that time, furlough allowed returning home and marry. During his first year in India, Henry Beveridge, a Bengal Civilian received a letter from his sister Phemie 'admonishing young Henry not to be taken up with the soft blandishments of any of these white roses in Calcutta, but to remember the brighter ones growing up for him at home'.[10] Henry waited for eight years before availing furlough to return home and got married. His first marriage, however, turned out to be short-lived as both his wife and baby died more or less at the same time. Distraught Henry lived solitary life at Backergunge before successfully wooing Annette Akroyd. This match perhaps was made in heaven and produced long blissful period both for Henry and Annete. George Campbell, a Haileybury Civilian who later became Lieutenant-Governor of Bengal also got married while availing first furlough in home. Subsequent furloughs were no less attractive, even to the Indian members of the service. Romesh Chunder utilised the furloughs for indulging on his creativity. Others gainfully utilised this period for visiting Europe, affording their family to familiarise with western society. Few were like Bartle Frere, enamoured of the service and its sacred trust. Frere served as member of the Governor-General's Executive Council and subsequently became Governor of Bombay. He served in India for 32 years without availing a single furlough. John Beames lacked the addiction perhaps only a shade less. Beames availed only the two home leaves in his thirty five years' service.

What was equally attractive to ICS men as pay and prospect was the absence of carping and pining spirit of discontent. This was invariably observable in all other services. It was impossible for a member of the ICS to have any misgivings regarding the dignity and importance of his work. His power for good and evil was almost unlimited, and he was fully aware of this. He was a member of official aristocracy owning no social superior, bound to no men and fearing none. He was fully conscious that his advancement did not depend on the will and pleasure of any individual but was regulated by the opinions entertained of his ability and character by the service in general. He thus worked fearlessly, trusting for his reward to the sense and public spirit of his chief. Vigorous men were needed for nurturing the Empire and the Civilians fitted the role. They were stately, dignified, courageous, and unyielding in their pride, all at a time.

Impression of Evan Maconochie about the ICS career echoed in harmony as he observed 'Few Englishman would belittle the attraction of a career that offered no more than daily occupation to suit every taste, the opportunity to service to the Empire, advantages to the adventurous and the chance of highest personal distinction'.[11] Title and awards were very much coveted by the Civilians. But the one which came silently to Henry Cotton was very rare. He wrote in his memoir 'my departure became, like Lord Ripon's had been, but of course on a smaller scale, a triumphal progress'.[12] Cotton's last assignment was Chief Commissioner of Assam from where he arrived at Calcutta and found that Sealdah terminus was crowded to suffocation. His long railway journey from Calcutta to Bombay witnessed further deputations at every railway station where they halted. Cotton had only a couple of hours at his disposal at Bombay to catch the steamer, but he was 'simply swept away by the work of popular enthusiasm from men'[13] who had no personal relations with Cotton, but showed in this remarkable demonstration their sympathy with his public career. Henry Cotton, born at Madras in September 1845, was identifiable among the race coming out successful in the examination of 1865 and reached India more than two years later in October 1867. He served India till April 1902 for full thirty-five years earning far more native admiration than official recognition. He came to be described by his opponents in the Ilbert Bill controversy as a 'white babu'[14] and a slightly junior contemporary delineated his role as 'I never met such a man more enthusiastic for Indians and their cause'.[15] He perhaps loved Indians 'not wisely but too well'.[16] His great grandfather and grandfather had both in turn been Directors of the East India Company. His father maintained the link having been for thirty years in the Indian service. Two years after his retirement from service, he was called back in 1904 to preside over the twentieth Indian National Congress. Sir Henry Cotton, KCSI had thus the rare distinction of being honoured both by the Government of India and by Indian nationalists.

The service thus richly deserved all the epithets attached to it. The exclusive class was certainly full of 'sun-dried' known for their experience and imagination and constituted the 'steel frame' of the imperial administration. The official term 'covenanted service' inadequately described their role, as the service belonged to the 'heaven-born'. Lesser mortals, more so the Indians, acquired the position through real ordeal which was in no way that of ordinary 'servant'. It was the Crown or the Empire at its zenith that requisitioned their service. News of the Indian prize spread far and wide and crossed continents. Colonists from other parts of the Empire were also enticed by the unmatched prospects of the service. Towards the end of 1886, Governor of New Zealand forwarded a representation received from his ministers to the India Office requesting reservation of a small percentage of the appointments to the Indian Civil Service for the Australasian group of Colonies. The measure, it was indicated, would induce the Colonies to take a greater interest in the Indian Empire. Alternatively, it was proposed that the examination should be held simultaneously in those Colonies for the admission of local candidates. India Office forwarded the suggestions to Civil Service Commissioners who maintained characteristic aversion towards any idea that may subvert their authority. They rejected the proposal pointing out the impracticability of the scheme of simultaneous examination. Oral tests which in all the subjects formed a part, the Commission opined, could not be conducted by the same examiner for all candidates in England and Australia. The proposal for reservation of posts was also not consistent with the regulations of the service. The demand never died as Indian prize induced Professor Morris of the Melbourne University to put forth an appeal in 1901 for the establishment of an Imperial Service. Morris most fervently desired the opening up of the Indian Civil Service to competitors from Australia by means of simultaneous examination. Indian press welcomed the idea, observing that 'simultaneous examination in India must of necessity follow'.[17]

Civilians on the Bench

In all the provinces, the executive service was preferred to the judicial service and had been manned by officers of better stamp. In spite of identical and even better emoluments, in case of a High Court judge, the judicial line was regarded with contempt. There was scramble on the part of ICS officers to get out of judiciary with variety of stories going round of the convolutions to attain it. One such story went as far as reporting that the Civilian had 'threatened to cut-off his right forefinger to avoid the judiciary'.[18] As short hand was little in use at that time, writing was unavoidable in judiciary. The branches varied greatly in their function so also the expertise called for to man them meaningfully. The observation that the departments be segregated to function more efficiently, later on became a demand of Indian nationalists. An attempt was made in Bengal to allow Civilians to choose between judiciary and executive line after a service of seven years and then stick to it. But no major success could be achieved. *The Times* was not far from truth when it reported that until recently, Civilians had the option, after seven years' service, of making a declaration whether they elected the executive or the judicial line. But this was done away with and officers were transferred from the executive to the judicial line by way of punishment as well as on other grounds. Civilian Judges rising to the post of Lieutenant-Governor which the Civilians supremely coveted had been very rare. The career of Sir George Campbell and Sir Dennis Fitzpatrick, whose elevation from a Judge of the Punjab Chief Court to the Lieutenant-Governor of that province remained the only exceptions. In 1903, Rampini speaking in the Indian Legislative Council on the budget debate admitted the relative unpopularity of judicial branch. The measures to make the judicial branch more attractive by quicker promotion to High Court and creation of new grade of District Judge, Rampinin told, had apparently failed. Rampini observed that this was perhaps due to judicial work being less varied and more monotonous and laborious than executive work. John Beames attributed 'the great charm of the work of civil officers in India'[19] to 'its variety'.[20] The job always presented some new feature of interest keeping away the weary of a monotonous routine. 'So that if one goes to bed very tired at night'[21] Beames continued, 'it is not the depressing weariness of sameness or drudgery, but the healthy fatigue of keeping mind and body on the stretch with a multitude of ever-varying calls on one's attention.'[22] An executive job could provide the 'joy of feeling that one is working and ruling and making oneself useful in God's world'.[23] Lee Commission constituted in 1923, to recommend means of Indianisation of superior service zeroed on the disinclination of Civilians to opt for judicial career. The Commission unerringly observed that officers appointed to the judicial branch of the Indian Civil Service had for many years received additional pay. Since the reorganisation of 1919, it was fixed at Rs 150 a month. This advantage in pay was given in view of the fact that in the past, the general attractions of the judicial work were inferior to those on the executive side, requiring that a higher rate of pay had to be offered to induce men to enter the Judicial Branch voluntarily. Commission pointed out that the duties of officers on the executive side had become so onerous that the judicial side had by comparison become the more attractive of two. Continuation of any special inducement, the Commission opined, need not be maintained to attract officers to enter judicial line.

Distinction between the executive and judicial line of the Civil Service was far more deep rooted than what judicial allowance was hoped to allay. Civilians, most often the Indians were often crimped and forced into the service, and it remained no secret that the judicial line was shunned both by the Government and the Civilian. The best or the most favoured lot of Civilians was reserved for the Executive Service, entrusted with the onerous job of maintaining the Empire. The least competent or the least favoured, the two being usually convertible qualities, were drafted into the judicial line. Alongside this sharp division continually deteriorated the relationship between the Bar and the Civilian Judges. Equipped with the legal education and increasing membership of Barristers, the Bar attempted to expose the lack of legal knowledge of Civilian Judges. Admittedly, the Civilians recruited under prevailing regulations in a majority of cases found wanting in the specialised knowledge in legal theory or legal principles. Neither law of any description was a compulsory part of the open examination nor did the study of the same by the selected candidates for the final examination could adequately replenish the deficiency. Civilians while serving as Magistrate got the opportunity to acquire the necessary knowledge and experience of criminal law and practice. As subordinate revenue officers, they had some experience and knowledge of complicated revenue system. But in his first appointment of district judgeship, the Civilian had to labour under great disadvantages in the areas of civil laws and the practice of the court. He had perhaps never read law reports, through which law of the land in its letter and in its interpretation was expressed. Before 1892, when the successful candidates had to undergo probationary course of two years, attendance at civil, police and criminal courts formed an integral part of the training. They watched the proceedings of courts, all and sundry, trying cases civil, police and criminal and wrote reports with analysis and notes. In the final term, before setting out for Indian career, they attended the Judicial Committee of Privy Councils on appeal cases from India. Their successors were deprived of this element of practical legal training which equipped the Civilians by no small measure. As the duration of probation was curtailed by one year, the practical training was first to be sacrificed. Civilians of 20th century thus started their Indian career without adequate legal training and ill equipped to match the knowledge of law possessed by natives of India. Legal profession in India at that time had acquired the subtlety, beyond the reach of a class of dilettante. Civilian Judges on their part were accustomed on the whole to look upon the Bar as a nuisance. Their conduct characteristically lacked the sensitivity and toleration which could have alleviated the feeling of attrition. There was no love lost and administration of justice which relied heavily on the wholesome relationship between Bench and the Bar, suffered the most. But along side general corpse of Civilians, existed a miniscule of sensitive individuals. One of them, Sir James Stephen, the Law Member of the Governor-General Council in 1872, could diagnose the cure of the situation. In a well-known minute, he expressed the need for the legal training of Civilians once they adequately familiarise themselves with local condition. Government, headed by omnipotent Civilians, did not appreciate such precise diagnosis of the ailment. The division of Civil Service into two separate departments appeared to them as the immediate solution. The scheme was awkwardly uneven with prospects of official advancement clearly in favour of the executive. Naturally enough, candidates for judicial service were few, and as a rule represented the least capable in the Civil Service. The situation was manifestly the worst in Bengal where even a judgeship of the High Court was regarded as 'cul-de-sac'. It was virtually a bar to higher office under Government either in India or in England. Madras and Bombay presented relatively better opportunity for judicial line, often reserving a seat in the local Council, and even to the Council of the Governor-General.

The situation deteriorated so fast that Indian authorities could no longer afford to overlook. Correspondence began in 1903, between the Government of India and the Secretary of State. The same year Indian National Congress in its annual session recorded its firm conviction of the need for reorganisation of Indian Civil Service. Financial and administrative evils of the country, the delegates felt, could be cured only through reconstitution. On judicial administration, the resolution observed, 'it's judicial functions in the meantime being partly transferred to persons who have been trained in the profession of Law'.[24] Governor-General Lord Minto recorded his concern for political dangers of the prevailing situation warranting material improvement in the capacity, training and status of the Indian Civil Service Judges. During the last two decades of 19th century, the law which the Civilian was called upon to administer became far more complicated. The departmental proceedings on many occasions surprised the administration, exposing ignorance of Civilian Judges. Government observing that incompetent men could not retain their position in the face of a well founded criticism, acknowledged the need for drastic steps to remove the blot on the judicial administration. The reform which Government conceived was by effecting bifurcation of executive and judicial branch immediately after the open competitive examination. From that stage special training was proposed with a view entirely to the requirement of judicial officer. Correspondence continued between Government of India and Secretary of State, intermitted with deliberation at various stages. Nearly a decade lapsed before the Secretary of State in Council could frame the scheme of facilities for legal studies by officers on leave. The Home Member in September 1913, confirmed the Imperial Legislative Council of the decision of Secretary. Government of India decided the issue of leave and finally notified the regulation in October, 1914. It provided for Government advances to the Civilian to cover admission fees to an Inn and fees for reading in a Barrister's chamber. No special leave was allowed and the officer had to avail leave due to him under ordinary rules. The regulation stipulated that Civilians wishing to avail the facility ought to have passed the final examination of law before he had completed fifteen years' of service in India. As a means of encouragement, Government announced prize of £ 25 for each first class obtained in any of the four examinations comprising part one, and £ 50 for a first class in the final examination. Soundness of the arrangement, however, remained questionable as the appointment preceded the essential endowment of expertise. As the scheme recognised the need of good legal education for judicial assignment, it was imperative that full complement of qualification be made a prerequisite to their selection. Besides the officers, it was pointed out, who could do 'without this additional qualification during fifteen long years of their service',[25] would hardly be tempted towards its fag end.

Reforms in the Civil Service

Indian agitations both at home and abroad in the mid 1880's caused Kimberley, the Secretary of State for India to reconsider the age limit. In March 1883, he sought suggestions from the Government of India. Viceroy Ripon seized the opportunity. He had already received a letter from Benjamin Jowett outlining the difficulties. Contrary to the hope that the lower age would give a choice of the best students from the public school, Jowett remarked that 'the best boys from the public schools have rarely accepted for the ICS; and the present class of candidates are not at all superior, if equal in natural ability to those of the year since'.[26] Many suggestions were considered on age limit and even on simultaneous examination in India. Ripon, supported by his Law Member C P Ilbert, was strongly pitted against the opposition of other members of the Governor-General Council.

Opinions of the Council remained strong against simultaneous competition in India.

When the Ilbert Bill controversy settled down, Government of India invited the opinion from local governments on a set of specific issues formulated on the basis of general agreement reached in the Council. Reports of the local governments though varied in content, called for a radical review of the Statutory Service and contained reference to age reduction. Ripon recorded a strong minute which started with 'I entirely sympathise with the present agitation among the natives to raise the age'.[27] All papers connected with the working of statutory rules as well as the representation received from various associations were sent to the Secretary of State in September 1884. Lord Randolph Churchill, the Secretary, while accepting the opinion suggested that Dufferin who had meanwhile succeeded Ripon as Viceroy, might openly revive the debate.

Open debate on Indianisation appeared practicable as a substitute for a non-materialised parliamentary investigation of Indian affairs. At that point of time, Irish dilemma engrossed all attention and paralysed the Parliament. Agitation of less than five million people pushed the great imperial interest to background. But the popular agitation in India made it desirable both at Home and in India, to offer a palliative for disaffection. In July 1886, the Secretary of State sent a dispatch to India calling for the appointment of a Commission to devise a scheme – which might reasonably be hoped to possess the necessary element of finality and to do full justice to the claims of India to higher employment in the public service. Governor-General in Council appointed the Commission through two Resolutions dated 4 October and 4 November of the same year. It desired the Commission to enquire into the appointment of native Indians through competitive examination for the Covenanted Service. At the same time, the Commission was advised to cover the Statutory Service, its mode of appointment and function, in its entirety. European interest was, however, safeguarded by clearly indicating that 'All questions connected with the provisions on which English candidates are admitted to the Indian Civil Service Examination in England were excluded from enquiry'.[28] The object of the enquiry was declared to 'devise a scheme which may reasonably be hoped to possess the necessary elements of finality'.[29] 'To do full justice to the claims of natives of India to higher and more extensive employment in the public service',[30] the resolution continued to notify. As a final point, the investigation of the Commission was purported to be preparation for a Parliamentary enquiry into Indian affairs.

The Commission was constituted with President, fifteen members and a Secretary. Duffrin's choice to head the Commission fell on Sir Charles Aitchison, then Lieutenant-Governor of the Punjab. Aitchison's unpopularity among his own covenanted colleagues, Dufferin hoped, would lend greater credibility to the Commission's proceedings among Indian observers. Besides the President, it included a trained English lawyer of judicial experience, five members of the Covenanted Civil Service. Civilians were selected as they possessed adequately varied and extensive practical experience of the actual working of district administration which entitled them to speak with authority for their own provinces. Europeans were natural choice for representing the Covenanted Service, but surprising was the selection of a European as the lone member of Un-covenanted service. One member each represented the non-official European and the Eurasian community. Six native members selected from various provinces were a poor minority but equally poor was the selection lacking broad-based representation. Selected members did represent different parts of the country but they hardly represented the different classes and modes of thought in India, far less commanding the confidence of their fellow-countrymen. With Romesh Chunder Mitter, the High Court Judge of Calcutta and Ramaswami Mudaliyar of Madras, joined Sayed Ahmed Khan and Raja Udhai Pertab Singh of Bhingra, Oudh. Kazi Shahbudin Khan Bahadur, late Dewan of Baroda and Krishnaji Lukshman Nulkar, Poona represented the Bombay Presidency.

British officials considered the reference of the issue to the Commission as an attack on their right. Rank and file of the Covenanted Civilians constituted a committee to look after their interest. Apprehension of the Covenanted Civilians became evident in the preliminary stages of organising the Commission. A P Macdonnell, the Home Secretary, emerged as self appointed guardian of the Covenanted Service. With the support of his colleagues both in the Secretariat and Governor-General Council, Macdonnell started his campaign through suggesting measures to constrict the scope of the Commission's enquiry. His desire to secure seat in the Commission though failed, C H T Crosthwaite, the member in the Commission, had practically identical opinion. The only concession considered feasible by them was a rise in age limit for the competition in London, from 19 to 22 or 23. This change, European Civilians thought, would mollify Indian opinion without seriously endangering the British monopoly of the covenanted posts. European members of the Commission favoured a drawn out session so that a new President would actually finish in place of Aitchison. It was widely known that Aitchison had planned to take leave in Europe between spring and summer in 1887. Aitchison reacted smart, expressing his desire to resign in case a summer adjournment was disallowed. Dufferin, apprehending Indian reprisals, was not prepared to accept the resignation. Governor-General hastened to inform Aitchison that summer adjournment would be suitable to allow a careful analysis of the massive testimony. Commission carried out an extensive work, visiting different parts of the country and calling witnesses for interview. Remarks were called from different branches of administration. The report was submitted in 1887, endorsing the soundness of the arrangement of competitive examination. The examination held in England for appointment to the Covenanted Service was presented as indispensable. At the same time, simultaneous examination in India and England was felt to be inexpedient. Commission, however, supported the popular demand of upward revision of age of native candidates. The minimum and maximum age for the open competitive examination was raised to 19 and 23 years respectively. Commission found no ground for admitting chief vernacular languages of India and the Persian language to the subjects of the open competitive examination in England. But these subjects, it felt, could be included for the probationary course of the successful candidates. The Commission wanted to transform the Covenanted Civil Service to a *corps d'elite* by limiting its numbers to what was absolutely necessary to fill the chief administrative appointments of the Government. This was to be supplemented by smaller number of appointments to ensure a complete course of training for junior Civilians. The posts thus released were transferred to Provincial Civil Service which it proposed to create. Furthermore, the Commission desired to replace the term 'Covenanted Civil Service of India' by the title 'Imperial Civil Service of India'. Its members were bound to serve where-so-ever and in whatsoever capacity the Government may deem fit. Commission observed that the statutory system had failed to fulfil the expectations anticipated from it and recommended for its abolition. The posts reserved for the statutory service were merged with the posts transferred to Provincial Civil Service and were recruited separately in each province.

The recommendation of the Commission to raise the age was accepted by the Government and the first examination under new regulations was conducted in 1892. Statutory service was wound up and Civil Service was partitioned into an All India Service and the Provincial Civil Service. Kimberley did not agree to the term 'Imperial Civil Service' and introduced the term 'Indian Civil Service'. The reforms, however, did not fulfil the aspiration of Indians. In its annual session in 1892, Indian National Congress recorded that 'full justice will never be done to the people of this country, until the open Competitive Examination for the Civil Service of India is held simultaneously in England and in India'.[31] Another two decades passed without any major change being initiated other than increasing the upper age limit to 24 years and restricting the number of subjects to be chosen by the candidates so as not to exceed a total of 6,000. The open competition remained a virtual monopoly of the leading universities of Great Britain. In March 1911, Subba Rao, an Indian representative of the Presidency of Madras on the Governor-General's Council, moved for the appointment of a Commission. Consideration of 'the claims of the Indians to higher and more extensive employment in the public services connected with the civil administration of the country'[32] had become long overdue, the member observed. Notwithstanding the repeated declarations made by the Imperial Government of its intention to admit Indians freely to higher offices in the public administration, the progress was affected by considerable disabilities, mainly imposed by artificial arrangements. The resolution gathered momentum and in 1912 the Under Secretary of State for India announced the appointment of Royal Commission. 'The problem before us when we have educated Indians',[33] House of Commons was informed, 'is to give them the fullest of opportunity in the government of their own country to exercise the advantages which they have acquired by training and by education'.[34] But in reality, the scope of enquiry expanded to include issues such as methods of recruitment, the systems of training and probation. Along with this was added, much to the delight of European Civilians, the condition of service, salary, leave and pension. Existing limitations in the employment of non-Europeans and the discord arising out of division of services into Imperial and Provincial were subjugated to the predominantly European and evidently secondary issues.

Notification, constituting Her Majesty's Commission was issued on 31 August 1912. John Poynder, 1st Baron of Islington, was the Chairman of the Commission formed under the Liberal Government. With eleven members, it was smaller than the earlier Commission formed by Lord Dufferin in size but varied in representation. Seven members were Europeans, two of them viz. Murray Hammick and George Sly represented the Civil Service. Ramsay Macdonald, the Labour Party chief, long before becoming Prime Minister of England, was inducted presumably for checking the 'sun-baked' Civilians from feathering their own nest. The other members were Lord Ronaldsay, a Conservative politician with experience of India and Valentine Chirol, representing British media, with knowledge of eastern affairs. Theodore Morrison was possibly chosen for his Aligarh College connection and Laurence Fisher who served as Civil Service Commissioner for his expertise in training and education of Civilians in England. Indian representation on the Commission included the public men Gopal Krishna Gokhale and Mahadev Bhaskar Chaubal. Other members were Abdur Rahim, Judge of Madras High Court and Walter Culley Madge, a member of Eurasian community. The list of members appeared very comprehensive, indeed, but certainly was not a very harmonious composition. Strange was the response of Government of India as the Home Secretary promptly declared from his place in the Imperial Legislative Council that a Royal Commission was neither necessary nor would be useful.

Coming in the wake of Morley-Minto reform, the Commission was generally welcomed in India. Dissension and discord notwithstanding, it drew up a scheme of proceeding far more extensive than its predecessor. Communication was initiated with different branches of Indian administration and witnesses were examined both in England and India. Academicians connected with leading English universities and public schools attended the Commission and deposed their views. It was insinuated by numerous European witnesses, both official and non-official, that Indian Civilians generally lacked force of character, organising power and readiness of resource, when confronted with an unforeseen emergency. Indian National Congress in its annual session in 1912, at Bankipore, recorded its indignant protest and emphatic repudiation of these utterly unfounded charges. On the other front, it fell on Jnanendra Nath Gupta, a rising member of the Civil Service, to take up the cudgels on behalf of his much-maligned brother officers. Appearing before the Commission, he pointed out that the ability of Indian Civilians had not yet been tested as very few of them had actually been given charge of important districts. Furthermore, they were given such districts the charge of which was ordinarily given to members of the Provincial Civil Service. Indian Civilians, Jnanendra Nath felt, were treated more like Statutory Civilians than as members of the Covenanted Civil Service. He viewed that comparative worth of European and Indian Civilians could appropriately be assessed by minutely examining the records of such districts which had been served by members of both classes. The evaluation, however, should not be limited to official documents only but should extend to check the useful schemes such as schools, dispensaries, village roads, excavation of new tanks that had been undertaken. The unassailable attitude of Jnanendra Nath was universally hailed by Indian press who prided with his ability, independence and courage. The debate continued and eventually a far greater war broke out. The Commission did not stop work and struggled through the uncertain days. Before it could complete the report, Gokhale breathed his last on 19 February 1915.

The Commission deplored the loss of its member who though ill for some months, did not hesitate to take a prominent part in the proceedings. Perhaps, the only class of people who were left out for examination by the Commission was the Civilians in retirement. Henry Thoby Princep, a Haileybury Civilian, retired from service in 1904 but lost neither passion nor zeal. Princep the last Haileyburian to retire from Indian service, intended and did actually volunteer to give evidence before the Commission which, however, was not granted. Princep served India for nearly half a century and acquired thorough and practical experience in all the three branches of the administration viz. Executive, Revenue and Judicial. He served as Judge at Calcutta High Court and was a member in the Governor-General's Legislative Council. Princep was one of the few Civilian Judges who commanded unbounded confidence not only of the legal profession, but also of the litigating public. The Commission, it was believed, did not avail the opportunity of sharing such invaluable experience. Dejected Princep penned his opinion through the columns of the periodical *Nineteenth Century*.

Without conceding to the demand of simultaneous examination in India and England, Commission reserved nine direct appointments to be made annually in India from amongst the natives of India. Two of these recruits would be nominated by the Secretary of State with the advice of the Government of India from amongst the graduates of the various universities. Remaining candidates would be selected on the results of a competitive examination conducted in India by the Civil Service Commissioners. The two examinations conducted in England and India would remain distinct. Indian educational curricula would form the basis of the examination, and limited to university graduates within the age limit of 20 and 22 years. In order to maintain the provincial representation, only a specified number of candidates from each university area would be nominated to appear in the examination. The selected candidates would go through the same three years' probationary course along with the candidates selected at the examination in London.

Commission was, however, retrogressive in its recommendation to reduce the age limit which could practically shut out Indian candidates. Minimum and maximum ages were prescribed as 17 and 19 years respectively with three years' of probation for selected candidates. Candidates wishing to appear in London examination ought to furnish a certificate of attending the course of a recognised secondary school for a period of three years up to a time within six months of the examination. In case, he left school prior to this and had gone to a university, the candidate must have pursued regular course at a university extending over an academic year. The curriculum of the examination was proposed for thorough revision. The absolute free choice of subjects was to be replaced by a scheme with both compulsory and elective elements. English would remain mandatory, so also the oral examination. The candidate would have option to choose a group of subjects from three alternatives. Subjects were grouped in three distinct categories of which one would be chosen by each candidate. Classics, Modern Languages and Mathematical and Natural Science formed the groups to choose from. Classics contained Latin and Greek while Modern Languages had English history and literature, French, German, Spanish and Italian. Mathematics, both pure and applied, Physics and Chemistry formed the third option. Candidate was also required to offer another subject besides the alternative opted for.

Objection to the majority recommendations chiefly came from Abdur Rahim, the Judge of Madras High Court. He viewed that allegation of Indians wanting in initiative, driving power, resource, and the faculty of control, depended much on a priori assumptions. These ought not to have affected deliberations as Indians had rarely been tested in high executive posts. Absolutely fearless and forthright, he dwelt on the need for simultaneous examination in India and England. These would be conducted on the same papers, by the same Civil Service Commissioners, the results being embodied in common list. Appointment through nomination appeared absolutely invidious to Rahim as he advocated the need on recruitment through competitive examination in India. He ruled out the proposal of lowering of age to 17 and 19 years as much as the plan of extending the probation to three years. He prescribed the age limit of 21 years and 23 years with two years' training in England for the selected candidates. On the syllabus of the open competitive examination, Rahim insisted on inclusion of Persian as a modern language and Sanskrit and Arabic being marked on the same scale as Greek and Latin. Chaubal was with Rahim in objecting the reduction in the age limit and viewed that Sanskrit and Arabic should be included in the classics group. Civilians Hammick and Sly dissented on the appointment of natives of India in the province of Burma and proposed giving Lieutenant-Governor the power to recruit Burmans to those positions. They also wanted to safeguard European exclusivity keeping superior posts of foreign department outside the scheme of proportionate appointment of Indians.

War continued and the report, though presented in 1915, was not published till 1917. Its recommendations were not carried out till 1920. Government did neither accept the suggestion of lowering the age nor did it agree to the revision of probation to three years. The scheme of direct recruitment in India, operating in parallel with competitive examination in England, appeared to be a complicated proposition. Far simpler was simultaneous examination in England and India, which though opposed by the Commission, was introduced in 1922 as sequel to Montague Chelmsford reform. Major changes were made in the curriculum of the examination reducing the total marks to 1800 and bringing the syllabus more or less in line with that of the great English universities. Viva voce examination, intending to test a candidate's 'alertness, intelligence and general intellectual outlook',[35] carried 300 marks — an important addition in 1921. On the financial front, Government was bountiful to the European demand and granted the service an important concession by taking on itself the full pensioners charge. The Civilian was relieved of his contribution of four per cent of his pay to the pension fund. At the same, the Government instituted an ICS provident fund into which each member paid not less than four per cent, not more than twelve and half per cent of his pay. Government of India paid interest on the accumulation of fund, the sum at a member's credit being payable to him on his retirement or to his heir at death.

Universities and Open Competition

Indian Civil Service was opened to competitive examination, chiefly for attracting university men who would be chosen for competence and ability. Besides intellectual ability, they ought to have possessed moral integrity. Benjamin Jowett, later Master of Balliol College, Oxford, who served on Macaulay's Commission, was obsessed with filling Indian appointment with university men. 'I cannot conceive',[36] he wrote, 'a greater boon which could be conferred on the university than a share in the Indian appointments'.[37] With this scheme, he desired to provide the college tutor 'an answer to the dreary question'[38] which very often came from the students 'what line of life shall I choose, with no calling to take orders and no taste for the Bar, and no connection who are able to put me forward in life?'[39] Jowett could justifiably rejoice the success of his scheme as the initial years of competitive examination successfully attracted university men. During the initial years, 70 per cent of the successful candidates were graduates from Oxford and Cambridge. Of these, 101 had been educated at Oxford, 80 at Cambridge, 37 at the University College of London. Trinity College, Dublin by providing 76 successful candidates was ahead of Edinburgh University who provided only 27. Irishmen, rare among Haileybury Civilians, secured the Indian prizes by no small measure. The Irish link was particularly marked as Queen's College, Belfast accounted for David Belford, selected in 1862 and Queen's College, Galway sent Antony Macdonnell selected in 1865. Irish ascendancy did not please Wood and must have perturbed Scotsman J Wilson who topped the open competition in 1873. He started writing a chronicle in *Edinburgh Review* glamorising the service, presumably with an intention to attract his countrymen. Appropriately meaningful was his preface as he remarked, 'I may thus induce more young Scotsmen to compete, and so help to secure more of the life prizes for Scotland, and to obtain a still better class of men for India, as, in that case, I shall have done some good both to my native and adopted country'.[40] The attraction of ICS among university men wore off significantly after the first decade. By the middle of 1860's, men other than university graduates began to appear in increasing numbers and by 1878, the majority were from non-university. Rivett-Carnac, a Haileybury Civilian explained, 'By degrees, as the first surprise of the change wore off, the position was readjusted by the service being recruited largely from the old class that had supplied Haileybury, by sons and relations of those who were of an Indian Service'.[41] Number of competitors, however, rose sharply from the mid 1860s. In the year 1869, 325 candidates sat for 50 appointments and the following year saw 332 candidates vying for 40 positions. An examination fee of £ 5, introduced in 1871, was thought to be the reason of weeding out the non-serious candidates and number of competitors thereafter crossed 200 only on few occasions.

Declining interest of university men for Indian career put the existing system into question. Universities were dismayed, so was the British public opinion, observing in this trend a major departure from Macaulay's plan. Tales of 'an ever increasing proportion of discontented men'[42] started reaching home. Promotional stagnation was the source of this growing resentment. While opening up the Civil Service to competition, Government notified through resolution in 1856 that half the administrators of non-regulation provinces should be appointed from covenanted Civil Service. The provision, however, was not complied and in 1870, the proportion of Covenanted Civil Service in three non-regulation provinces of Oudh, Central Province and Punjab were 27, 30 and 42 per cent respectively. The immediate effect of dominance of military personnel in the administration of the provinces created bottlenecks in promotion for the covenanted Civilians. In Berar, there was only one covenanted Civilian. The Civilians of North West suffered the most. The disparity in position was so heavy that the Civilians who went to Madras in 1858 had in 1872, on an average, an income twice as much as that of his contemporary who, obtaining higher marks in the examination, selected the North West Provinces. Situation deteriorated very fast in the province as the Civilian who in 1862, completing ten years' service, drew an average income of £ 1,200, while the man who in 1872 was, of ten years' standing received £ 660. News of the promotional stagnation did reach England and might have contributed in lowering the attraction of ICS among university graduates. John Beames passed out from Haileybury and arrived in India in 1857. He served in Punjab for four years before being transferred to Bengal with an unhappy experience of working under 'soldier civilian'.[43] He recorded the prevailing feeling 'We junior civilians resented the presence of these men, because they stopped our promotion'.[44]These military men in civil employment were known as 'Cutchery Captains'[45] who oftentimes were harsh and stuck up. Beames was critical of their overbearing attitude and tendency to introduce 'military ideas of subordination instead of the genial brotherly relations which subsisted between members of our own service'.[46] Such attitude never allowed perfect harmony to develop among Civilians ultimately affecting *esprit de corps*, the binding force in the service to support each other. The Haileybury Civilian Beames stored his resentment to record in his memoir but the successful university men promptly ventilated their grievances. A letter from Oxford graduates who joined Bengal Civil Service to the Vice-Chancellor of the University demonstrated the resentment quoting as 'We feel it to be our duty to ask your, as resident head of the University, to take measures that full and accurate information as to the state of the Indian Civil Service is laid before intending candidates, in order that none may be induced to compete by false expectations. In a country like India, divided into many different provinces under different Governments, such information is by no means easy to obtain. We inform that such information has not, at any date till recently, been laid before Her Majesty's home Government, to whose wishes we understand that gradual depreciation in the value of the appointments held by the Civil Service which has taken place of late years in entirely opposed, and it is clear that the Civil Service Commissioners have not been in possession of such information. The expectations held out by these officers – expectations on the faith of which we and many others were led to enter Her Majesty's Indian Civil Service, have not been, and seem less likely to be realised.'[47]

Many letters appeared in *The Times* starting from 1873, accusing the Government that 'the best of our youth are sliced off, stimulated, sharpened and then left to rot and ferment'.[48] It was alleged 'in order to attract flower of our youth to the service of India, officials tables were published, showing the rates of pay to be expected after specified period of service. The arrangements were based upon a pledge which had been given by Lord Dalhousie, that the appointments in the Punjab and Oudh should be filled in equal proportion by civilians and military men'.[49] But the non-regulation provinces still belonged to the old domain of patronage with ten out of eleven Deputy Commissioners as military men. This controversy along with other reasons prompted Salisbury to initiate an enquiry in 1874 which caused further reforms in the process of selection and training of candidates.

Reduction of the maximum age to 19 was intended to attract the best boys from English public schools before they were lured by other opportunities and send them to India after two years of refinement at the universities. Residence at university was mandatory for the successful candidates to avail the allowance from the government. Both Oxford and Cambridge created separate facilities. The upper age limit was raised to 23 in 1892 reviving the hope of attracting university graduates. Seventeen Oxford and six Cambridge men were successful in the first examination under this scheme. To 'Fathers and Mothers of English son'[50] urged a retired Indian Civilian to encourage their wards 'to enter the Indian Civil Service'.[51] For the first three years of new regulations 1892-94, when examination was conducted with maximum age of 23, Oxford alone contributed 73 successful candidates and Cambridge 28. No non-university man succeeded in these three years. But paucity of candidates was rather stark. Only 274 candidates sat for 140 appointments. In 1895, the class-I examination for Home Civil Service was combined with the examination of the Indian Civil Service, a move viewed as a measure to increase the attraction. The following year, the examination for recruitment of colonial officials for Eastern Cadets was also merged. With this scheme, the number of candidates competing for the appointments did rise to an average level of four candidates for each appointment, but it never recovered the high level of 1860's. Home Civil Service remained the preference of the successful candidates and barely two or three successful candidates who stood in the first ten in order of merit opted for Indian Service. The trend belied Lord Dalhousie's epigram that 'a member of the Civil Service in England is a clerk'.[52] Home career remained more attractive than becoming a member of the Indian Civil Service whose prospect 'may be a pre-consul'.[53]

During the last decade of 19th century, the examination was marked with increasing severity with every passing year. In the year 1898, it was observed that eight candidates had secured more than 3,000 marks, contrasted with barely a candidate with the same distinction five years back. Though the standard of examination paper had not fallen off, 54 candidates crossed 2,000 marks. This trend continued till the Great War when the two universities competed with each other, thus monopolising the Indian prizes. Oxford obtained 52 per cent of the places between 1892 and 1894, compared with 20 per cent obtained by Cambridge whose tutors complained bitterly that the system of marking unduly favoured Oxford. Cambridge no doubt trailed behind its rival, but on odd occasions triumphed remarkably. The year 1907 presented one such case when Cambridge graduates monopolised the top position securing first, second, fifth and seventh places. The three Indians selected that year were all Cambridge boys. Oxford students enjoyed the benefit of the examination scheme as one who read a four-year course could compete for a far higher number of marks than a student of Cambridge pursuing three years' Tripos.

The pattern might have continued but for the war which upset the recruitment to the Civil Service. The competitive examination was held regularly, but the number of appointments greatly declined. From 1915 to 1918, there were only 29 admissions, and in the first three years after the War, a shortage of 206 had to be made up by special measures. In 1915, an Act was passed which allowed ex-servicemen to be appointed by selection subject to a qualifying educational test. They were also allowed an age adjustment on account of their military service. After the reform scheme of 1919 was introduced, the service, to a large degree, lost its popularity among the British youth. By the time specialist departments had usurped the district officers' functions, breaking up the union of powers which made the head of the district such a force in the land. The proliferation of set procedures curtailed the local officers' discretion and sucked decision taking into the provincial secretariat. Constitutional reforms, elected legislatures and Indian ministers delivered the final blow by subordinating British Civilians to Indian Ministers.

In spite of the provisions which were inserted in the Montague-Chelmsford Act to safeguard the Civilians, it was apprehended that political changes might cut short their career, and prevent from earning full pension. British politicians, the Civilians apprehended, were more interested in placating Indian nationalists than maintaining the morale of the service. The provisions contained in the Montague-Chelmsford Act to safeguard the Civilians could hardly allay their feeling of uncertainty about the career. Shortly afterwards some senior Civilians started claiming that the famous covenant between the Secretary of State and the Civilians had been breached by the introduction of diarchy. Accordingly, the right to retire prematurely on a pension proportionate to length of service was claimed and was accepted. Under the provisions, about 350 senior British officials retired prematurely in the 1920's.

Careers of Bar, Medicine, the Church and literature in the country were emerging very fast, wooing the best of university men over those of the splendid prizes offered in a distant and unhealthy country. Round about the same time the members of 'Royal Commission on Service' were trying to figure out the underlying cause of disinclination among the top of successful candidates in choosing ICS over Home Civil Service. The probable reason that came out from the disposition of witnesses ranged from deteriorating impression of British public about ICS men to an Egyptian connection. The grumbling, the complaints about high-handed attitude of ICS men in India all swelled up against their reputation. As India passed fifty years under the Empire, ICS men by increasing number drifted from Plato's paternalist role. Sacred imperial trust became extraordinarily platitude, subordinating itself to British commercial interests. Growing nationalist feelings among Indians met with harsh official reaction often verging on brutality. How much of it the Indian authority countenanced was unclear, but British public was made acutely aware of growing resentment. A number of Indian representations had visited England drawing attention to the Indian affair. The harsh news reports, covering questions asked in the Parliament and the discussions exposed the performance of ICS men, miserably de-glorifying the service. Other reasons also contributed in varying degrees to the declining interest of British youth in Indian career. Headmaster of Fetles College, Edinburgh disclosed a plausible explanation of British youth joining services in African colonies. 'A very large number of boys at Fetles have been diverted to Egypt',[54] he deposed before the Commission, thus establishing, a link between the College and Egypt. The more plausible argument appeared to be the parental refusal to send out their sons to India. It was again the old Anglo-Indian families who set their heart in India that sustained the Indian administration.

The trend judged in the backdrop of prevailing British attitude was not extraordinarily uncommon. Indian Service viewed as Asiatic exile, fraught with risk of disease and stifling heat, had discouraged people to decline even the offer of Governor-General. When after the election of 1880 Gladstone returned to the office, he urged Kimberley to accept the post of Governor-General, believing it an unprecedented opportunity to erase the blot of the Lytton regime. Kimberley, however, declined where upon the Prime Minister sought to persuade Goschen, and only on the refusal of the latter, the post was offered to Ripon. On another occasion, Gladstone Government offered the post to Henry Norman, a soldier with experience of India. Henry declined and Lansdown was selected for the post of Governor-General. Elgin too at first declined, and was only persuaded with great difficulty by Roseberry to take up the Indian assignment.

Professional classes provided the maximum number of candidates followed by commercial classes and landowners with hardly any representation from working classes. Civil servants in those days were trained to idealise the role of Plato's 'guardian', doing what in their vision is good. N B Bonarjee in his autobiography, *Under Two Masters*, published in 1970, wrote on this. 'The analogy is an apt one inasmuch as the education given in the English Public School at the beginning of the century approximated in many respect to that recommended by Plato. It was not tailored specially for Plato's political purposes and it was not formulated precisely in Platonic terms; but certainly up to the end of first world war, the English professional, upper-middle classes were trained almost unconsciously, for their imperial duties under a system which stressed the humanities while simultaneously laying equal importance on physical fitness, on the development of the corporate spirit and on the inculcation of a high sense of duty and responsibility.'[55] Before the World War I, the public schools virtually monopolised the ICS. A limited number of names Marlborough, Winchester, Harrow and St Paul's constantly recur. A few grammar school boys slipped through the nets but they tended to be Scots or Irish. By the 1930s two-fifths of the British Civilians reaching India came from day schools. The last recruit from Eton admitted the choice of career was considered eccentric, India having fallen out of the school tradition.

Attraction to the Indian Youth

As for Indians, the service was, however, the most coveted career. What stood on the way was the religious restriction against sea travel, the heavy expenditure, stay in alien land with adverse weather and competing with the 'unconquerable' British youth. The religious restriction, however, started subsiding with spread of western education. Satyendranath, the first native Civilian appearing before the Aitchison Commission, denied of facing any problem on his return. Sardar Bahadur Mahomed Hyat Khan of Statutory Civil Service told the same commission that three Mahomedans and eleven Hindus had gone from Punjab to England during the last six years. The Hindus belonged to various classes and on their return had all been taken back to their caste and honourably treated except in one case, where the man married an Englishwoman. When the three Bengali Civilians returned home in 1871, they were readmitted into their homes without undergoing any expiatory ceremony. *Indian Mirror* reported it as 'strange, but not unaccountable, for natural affection may prove stronger than religious prejudice'.[56] It, however, could not rid itself of the doubt that the other caste fellows would show similar indulgence.

The act of crossing the *kala pani* appeared to be a great sin which members of Hindu community could hardly overlook and condone. Expressing full sympathy with the young Civilians, the newspaper urged them to 'stand firm amidst all their trials, and make no concession, though they may have to face the strongest opposition or forfeit all social privileges'.[57] The religious prohibition thus slowly waned only to be overcome by the resolute youths. Brahmins of Madras province perhaps had the strongest social objection of crossing the sea. That perhaps explained that Rajappaya Narayanan Aiyer selected in 1899 was the first Brahmin from the province. Rajappaya was third native Civilian from the Madras Presidency. The earlier two belonged to the Chetty community. Pulicat, the first Civilian died prematurely. The next successful candidate Venugopal was a student of Madras Christian College where his father also taught. Rajappaya had the same *alma mater* and secured the Government of India Scholarship. He proceeded to England and joined Cambridge University on the advice of the Reverend Kellett, a distinguished graduate of the Cambridge University, and under whom he studied History and Political Economy in the Madras Christian College. Rajappaya passed Historical Tripos and the open competition of the Civil Service. His brother, R Swaminathan, was with him in England utilising his time in qualifying himself as a Diploma in Agriculture at Cambridge. As Rajappaya was selected for Government scholarship and was planning to proceed to England, Indian press observed 'Mr Narayanan is a Brahmin of Tanjore District, and a brilliant graduate of Madras University. Last year Mr Swaminathan, M A of Malabar, also a Brahmin and a member of the Social Reform Association, went to England as Gilchrist Scholar'.[58] The press was delighted that 'The examples of those men ought to prove a stimulus to other young Hindus'[59] more so because 'The Brahmins of this Presidency are a conservative class, and those of the Tanjore and Malabar Districts are perhaps the most conservative of those conservatives'.[60]

Mahomedan and Parsee students were, however, free from any religious taboo. Parsee community known for their keen interest in western education sent their youths to England quite early, their number being disproportionately high compared to the small population size. Mahomedans were slow in realising the need of western education. Very few Mahomedan students proceeded to England before 1880.

Eminent Indians-Infatuation and Reminiscences

Motilal Nehru sent his son Jawaharlal, brother Brijlal and nephew Sridhar more or less at the same time to England for education. His ambition for them was that they would become members of Indian Civil Service. Commenting on this, Brijlal's son B K Nehru, himself an ICS wrote, 'This is nothing surprising. Till the first decade of twentieth century, this was the highest ambition that any Indian could think of his son'.[61] Motilal reminded his brother Brijlal in a letter written in 1905, 'You are, of course, fully alive to the vital issues which depend on the result of your fling at the ICS, both to yourself and to the community at large. Just one year of hard work and you can make yourself a hero'.[62] His encouraging words to the young man were 'I am looking forward to the day when Reuters will cable across the seas to India that Mr B K Nehru of Allahabad tops the list of successful candidates for the ICS'.[63] Brijlal, though unsuccessful in ICS, was offered appointment in the Colonial Service which, however, he declined.

Jawaharlal joined Cambridge, finishing his study in Harrow. He had to choose a career and for 'a little while the Indian Civil Service was contemplated'.[64] This was chiefly because, Jawaharlal continued 'there was a glamour about it still in those days'.[65] But this idea was dropped as he had not attained qualifying age. He had already spent long time in England and his family wanted him back in India soon. Work in ICS would have required him to stay at different places away from home which his parents did not like after his long absence in England. The die was, therefore, cast in favour of the paternal profession, the Bar, and he joined the Inner Temple.

Motilal had to wait till 1912 to rejoice the first success of a family member in the ICS examination. Sridhar Nehru brought the glory. He was the son of Motilal's second brother Bansidhar who was in judiciary. Bansidhar was a learned man with an eccentric mind that he passed, along with his learning, to his three sons. The youngest son, Sridhar, went to Cambridge and then competed for Indian Civil Service. Vijayalakshmi (Pandit), Motilal's daughter felt her cousin to be a misfit as 'his real love was not for administration, but for one of his several outside interests, among them his devotion to science and linguistics'.[66] Sridhar had been to the great continental Universities of Sorbonne and Heidelberg and had studied seven European languages. He wrote poetry in those languages that the rest of family members were not always able to appreciate.

Disapproval of family also made Dr Rajendra Prasad, the first President of independent India, to drop the idea of proceeding to England for competing for the ICS. After taking his degree from the Calcutta University and topping the list of all the candidates, he began thinking of a career. Government service did not appeal to him, but the glamour of the Indian Civil Service attracted him. As he said, 'I began to be obsessed by a new idea; to go to England somehow and pass the ICS examination'.[67]Several friends offered to help him with funds. As his trip to England was not likely to be approved by his family, he made secret preparations to leave, hoping that after his departure from India, his family would get reconciled to the idea.

But somehow the information leaked through and the family could not bear the idea of separation from him. Rajendra Prasad, therefore, reluctantly dropped the idea.

The ambition of the Indian student to become an ICS, more so of his parents' was confirmed by Subhas Chandra Bose also. At the age of 10, his teacher in school asked students to write about their ambition in life. Subhas had heard of the terms Magistrate, Commissioner, Barrister from his elder brother. But jumbling up the terms, he wrote 'magistrate' as his ambition. Teacher remarked that to be a Magistrate after being a Commissioner would be an anti climax, but he was too young to understand the status of the different professions and designations. Though he had no occasion to be worried by the thought of what he would aspire to be in later life, he confirmed of 'hearing in talks within the family circle that the highest position, one could get to was the Indian Civil Service'.[68]

Father's wish prevented another Indian from competing for ICS. Jatindra Mohan Sengupta, later president of Indian National Congress, joined Cambridge in 1905 and was induced by his British friend to sit for the competition. Jatra Mohan, an advocate himself wanted his son to take up his parental profession. His friend also could understand the mind of Jatindra Mohan and stopped pestering.

Means and Expenses

Finance often deterred the ambition of young Indian to proceed to England for appearing in the competition. Passage money and the expenditure for London residence for couple of years were quite heavy for Indian purse. W C Bonnerjee, the first and eighth President of Indian National Congress set foot in the shores of England towards the end of 1864. He deceived his family and left India surreptitiously during Durga Puja festivities. Pherozeshah Mehta and Woomesh Chunder were two Indians selected for Jamshetji Jeejibhoy Scholarship for higher studies in England. He, however, faced extreme financial hardship as the business declined following the termination of American Civil War in 1865 which upset Jamsetji's financial scheme. Writing about the expenditure of London in 1866, Woomesh Chunder said in a letter to his cousin that £ 10 a month or £ 120 a year, was enough for a man to live in London. But £ 15 a month would have allowed a person to live quite comfortably, of course, avoiding luxuries of riding and eating a lot of dinner every day as he humorously put it. With an exchange rate of 10 rupees for one pound sterling, living expenses alone was nearly 2,000 rupees a year. Kaikhoshru Navroji Kabraji, editor of *Rast Gofter*, founded by

Dadabhai Naoroji, gave an estimate of expenditure which nearly matched with the assessment of W C Bonnerjee. Kabraji's eldest son Jahengirji Kaikhosre left for England in 1883 to compete for the Indian Civil Service. Jahengirji's first attempt in 1884 was rather poor. In his second attempt in 1885, he greatly improved his performance but narrowly missed the mark. He stayed in London for two years and nine months incurring an expenditure of 11,000 rupees. Appearing before the Public Service Commission, Kabraji described financial condition as a great barrier to Indians for appearing in the competition in England. With his own case, he convinced the Commission as to how the ambitious missions had ruined many Indians. Lytton's scheme of Statutory Civil Service rescued him from absolute ruin. Jehangirji Kaikhosre Kabraji, on his return to India, was appointed a probationer under the Native Civil Service Rules in 1888. He was posted as Assistant to the Collector of Bombay.

Sir Herbert Edwards, the veteran Anglo-Indian, apparently figured out the difficult financial barrier for Indians to proceed to England. Shocked to find that only 25 Indians were completing their education in England, he proposed that five-year scholarships be awarded to Indians to enable them to proceed to England and study. Northcote, the Secretary of State was favourably inclined, more so owing to pressure both from outside by East India Association and the Bombay Association and the liberal elements in his Council led by Bartle Frere. Northcote quickly suggested the idea to Lawrence, who in 1868 announced nine scholarships of £ 200 a year for three years. The scholarship scheme had hardly been in operation for long enough for the scholars to leave India, when the Duke of Argyll, new Secretary of State suspended it. He justifiably confused Government of India that the Bill he had laid before the Parliament would obviate the need of scholarship by providing Indians admission into high offices without competitive entry.

Gilchrist Scholarship which was announced in 1868 for selection of two students annually for pursuing studies in England encouraged Indians. Anundoram Borooah won the scholarship and successfully competed for the examination in 1870. Mancherji Pestanji Kharegat, a successful competitor of 1877, was also a Gilchrist Scholar. In 1883, the trustees of Gilchrist Scholarship Fund decided to admit candidates from Ceylon equally with those from India to compete for the yearly scholarship of £ 150 to be held at the University of London. This step was taken, the Trust asserted, owing to the very small competition among natives of India for the scholarship during previous years. In 1889, the scheme was changed with the Trust deciding to withdraw the competition and delegating the universities to award annual scholarship of £ 220, tenable for three years in Europe. The Universities of Calcutta, Bombay and Madras were chosen in rotation, and a similar scholarship every third year was given to the Universities of Punjab and Allahabad jointly. Each scholar was provided a free passage to England by the Government of India. The Trust agreed to provide a return passage at a cost not exceeding £ 50.

Many Indians, both wealthy and generous public men, realising the financial difficulty devised schemes to assist Indian students. Inspired by the success of four Indian Students in 1869, eminent Hindus of the North Western Provinces, at the instance of Anjuman-i-Mirzapore, established 'Hindoo National Improvement Society' with one of its objectives of enabling a certain number of Hindus to go to England every year to compete for the Civil Service. The Society urged Hindu Chiefs and Rajahs, as well as the native public generally, to extend a helping hand to the undertaking. As early as in 1872, Maharaja of Patiala offered to endorse a civil service scholarship for the natives of Patiala educated at University of Punjab. The Punjab Government, however, cleverly declined the generous offer on the subterfuge that the Act of 1870 had already thrown open the high offices of civil service to all natives of India without the need for competition in England. While declining, it also questioned whether the candidates from this Indian state would be eligible for the competition, as they could not be called British born subjects. Syed Ahmed Khan in 1883 started a similar scheme for the establishment in Punjab of a Society. Its objective was to send promising Mahomedan youths to England, in order to enable them to compete at Civil Service Examination. The society was named 'The Mahomedan Civil Service Fund Association'[69] and membership required monthly payment of at least two rupees.

Indian Association headed by Surendranath announced a scheme of scholarship in 1883 to aid prospective civil service candidates. Young men under the age of 17 as on 1 January 1883 were eligible. The condition attached that the scholar, if successful, must send another candidate to England within five years of his entering the service was, however, severely derided by the native press. Jyotish Chandra Mitra proceeded to England with this scholarship in 1884. He competed unsuccessfully in 1885 thus ending the controversy.

Government of India, after a lapse of nearly two decades, revived the scheme it shelved in 1869. Lord Ripon recommended to the Secretary of State in March 1884, the establishment of six scholarships for Indian students to pursue studies at Indian Institute, Oxford. Monier Williams, the founder of the Institute, was in Calcutta in January 1884. In a meeting with the

Governor-General Ripon, he gave a graphic account of the Institute and hinted that the Government of India may nominate five Indian students annually for it. Ripon responded favourably and agreed to establish the scholarships to enable Indian students to proceed to England. The purpose was expanded beyond studying at the Indian Institute and included in general study for the ICS Examination. The measure foreshadowed by Monier Williams and indulged by Ripon became a reality. Secretary of State accepted the proposal, restoring the Indian scholarships established by Sir Stafford Northcote. In 1886, two scholarships annually for the natives of India were placed at the disposal of the Universities of Calcutta, Bombay, Madras and Punjab in rotation. One scholarship was given to each of the first two Universities during one year, and one scholarship to each of the last two during the next year. Each scholarship entitled the holder to an allowance of £ 200 per annum payable from the date of his arrival in England and was tenable for three years. The selected candidates were provided with free passage to and from England. In 1888, consequent to the establishment of the Allahabad University, Government of India modified the scheme to include the students of that university also.

Two fully native scholarships were introduced in 1892 to assist the Indian students. One of them, Joy Gopal Mallik Scholarship was intended for the students of Calcutta University only. Tenable for four years, the scholarship was intended for students who passed the First Arts Examination in first division. The award was £ 150 annually with passage advance of £ 70. An additional £ 60 was assured as return passage. Candidate had to be bachelor at the time of selection. The donor desired that the scholar would devote a portion of his time to physical exercises, such as running, gymnastics, riding and volunteering. In the first year of 1892, 14 candidates presented themselves. Eight graduate candidates were not considered, limiting the number of eligible candidates to six who passed F A Examination in the first division. The choice fell on Sarat Kumar Chakravarti of Presidency College, son of Pandit Behari Lal Chakravarti of the city. In the following years were selected Nalinikanto Nag and Amita Nath Mitra of the Presidency College.

J N Tata, the wealthy Parsee millionaire, published the outlines of a scheme for assisting studious youths of his community to enter the civil service and liberal professions. He proposed to advance them by monthly instalments the necessary funds to pursue their studies in Bombay, Calcutta or elsewhere, and then in England or European universities. The money is to be repaid as convenient to the fund for similarly assisting other Parsee youths. Pestonji Sorabji Patuck was the first Tata Scholar to have successfully competed for ICS in 1897 and many more followed thereafter.

Wealthy Indians also in a few cases, realising the national interest, supported the endeavour of ambitious Indian youth. Raja Surya Kant Acharya Chowdhury of Muktagacha defrayed the expenditure of the son of Dwarka Nath Ray, Deputy Magistrate. The young man Jnanendra Nath Roy competed twice for the Indian Civil Service but without luck. Dharma Dass Bose did not inherit a fortune and was only the Civil Surgeon at Mymensingh. But the humble position of the doctor did not discourage him to bear the expenses of sending a candidate to England.

The case of Gurusaday Dutt showed how keenly the community felt the need for Indian success in Civil Service Examination. Gurusaday, a native of Sylhet district, left for England to compete for the Civil Service in June 1902, with members of the Sylhet Association raising through subscriptions an amount of 6,000 rupees for his expenses in England. Association desired that Gurusaday, on his return from England, would refund the money, which could be expended in sending another Indian youth for education to England. Gurusaday, on his return as successful Civilian with his generosity and concern for the community, more than fulfilled the obligation.

During the first decade of the 20th century funds were organised in different provinces of India for the purpose of sending promising Indian youths to Europe, America and Japan for education. Hindu Education Fund of Bombay started much in the same line as that of Tata's scheme. Shankrao Dhavle, the first student sent by the Fund, successfully passed the examination in 1905. In the same year, similar fund was raised in Madras under the name of the 'Madras Hindu Forcign Education Fund'[70] aimed to provide scholarships for deserving Hindu students of the Madras Presidency to enable them to go to England and compete for the Indian Civil Service and other branches of the Indian Public Service. Rai Bahadur C Jambulingam Mudaliar, Dewan Bahadur Krishnamurthy Rao and P S Sivaswamy Aiyar formed the Provincial Committee. The fund started with collection of Rs 18,000 per annum from one hundred and fifty gentlemen contributing Rs 120 each.

Notwithstanding the various schemes, number of scholarships remained very few and fell far short of meeting the ambition of the Indian students. Wealthy families of course could support their sons in undertaking such formidable mission while uncertainty discouraged others. Many young saplings thus wilted under the tropical sun. Brave and resolute Brajendra Nath started from Lucknow about the middle of July 1872 with a sum of about Rs 1,300. Authorities of Canning College, Lucknow from where he passed out, awarded a scholarship of Rs 50 a month to him for about six months, a period barely adequate to appear in the open competition for the Indian Civil Service. His purse nearly dried as he reached London and could pay the taxi fare only with borrowed sum. He received a great deal of help from Srinath Dutta, and secured residence near University College. Srinath had been bracketed 4th with him, in the First Examination in Arts of Calcutta University in 1869. Srinath came to England as Gilchrist Scholar in 1871 with the intension of competing for the Civil Service. Srinath spent nearly a year in preparation of the examination, towards the end of which he developed a serious ailment. He consulted doctor who advised him to stop his study. Srinath thus could not appear in the competition. By the next year, he had crossed upper limit of the prescribed age. As he was unable to pursue his studies, the scholarship was stopped throwing Srinath in utter financial hardship. Brajendra Nath, however, was not deterred by any difficulty and his brave attempt could not but win the luck. As successful candidate, Brajendra Nath could subsist on probationary allowance and passed the final examination.

Cadre and Covenanted Service

Charter Act of 1793 stipulated that vacancies occurring in a Presidency be filled from among the Civil Servants of that Presidency only. This provision was reaffirmed in the Charter Act of 1833. There were three Presidencies in 1793, viz. Bengal, Bombay and Madras. As different territories were brought under British rule, they were attached to the Bengal presidency, so that in course of time it came to include the whole of British India outside the Bombay and Madras Presidencies. A Bengal Civilian might, therefore, serve in Bengal, Bihar, Orissa, Assam, Arakan and Tenasserium, the North West provinces of the Punjab. The members of the service in the three presidencies had separate pension fund and the service in each Presidency adopted its name as designation, i.e., Bengal Civil Service, Bombay Civil Service and Madras Civil Service.

The restriction of service to the limits of the different Presidencies naturally caused difficulties. In 1878, Lord Salisbury, the Secretary, accepted the suggestion of Government of India and directed abolition of the provision. It was laid down as a general rule that every Covenanted Civil Servant 'is bound to serve wherever the Government at any period of career requires him to go'.[71] The Order of 1878 by which the service became 'all-India service' received the legislative sanction after a gap of over thirty years. The provision was modified through Section 4 of the Government of Indian Act, 1912. Apart from the three Presidencies, no province came into existence till 1836, when the North Western Provinces were carved out of Bengal and put in charge of a Lieutenant-Governor.

Macaulay Commission while formulating the scheme of competitive examination recommended that the candidates be allowed to choose the presidency on the basis of the open competition. Successful candidates during their probation could, therefore, learn the vernaculars of the selected Presidency. Bengal Presidency was further divided into lower and upper province which the candidates could select. Cadre for lower Bengal included Assam and that for Upper Bengal contained United Provinces of Agra and Oudh, Punjab and Central Provinces. Thus ran the regulation of the Civil Service Commission stating that 'candidates shall be permitted to choose, according to the order in which they stand, as long as a choice remains, the Presidency (and in Bengal, the division of the Presidency) to which they shall be appointed'.[72] A new cadre for Burma was introduced from the open competition of 1881. Upper Bengal was the top most priority for Civilians followed by Lower Bengal. All attractive posts in the Imperial Government including the executive members of the Governor-General's Council, the posts of Lieutenant-Governors and Chief Commissioners were monopolised by the Bengal Civilians. This of course did cause a lot of heart burn among the Civilians of other provinces. But Bengal Civilians were strongly averse to sacrifice their privilege to any outsiders. Before 1881, Burma was not considered of sufficient importance to have men assigned to it after the open competitions. 'Men were sent thither for their sins, either permanently or for a term of years'[73] Herbert Thirkell White opined. The statement 'other provinces sent their worst men to Burma',[74] had indeed more truth than humour. 'However this may be, no doubt Burma was regarded as a place of banishment, a dismal rice-swamp where the sun never shone'[75] Thirkell, who himself served in Burma, concluded. Two native Civilians selected in the open competition of 1890 were sent to this province. Govind Dinanath Madgavkar could wriggle out himself from the land of Iravaddy on transfer but his compatriot Mohammad Yusuf served the province for nearly two decades. He came back to Bengal Presidency and was appointed District and Sessions Judge of Burdwan in May 1912. After a brief period, he was transferred to Rangpur in the same capacity. In the 20th century Arunachalam Thyagrajan and Vithal Sivaram Bhide succeeded in the examination of 1906 and 1914 respectively. These two native Civilians were assigned to serve the province of Burma, still an integral part of British India. Burma remained the least favoured province even for the Indians. Lee Commission while enquiring the position in 1923 observed the apathy of Indian Civilians to serve Burma. Though few Indians were appointed, only one remained in Burma at the time of the enquiry. All others had succeeded in obtaining a transfer back to India. Burma Government represented that Indians should not in future be posted to the ICS in the province. Commission endorsed the appeal for Government of India to accept the demand. At the same time, the higher education, both secondary and collegiate, was in very backward state in Burma. Burmese were also reluctant to attend the Indian colleges. It was only in 1923 when for the first time, a Burmese succeeded in the open competition.

The official confirmation of Partition of Bengal as 'settled fact' was reflected in the distribution of provinces among the successful ICS candidates. Starting from the open competition of 1909, the candidates could choose between 'Bengal' and the new province 'Eastern Bengal and Assam'. This arrangement operated for barely three years till the open competition of 1911. In three years' time, a total of 21 successful candidates, all European Civilians were assigned to 'Eastern Bengal and Assam'. As the decision of Partition of Bengal was unsettled, the provinces changed as 'Bengal and Assam' and newly created 'Bihar and Orissa'. Yeshwant Anant Godbole was among the six Civilians assigned to 'Bihar and Orissa' from the batch of candidates who joined service in 1912. Another native Civilian Balchandra Krishna Gokhale succeeded in 1914 and joined the province of Bihar and Orissa in 1915.

The Aitchison Commission recommended that the use of the term 'Covenanted Civil Service of India' should be discontinued and it should be replaced by the term 'Imperial Civil Service of India' in distinction from the proposed Provincial Civil Service. The suggestion was not acceptable to Lord Cross, the Secretary of State for India. He instead ordered that Covenanted Service should be designated as 'Civil Service of India', that each branch of the Provincial Civil Service should be designated by the name of the province to which it belonged, e.g., Punjab Civil Service, Madras Civil Service etc. It was decided to totally stop the use of the terms 'covenanted' and 'un-covenanted'. The term 'covenanted' originated from the requirement of signing long printed indenture by the candidates selected in England during the Company's time. The indenture drawn up in a form approved by the legal advisers of the Company, contained among many other things a document known as 'Covenant'. The 'Covenant' defined condition of service, rights and obligations which the Company and the Civilians would honourably follow. Members of other services, who were recruited in India, executed no covenant. The service thus ridded itself of the odious term 'covenant' but the whiff hardly evaporated. Execution of covenant remained a prerequisite to joining the service. Passionate Indian youths perceived the odious covenant as an invidious scheme of securing loyalty. None realised it more than the impassioned Subhas Chandra Bose who gave up the service against the wishes of his dear parents. It was not possible for young Subhas to convince his parents as they had nurtured the aspiration since the birth of the child. Subhas, therefore, wrote to his elder brother Sarat Chandra that 'joining the service was based on the fact that I would have to sign the covenant and thereby owe allegiance of a foreign bureaucracy which I feel rightly or wrongly has no moral right to be there'.[76]

Subhas met Jinnah who was in London and asked his advice. Subhas wanted to resign and work for his country. Jinnah said people like Subhas were required in the ICS. If they left the Service, the future of the country would be dark, since it would not have patriotic men serving the country. Subhas had a great regard for Jinnah and he was for a time influenced by Jinnah's opinion. Eventually, his strong conviction triumphed and quieted his mind. To Subhas, highest ideals of one's life were not compatible with subordination to the conditions of service which an ICS man had got to accept. Though securing the fourth place in the open competition of 1920, Subhas gave up the coveted job and returned home with his conviction that 'national and spiritual aspirations are not compatible with obedience to Civil Service conditions'.[77]

Gopal Krisna Gokhale, though not competed for the examination himself, had difficulty in agreeing with the idea that Indians could serve the national interest even while joining the Service. Shankar Pandurang Desai was successful in the examination of 1914. Before joining Cambridge University as part of his training, Shankar met Gokhale who was then touring England as a member of the Royal Service Commission. Veteran nationalist listened to Shankar patiently. He could sense the young man's objection to the invidious British strategy of keeping the Mahomedan from the current of national movement. Gokhale lost no time to urge him to join his 'Servants of India Society'. Shankar politely turned down the offer as his parents had sent him to England for getting entry into ICS. Gokhale, the founder of the society, was quite unhappy with this refusal and retorted that Shankar had placed the interest of his family above those of the country. Shankar was depressed, and a few months later, met Lala Lajpat Rai who came to Cambridge. Lajpat Rai did not quite agree with what his compatriot said. His words cheered up Shankar. Fiery leader of India thought it would be possible for Indians in the Service to serve the cause of the country. Conversation with Lajpat Rai helped Shankar recover from gloom and he joined the service with these words ringing in his ears. He conducted himself to become a true servant of India, not only in name, but in true spirit.

Bal Gangadhar Tilak concurred with the view of his compatriot Lajpat much the same way as they shared their political ideas. Chintamon Desmukh passed the examination successfully in 1918. Towards the end of the following year, Bal Gangadhar visited England in connection with the defamation he had filed against Sir Valentina Chirol. Young Chintamon still had doubt in his mind as to his duty to participate in the political struggle and met Bal Gangadhar seeking his guidance in regard to his future line of action. The great leader's words dispelled the doubt as he affirmed that India was sure to achieve independence soon. Experienced administrators would immensely help in reinforcing self-government. Bal Gangadhar, therefore, advised Chintamon to prepare himself for that role clearly observing that 'any good purpose will be served by your taking part in the political struggle'.[78]

Nearly two decades later, father of the Nation Mahatma Gandhi entirely differed from Subhas on the issue of Indians joining the service. Badr-ud-din Tyabji was the grandson of the great nationalist Tyabji who presided over the third National Congress at Madras in 1887. Badr-ud-din Tyabji met Mahatma Gandhi at Oxford University during the second Round Table Conference in 1931. Badr-ud-din was then preparing for Indian Civil Service and noted that Mahatma, far from trying to influence him to abandon preparations, rather encouraged him to do so. Perhaps 'free India of tomorrow' was visible to the great Indian mass leader. The visionary could perceive that the nation 'would need workers of every type, not the least the administrators with a knowledge of world outside India and with a capacity to utilise the knowledge and experience for the benefit of Indian people'.[79]

Chapter V
INDIAN ATTEMPT, INDIAN YOUTH

The Begining

The regulations of the competitive examination for Indian Civil Service till the World War I underwent a number of changes, chiefly for accommodating the requirement of the Empire. Colonial interests were carefully protected by the reforms and Indian demands were rarely incorporated. Sometimes, however, conflict broke out on home turf as the great English universities viz. Oxford and Cambridge fought with each other. No less important was the role of the British Public Schools. Appointment in the service, therefore, remained outside the reach of Indian students, who, by and large, faced the extraordinary difficulty in competing with their English counterparts. Only the handful Indians, both resolute and resourceful, could challenge the English exclusivity.

Set against this backdrop, the first Indian success came as late as on the ninth year since introduction of competitive scheme. The candidate belonged to none other than Tagore family, one of the leading Brahmo families of the Imperial capital, Calcutta. The family was one of the earliest to acknowledge the need for social reform. Its members had struggled in various forms for embracing western education and risked as much as social excommunication. In a fitting tribute, Satyendranath Tagore brought glory to the nation, becoming the first successful candidate. The news of native success cheered up the Indians, attracting many more candidates to England. The trend was cut short in the year 1878, by lowering upper age to 19. Governor-General Lytton introduced the scheme of 'Statutory Civil Service' which puzzled Indians for quite a long period. The first four examinations under the new scheme went off without any successful Indian candidate. Eventually, countrymen of India realised that the statutory scheme was a clever ploy, not at all intended to replace the competitive examination. Mancherji Pestonji Kharegat, a Parsee youth from Bombay broke the barren run and stole sole success after a gap of five years. Indian parents, thereafter, reconciled to the changed circumstances and started sending their sons at teen age. Many of them completed school education in England and their

England stay was proportionately longer. Following the recommendations of Aitchison Commission, the maximum age was restored to 23 in 1892. This allowed more matured Indian students to compete, many of whom graduated at the Indian universities and quite often completed MA also before proceeding to England. After this change, there was no further attempt to lower the maximum age.

During the period from 1862 to 1878, a total of 73 Indian candidates competed of whom only 12 succeeded. Gustasp Ardeseer, one of the successful candidates was, however, denied appointment on medical ground even after completion of probation. Selection of Satyendranath was chiefly due to his superior performance in Sanskrit and Arabic. In his total score of 1,574, these two subjects contributed as much as 728. His other subjects were Moral Science, French and English language and literature. The entire nation rejoiced at the news of success but had to wait for another six years before celebrating again. The occasion, however, offered a cause for bigger celebration as four Indian candidates successfully passed. Three of them were from Bengal with Romesh Chunder Dutt standing third and Biharilal Gupta thirteenth in the list. The third Bengalee Surendranath Banerjea and the Mahratta Brahmin Sripad Babuji Thakur occupied the consecutive places of thirty-eighth and thirty-ninth.

The celebration, however, turned into much melancholy as the Civil Service Commissioners disqualified Surendranath and Sripad Babaji on the ground of over age. A Bengali doctor residing in London, for quite some time and who was 'thoroughly denationalised'[1] advertised in *The Telegraph*, for the unsuccessful numbers 51 and 52 to come to him if they would 'hear something in their advantage'.[2] It received immediate response and finally the complaint reached the Civil Service Commissioners that on the basis of what Surendranath and Sripad Babaji averred at the time of their matriculation examination, they had exceeded the upper age limit of 21 years at the time of open competition. The Civil Service Commissioners without further enquiry disqualified both the successful candidates and admitted in their place the candidates who stood as fifty-first and fifty-second in the list. Surendranath was of different composition and never gave up on unjust ground. As a youth of 21 years, he had ample confidence in British tradition of justice and appealed to the Commissioners trying to explain the difference between Hindu practices of calculation of age from the English custom. The issue snowballed to a major controversy drawing attention of House of Commons through the question of Eastwick. Grant Duff could provide only a mild reply, expressing his position of helplessness owing to legal obligation. The young Indian, however, could generate wide interest both at home and abroad. James Bruce and Sir J W McCrindle, respectively Head Master and Principal of Doveton College, where Surendranath studied for seven years gave him testimonial. Charles Dickens wrote an article in his periodical 'all the year round' and Professor Henry Morley sent off a spirited letter to the same magazine, attesting his pupils as 'They came to this country well educated, were liberal in mind, most friendly to England'.[3] He marked them for their qualities 'amiable, upright, and indefatigably hardworking'.[4] The considerate professor did not forget the painstaking effort taken by the students, working 'steadily for at least twelve, usually fourteen, fifteen, sixteen hours a day'.[5] Professor Morley was aware that the young men staked very much on a terribly bad chance of success in the examination that could be derived only through 'beating two or three hundred Englishmen on their own ground in their own subjects of study'.[6]

Surendranath engaged Mellish as his advocate who moved at the Court. Dwarkanath Mitra, Judge of Calcutta High Court, had already sent a certificate attesting the deposition of Surendranath's father. The Court order re-instating both the candidates finally reached India in February 1870, late by a day or two only, for Surendranath's father Durga Charan to know. The medical practitioner with whose encouragement, Surendranath proceeded to England died in great anxiety. Durga Charan was the man who readily assented when John Sime strongly urged him to send his son to England for competing in the Civil Service Examination. Sime was the Principal of Doveton College, Calcutta from where Surendranath passed out and this was the parting advice from the Principal at the time of Surendranath's leaving the college.

Sripad Babaji Thakur who studied in Elphinstone College, Bombay was the first Indian Civilian from Bombay Presidency. Sripad was a fellow student of the Hon'ble Kashinath Trimbak Telang, with whom he rivalled for many a scholastic honour, albeit maintaining friendly attachment till his dying day. He joined Elphinestone College at Bombay in 1866, when the pre-eminent philosopher and Greek scholar, Sir Alexander Grant, was principal. Great as his learning was, the principal never failed to recognise merit and ability in his Indian pupils. Sripad graduated in Greek and Sir Alexander then Director of Public Instructions appointed Sripad as Deputy Educational Inspector of Marathi Schools in Bombay. He worked in the post till he left for England in September 1868 as Mangaldas Nathubuoy Travelling Fellow of Bombay University. Game of chess was Sripad's fascination which he could not sacrifice even on the face of approaching examination. Though he bothered little about his disqualification, both he and Surendranath were re-instated at the same time. Commissioners being of perfect bureaucratic mould, decided not to repeat the mistake. Swallowing the bitter pill, they brought out a condition in 1872 that in the case of natives of India, the age must be certified by the Government of India or of the Presidency or Province in which the candidate had resided.

Surendranath had lost a year in his fight for re-instatement, but managed to complete the two year probation course in one year. Brahmo reformer Keshub Chander Sen embarked on his England trip in February 1870. Five young Bengalees accompanied Keshub to England for educational purpose, one of them being Ananda Mohan Bose. Keshub had quite a large number of English friends who eagerly offered their hospitality and pressed him to stay with them. But Keshub preferred to stay on his arrival with 'B & R'[7] as he wrote in his diary. 'B' was Beharilal Gupta, his cousin, and 'R' was Romesh Chunder Dutt. Passing the final examination, three friends made a hurried tour of Europe on the way to returning home. A surprise waited for them as they crossed the English Channel. French security men with their poor knowledge of English could not make out their identity. French Police detained the friends in prison for a night suspecting them to be Prussian in origin and communists by nature. Their detainment was cut short as a Frenchman, adequately familiar in English language arrived on the following morning. He could make out the identity of the Indian Civilians and set them free. The friends waited no more and crossed the French border in a hurry. Entering Italy the friends boarded the home bound steamer at Brindsi. They arrived at Bombay and came straight to Calcutta by train. The train journey was broken at Allahabad where Indian community arranged a reception for them. At this reception Surendranath made his first public speech in the Indian soil. When the train rolled in at Howrah station the Indian Civilians were received by great applause from a cheering crowd. A great garden party was given for the three ICS probationers on their return to Calcutta by Keshub Chunder Sen and other progressive Bengalees at Seven Tanks Villa, Belgachia. Romesh by that time had attuned himself to hard reality. His speech sounded with characteristic practical sense of sun-burnt Civilian. He made full use of the occasion to share his western experience. In his words, he neither bragged of his achievement nor prostrated himself to western manners. Romesh rather prescribed what he felt to be the right course of action for his countrymen. Expressing his feeling plainly, he uttered, 'If, indeed, we have done anything to merit your approbation, we shall consider ourselves amply rewarded if our countrymen were to follow our example'.[8] Romesh's words clearly indicated that he would not slavishly imitate everything English. But, he acknowledged that there were many things estimable in English manners which Indians with advantage could introduce into their own social institutions. 'I would therefore beg of you, gentlemen',[9] he concluded 'to try your best to send as many young men as possible to England, for the fact they would initiate ideas of liberty and equality between men and women'.[10] Romesh himself also helped prospective Indian candidates with his first hand experience. Brajendra Nath before proceeding to England came down from Lucknow to Calcutta to meet Romesh. Assistant Magistrate and Collector, stationed at Alipur, Romesh did not disappoint his aspiring countryman. Brajendra Nath received great deal of information about the procedure that he would follow on arrival in England.

Next year 1870 marked the selection of Anundoram Borooah from Assam. Anundoram studied at Presidency College, Calcutta and proceeded to England in the spring of 1869 with H Woodrow who served as Director of Public Instructions in Bengal. Being counselled properly, he joined one of the civil service coaching institutions in London and studied science in the London University and law in the Middle Temple. His aptitude for scientific studies was so great that Dr Carpenter, Professor of Zoology in the London University and Principal of the University College, London once remarked that 'Mr Borooah was the most inquisitive student that I have ever come across'.[11]

Two more Indian candidates were selected in 1871 and 1873. They were Krishna Govinda Gupta from Pogose School, Dacca (now renamed Dhaka) and Brajendra Nath De from Canning College, Lucknow. Krishna Govinda made a friend for life in a characteristic way. Henry Beveridge, a Bengal Civilian was standing in a crowd one morning when he was a newcomer, looking at a passing show. There was a very small unknown Indian boy standing near him struggling hopelessly to get a view. Henry hoisted him on his shoulder, where he watched it all above the heads of the other spectators. This was the beginning of a life-long friendship. The little boy turned out to be Krishna Govinda Gupta who perhaps started aspiring to join the 'heaven born service' from that very day. The year 1874 produced two more successful Indian Civilians. One of them was Pulicat Ratnavelu Chetti, the first Indian Civilian from Madras Presidency and the other was the first Parsee successful candidate RustomjeeCursetjee. The Parsee young man was the son of a well known Calcutta merchant and had reached England at the age of eleven. Two more students of the same community, Kavasjee Jamasjee Badshah and Gustasp Ardeseer were selected in 1877. Ardeseer, however, had the misfortune of rejection on medical ground even after completion of his training. Of the eleven successful native Civilians during this period, six were Bengalees and two from Parsee community. The remaining three were Mahratta, Assamese and Tamil.

Teens in the Fray

During the period 1878-1891, the open competition was conducted with upper age limit of 19 years. Indian students in their teens, though shrunk in number and no better in maturity, reached England for realising the dream. A total of 54 Indian candidates appeared during this period with 15 success, five of which coming in the single year 1890. One of these successful candidates, Aravind Acroyd Ghose, did not appear for riding test and was denied appointment. Destiny perhaps decided his course of action as the world could ill afford to miss such a prodigy.

The year 1884 brought glory to India as Arthur Goodeve Chuckerbutty headed the list. He was the son of Dr Soorjo Coomar Chuckerbutty the first native to join Indian Medical Service. Securing a total of 2,034 marks, Arthur was ahead of the second candidate, Norman S Brodie, by 129 marks. In the preceding year, he stood at the head of the list of 50 successful candidates at the public competitive examination for admission into Royal Artillery and Royal Engineers in the Royal Military Academy, Woolwich. This Academy conducted the technical training of officers in the British Army, and Arthur was expected to be the first Native Commissioned Military Officer in any Royal Artillery. Racial discrimination denied him the entry. Undeterred, the young man competed for Indian Civil Service and delighted the whole nation by coming on top. Another Calcutta boy Lokendra Nath Palit was selected in the same year. Lokendra Nath was the son of Taraknath Palit, renowned Barrister of Calcutta Bar. Lokendra Nath and great poet Rabindranath Tagore together joined University College, London in the year 1880. Rabindranath did not continue for long but Lokendra Nath stayed back in London. In 1885, before the first Indian National Congress met at Bombay, Mohsin Badr-ud-din Tyabji, the first Mahomedan candidate succeeded in the open competition. His father Badr-ud-din Tyabji subsequently presided over the third national congress at Madras in 1887. Mohsin, a student of Bombay St Xavier's School reached England six years back. Mrs Wadia's congratulation to Badr-ud-din was most appropriate as she observed 'the sacrifice involved in such long parting had been so well rewarded'.[12] Badr-ud-din himself was no less uncertain about the prospect of his son. During this time, he received the letter of 13 April 1884 from His Excellency the Viceroy Lord Ripon, seeking his views on the subject of the extension of the age of the candidates for the Indian Civil Service. In reply, Badr-ud-din forwarded his memorandum and later called a special meeting of the Anjuman, and strongly urged that the limit should be extended. Badr-ud-din replied to the Viceroy, 'I have had the hardihood of sending my son to England to go up for the Examination to be held on the 3rd proximo. What the result may be I don't know, but in India he was considered a lad of great promise being always at the top of his class and carrying off almost all the prizes in the St Xavier's College, receiving no less than seven or eight last year at the hands of his Excellency the present Viceroy, Lord Ripon'.[13] Indian candidates drew blank in the examination of 1886. But the next three examinations returned four successful candidates. Among them three were from Bengal while Venugopal Chetti was the second successful candidate from Madras Presidency. William Goodeve Chuckerbutty was the brother of Arthur Goodeve Chuckerbutty, a Bengal Civilian.

The year 1890 was bountiful for Indians as five candidates passed. One of them, Aravind Ackroyd Ghose, however, did not appear for riding rest and was denied appointment. Mohammad Yusuf, a lad from Bankipur was the second Mahomedan successful candidate. Along with them were selected two Bengalee candidates Satischandra Mukherjee and Mahimohun Ghose, and a Mahratta boy Govind Dinanath Madgavkar. The following year was, however, much less productive. Only two Indian candidates were selected, one of them, being Satyendra Nath Palit, the youngest son of Taraknath Palit. He maintained the family tradition and joined Bengal Presidency where his brother Lokendra Nath Palit was already serving. During this period, Bengal had absolute monopoly in the success of native candidates sending ten out of fifteen successful candidates. This included Arthur and Alfred, the two sons of Dr Soorjo Coomer Goodeve Chuckerbutty. The doctor, however, did not live long to see the success of his sons. Dr Soorjo Coomer was the first native of India who appeared at the competitive examination in England for the Indian Medical Service, and stood second in the list of successful candidates. Eventually, he became the Professor of *Materia Medica* at the Calcutta Medical College and passed away in October 1874.

Besides the students from Bengal, among the other successful candidates two were Mahomedan and one was Parsee. Of the remaining two, one was a Mahratta and the other was a boy from Madras. Both these candidates came from middle class background. Venugopal's father was a teacher at Madras Christian College and the young Mahratta was the son of Dinanath Vishnu Madgavkar, Secretary to Bombay Prarthana Samaj. This was the

period when the Indian teens spent long years in England in finishing their school education and preparation of examination. The Palit brothers were in England for four years prior to the competition and so were the sons of two nationalist Indians Badr-ud-din and Manomohan. But very few Indian parents could endure that emotional ordeal, more so their sons at such tender age. Only exception to this trend during the period was perhaps Birendra Chandra Sen, who aided by Gilchrist Scholarship, reached England only seven months prior to the examination. Successful candidates with their English education and long residency in England studied continental languages, French, German and Italian and also Latin and offered them in the competition. Their scores in these subjects in the open competition manifestly established the proficiency acquired, more so the ability of Indian students to learn foreign languages.

Matured Young Men

The upper limit of age was restored to 23 and more matured Indian students started competing from the year 1892. The number also proliferated as a total of 220 Indian students competed during 1892 to 1904 of whom 42 succeeded. One of the successful candidates, Jotindra Nath Ray, was rather unfortunate to miss the appointment. He succeeded in the open competition twice but was rejected on medical ground on both the occasions. The other tragedy was the death of the Parsee candidate C N Cama in riding accident. He along with his twin brother B N Cama had succeeded in the year 1901 and met with the accident while practising riding, a requisite for final examination. The number thus shrunk and 40 Indians could join service after completion of training. By this time education had expanded in India with foundation of new universities at Punjab and Allahabad. The young men, graduating from these institutions, were equally attracted to an ICS career.

The year 1893, 1895 and 1902 had been relatively depressing for Indians when selected candidates numbered 1, 1 and 2 only. Jamshedji Barzore Dalal, selected in 1893 was a Parsee from Bombay. His father Jamshedji Dalal was a Professor of Mathematics in the Elphinstone College, Bombay, and subsequently joined the Education Department of the Baroda state. The year 1892 produced three successful Indian candidates, two of them from Bengal and the first Eurasian candidate from Mangalore. Francis Xavier D'souza, the first Indian Christian studied at St Aloysias' College, Mangalore, followed by St Joseph, Trichinopoly. From middle school to BA degree, D'souza was first in every examination and proceeded to England on

Government of India Scholarship. He joined Cambridge University and stood fourteenth in the open competition. John Joseph Platel was another Eurasian who studied at St Xavier's College, Calcutta and succeeded in the same year. An orphan lad, Platel was brought up at Murgihata Orphanage and like D'souza, secured Government of India Scholarship. After rather dismal performance in 1893, Indian candidates did well again in 1894. Six candidates were selected representing all the major communities and regions of India. Two of them were Mahomedan, three were Hindu and one came from Parsee community. Of the three Hindus, Bengal sent up two and Punjab one. Bengalee student Albion Rajkumar Banerjee was born at Bristol when his parents were touring England. This being the 'first Brahmin subject of her Majesty Queen Victoria born on British ground',[14] he was named Albion. Queen, known for her keen interest in the female position of her Indian subjects, was apprised of the event by Miss Mary Carpenter. Atul Chandra Chatterjee, coming out first in 1896 sensitised the whole country. Earlier Arthur Goodeve Chuckerbutty had headed the list in 1884 but many Indians did not consider Arthur to be natural-born Indian. Atul Chandra secured the highest number of marks in four subjects, viz. English Literature, English History, Indian History and Political Economy and missed the distinction in Sanskrit by a solitary mark. His poor performance in Mathematics, a subject in which he was known to have possessed good knowledge, disappointed many. The reason slowly surfaced that on the day of the examination he fainted for a time. His score of 216 out of maximum of 1800 marks in Mathematics was in stark contrast to his proficiency in the subject. Atul Chandra was a resident of Santipore, in the District of Nadia, Bengal. His father served in the Public Works Department. Atul Chandra studied at Presidency College, Calcutta and went to England as a Government of India Scholar. A few days before starting his sojourn, he married in order to satisfy his mother and relatives. Atul Chandra entered King's College, Cambridge in October 1893 and studied for the Historical Tripos.

In 1898, eight Indian students passed out successfully. The list included the two Rays from Bengal phonetically in perfect identity. One of them, Jotindra Nath Ray, was rejected on medical ground. The other Ray represented Narail Zaminder family who also fell into the charm of 'heaven born service'. Rajappaya Narain Aiyar of Madras selected in 1899 was again a Government of India Scholar. He scored the highest marks among all candidates in English. In 1904, a candidate from Ceylon passed out successfully. Tempoe Alfred Mcgowan Coomarswamy was a Tamil Christian. Their family lived in Ceylon for many generations, retaining, however, a branch in India. While his father served as Police Magistrate, Jaffana, Ceylon his uncle was Chief Superintendent, Accountant-General's office, Madras. Tempoe was educated at St Thomas' College, Colombo, and preceded to England with the Ceylon State Scholarship in 1899 at the age of 17. In England, he studied medical science for short while before changing his decision to sit for the open competition. He then entered Clare College, Cambridge where he graduated second Senior Optimo in the Mathematical Tripos in June 1902. Coomarswamy also took a good place in the National Science's Tripos in 1903. He passed out successfully in 1904 and joined Madras Presidency to which his ancestors belonged. Though Bengalees, securing 15 out of 40 successful candidates retained their dominance, other communities were emerging fast. There were seven Parsee and six Mahomedan students among the selected candidates. Before the close of 19th century, Punjab had sent four successful candidates. Dewan Tek Chand passing in 1893 marked the beginning. The second Indian Civilian from the Province was Ashgar Ali who passed the examination in the following year. Gokal Chand Badhwar and Balak Ram became the third and fourth Civilian from Punjab. Joseph Vas of Karachi passed the examination in 1897. Mahratta land rejoiced the glory with success of Hariganpat Rao Gharpurey of Nagpur, Joseph William Bhore of Nasik and Vombatkere Pandurang Row, a Konkani of South Canara. The west-coast Civilian Pandurang was a member of the Saraswat Community which boasted of its illustrious sons Narayan Ganesh Chandravarkar of the Bombay High Court and Dr Row, the only Indian MD of the London University. Pandurang studied at Presidency College, Madras before proceeding to England. He joined St John's College, Cambridge and stood second in the examination of 1902.

Selected in the same year, Jagdesh Prasad fulfilled the aspiration of his father Jwala Prasad, a Statutory Civilian himself. The young man was grandson of Raja Jai Kishan Dass of Moradabad for whom it was a greater honour than the decoration bestowed by the Crown. The honours were equally distributed among the land-owner and professional classes, though both were pre-eminently wealthy. The boys from middle class families never despaired and often competed successfully. Anglo-Indian press kept watch and perhaps sensed the danger in progress of educated middle class. Commenting on the success of Jotindra Nath Ray, a member of Zamindar family of Narail in the Jessore District, *The Pioneer* observed, 'We want men of this stamp as they will command the respect and confidence of the people in a higher degree than the sons of Vakils and petty traders'.[15] The paper reminded that this family was known for their long history of collaboration with the Government of North Western Province also.

Great Awakening

The decade immediately preceding the World War I was characterised by intense passion that built up against the racial discrimination and revolted not very infrequently. The student community could rarely disassociate themselves from the social and political development in India and elsewhere. The idea of joining a service which would bind them to a foreign yoke distressed the tender mind and set them thinking. Quite a few of them reached the land of Albion but the conflict did not leave them. Hardayal gave up the government scholarship and left for the motherland as the Indian students gathered at London to celebrate the fiftieth anniversary of Indian Mutiny. Equally active was Shyamaji Krishnavarma who stepped up his activity in British soil before being forced to move out of the Empire. The murder in 1909 of Sir Curzon Wylie, the student advisor of the India Office by an Indian student was the flash point. The murder taking place at the reception organised at Imperial College, London caused such revulsion that several Oxford and Cambridge colleges closed their doors to Indians. But nothing deterred the Indian students who flocked to England for prosecuting studies and compete for ICS. No doubt, the revision of maximum age to 24 in the year 1906 and the curtailment of free choice of subjects to a maximum possible of 6,000 marks were welcome changes. But the scheme still favoured the English students and the hard labour of Indian candidates echoed in the resolutions of the Indian National Congress. During the period 1905 to 1914, a total of 204 Indian candidates had competed of which only 35 were successful. The number dwindled further as Kannanthot Padmanabhan Padmanabha Pillai, selected in 1913, was dismissed from service even before the final examination, on charges of falsifying his age. Hassamal Baharmal Shivdasani, a resident of Sind joined the Service in 1915, only to resign after a period of barely six years. The Indian performance stood nowhere near the success of 502 Europeans during the same period. The small figure notwithstanding, all the regions of the country with possible exception of Burma, secured their representation.

In the year 1905 was selected the first Gujarati Covenanted Civilian of the country, Vinayak Nand Shankar Mehta. He cleared the final examination and returned home at a time when *Karan Ghela*, a semi historic novel composed by his father, achieved a wide and well deserved reputation. During these years, the preponderance of Bengali students disappeared much to the consternation of the community. Only two Bengali students were selected during the years 1905 to 1911, prompting many astute to correlate this temporary eclipse to Partition of Bengal. The storm raised by the division never really subsided but a sort of calm descended with annulment of

Partition. Happily enough, three Bengali students featured among the seven successful Indians in the open competition of the year 1912. The connection, the optimist felt, was mere coincidence and hoped that the sun, emerging from the eclipse, would not pass into the shadow again. The students from Bombay and Madras Presidencies were successful in greater number than before. Among the selected candidates were the brothers Benegal Raus from Madras, elder Narsinga, the lone candidate of 1909 and younger Rama following his predecessor, three years later. The luck of Ameer Ali, the renowned Barrister, proved mixed as he rejoiced selection of his elder son Warris in the year 1910. This success must have infinitely pleased Ameer Ali, who reached England for the first time in 1869. He had completed MA from Calcutta University and among other things, competing for ICS, was in his mind as he left India. Age was, however, against his candidature and he passed as Barrister in 1873. He practised at Calcutta High Court and settled in England in 1904. His younger son missed appointment though placed 90th in the list of 1914. The dejected father at that time was officiating in the Privy Council.

United Province secured its share through Panna Lall and Girija Shankar Bajpai selected in 1906 and 1914 respectively. The students had one honour in common, that of heading the final examination. Girija Shankar, a Government of India scholar was the son of a well-known and highly respected subordinate Judge of the Provinces. With selection of six candidates, the representation of Parsee community remained high compared to their size of population. The dismissal of Kannanthot Padmanabhan Padmanabha Pillai who was selected in the year 1913 became a sore point. A resident of Travancore, Padmanabha completed his matriculation in Church Missionary Society (CMS) College at Kottayam before taking admission in Presidency College, Madras. On obtaining BA degree from the university, he proceeded to England and joined Trinity College, Cambridge. At that time, ICS examination regulations required each Indian candidate to produce certificate of age and character. In case of Padmanabha, the certificate was not issued by Madras Government but by the Resident of Travancore and Cochin. Government of Madras in a routine communication to Secretary of State indicated the mismatch in his birth records as submitted at the Kottayam College, Madras University and Civil Service Commissioners. Padmanabha's father was a retired Tehsilder of Travancore State and aspersion was cast on his conduct also. A Commission consisting two Judges, was appointed who found a discrepancy between his ages as entered in the school register and when he appeared for the ICS. There was no reason to think that there was any deliberate dishonesty on Padmanabha's part, but the Secretary of State rejected him on the ground that 'an ICS man must be above suspicion'.[16]

The Charter Act of 1833 conspicuously declared to remove all obstacles, from admitting the native of British India or natural-born subject of His Majesty residents therein, in the appointment of any place or office in the Company's Government. Disabilities arising out of religion, place of birth, descent and colour were purported to be abolished by this Act. Indians, however, had to wait till the year 1855, when following the renewal of the Charter, competitive examination was introduced for appointment into the Company's Covenanted Service. Three years later, the administrative power was transferred to the Crown, which marked the memorable proclamation: 'We hold ourselves bound to the Natives of our Indian territories by the same obligation of duty which bind us to all our other subjects; and those obligations, by the blessings of Almighty God, we shall faithfully and conscientiously fulfil.'[17] Education, ability and integrity thus formed the requisite qualification for the appointment into Her Majesty's Service. The proclamation proved less equivocal in practice than it sounded. Colonial authorities interpreted the regulations much to their convenience and denied the rightful admission of Indians. Perhaps most ambiguous was the question of eligibility of the candidates from numerous Indian States. The allegiance of these States to the Crown, unfeigned and clear, could hardly secure the eligibility of its residents into the Indian Civil Service. This happened when the Great War was continuing and Indians, by and large, stood by the Crown, swearing their allegiance. In the southern part of the country, Mysoreans complained of the denial of their just claim. Subba Rao, a Barrister-at-Law, while studying at Oxford sought admission to the ICS. He was refused as the subject of an Indian State and came back to India to join the post of Professor of History at Maharaja's College, Mysore. Entire nation viewed the position as an extraordinary one but the Imperial authority was hardly perturbed.

Oriental Attitude – Tenacity and Fortune

Indian students reaching British shores clung on to their youthful aspiration. Manomohan's attempts in the competition, though unsuccessful, were proverbial in motivation. Equally tenacious were his fellow countrymen. Anundoram was disappointed with his first attempt in 1869. He never gave up the hope and proved his competence in 1870. Krishna Govinda was intoxicated by the charm of ICS quite early in his life and did not bother for his failure in 1870. The competition of the following year did not disappoint Krishna. No less tenacious were the Indian students who left home in their teens. Satyendranath Palit failed in the competition of 1890. He had imbibed the ideal of his elder brother Lokendra and came out successfully in 1891. Starting from 1896, appointments in Home Civil Service and Eastern Cadetships were also offered through the same open competition. Indians by and large turned out to be truly imperial citizen, marking out their option as HIC viz. Home, India and Cadetship. But their inclination did not remove the barriers, set out by the authority. They were debarred from joining Eastern Cadetship and appointment to Home Civil Service was truly exceptional. Nirmal Chander Sen, son of a well-known physician of Calcutta, left India as a Tata Scholar. He appeared for the competition in the year 1903 and was offered an appointment in Colonial Civil Service. Though a couple of Indians had earlier turned down the offer, Nirmal Chander went to the Straits, recording the first occasion for an Indian to serve as member of the Covenanted Civil Service in the Colonies. The same year had more surprises to come. Silendra Ghose despaired for a month after the results were announced and the competition seemed closed. Providential was his lot that three new vacancies occurred in Home Civil Service, and Silendra was selected for one of them. He almost accidentally became the pioneer in a new line, entering the hallowed precincts of Home Civil Service.

Indian National Congress and ICS

Public service in India in general and appointment of Indian into it in specific, featured with remarkable consistency in the resolutions of the Congress in first thirty years of its history. It chronicled the aspiration of Indians for deserving role in the administration of their own country. The issues were deliberated at the annual session of the Congress, the resolutions reflecting the changes introduced in the scheme of appointment and the competitive examination. In its maiden session, Congress highlighted the need for simultaneous examination in India and England for the Indian Civil Service. As the Public Service Commission was constituted in 1886, a committee was formed in the Congress session at Calcutta held in December 1886. The committee headed by the President, Dadabhai Naoroji, had Surendranath Banerjea of Calcutta, Subramaniyan Aiyer, both S and G of Madras, Rahimtulla Sayani of Bombay and Rao Madhaw Chitnavis of Nagpur among its members. Besides reiterating the demand for simultaneous examination, the committee urged for upward revision of age and fair consideration of Arabic and Sanskrit among the subjects. When the age was revised to 23 years, Congress in the year 1889 did express thanks to Her Majesty's Government. But at the same time, it recorded the universal disappointment, created by the denial of the demand for simultaneous examination. Civil Service was now divided into two categories, one the 'All India Service' and the other 'Provincial'. Government, however, did not transfer the posts that the Commission recommended to the Provincial Service. Congress in 1892 pointed out that only 93 posts had been thrown open against recommendation of 108 posts. Government did not put into effect the recommendation of shifting the senior executive posts of Membership of Board of Revenue and Commissionership of a Division. In Judicial branch, the number of posts transferred was less than the recommended level. By the year 1894, Congress was convinced that the Provincial Service in its prevailing constitution could not meet legitimate aspirations of the people. Meanwhile, a resolution was passed in the House of Commons on 2 June 1893 for introducing simultaneous examination in India and England for ICS. Congress followed with keen interest the subsequent development on the issue. It was disappointed when Government of India, in reply to a reference made by the Secretary of State, opined that minimum of European officials in the Covenanted Service was indispensable. Further dejection was in store as the Secretary of State supported the views prompting Congress to record its respectful but firm protest. This resolution of 1894 remained the core issue for deliberation in the subsequent Congress sessions till 1903. Congress felt that the labours of the Public Service Commission had practically proved void of any good results to the people of this country. It kept on uttering its old demand of simultaneous examination now supported by the resolution of the House of Commons of June 1893, of which the Government had no intention of giving effect. Very soon the demand for simultaneous examination expanded to cover other branches of civil administration also viz. Medical, Police, Engineering, Telegraph, Forest and Accounts for which recruitment was done only in England. The principles and policy enunciated by the Government of India in their sesolution of 24 May 1904, discouraging employment of Indians in the higher grades of Public Service, further upset the Congress. Partition of Bengal and the internal dissension shifted the attention of Congress for the years 1905 to 1908, pushing public service issues to relative obscurity. In 1909, Congress met in far more favourable environment created by Morley-Minto Reform. Appointment of two Indians in the Indian Council of Secretary of State and an Indian Member in Governor-General's Executive Council, coming after a long wait, was expected to be a turning point in government policy. Congress reciprocated the gesture by gratefully recognising the efforts that had been made during the last three years both by the Secretary of State for India and the Governor-General. The authorities were after all giving gracious effect to the policy laid down in the great Charter of 1858.

Next two years passed without any major event or significant change being incorporated. Before the Congress met at Bankipore in 1912, Royal Commission on Public Service, already constituted, had started examining witnesses. The notification of the Commission must have pleased the Congress but not the unfounded deposition of the European witnesses, both official and resident. The way some of the highest administrative officers, all European, without definite evidence, were levelling charges against Indians of general incompetence, lack of initiative and character could not but raise Congress to protest. It reminded the Commission that justice, national progress, economy and efficiency all were heavily in favour of the Indians for increasing their poor representation in the administration.

By this time, it sensed a sinister move to lower the age limit, and recorded in its resolution that it would operate to the disadvantage of the Indian candidates as well as prove detrimental to efficiency. Its urge to the Commission was for the abolition of division of Services into Imperial and Provincial and equalisation of the conditions of services between Indians and Europeans. The other important issue that it pointed out was the disproportionately high scale of salaries admissible to the Civilians, urging the Commission not to increase it further. At the same time, exchange compensation allowance, founded on a Statute, appeared to be a costly anomaly and was long due for abolition. The appointment of people of various dominions of the Crown in Indian services, where Indians were not accorded the rights of British citizens irked Congress for a long time. This remained a vexing issue of which Congress was bitterly critical. Deliberations of the subsequent two years on public service issues remained much the same. Royal Commission continued the enquiry amidst serious conflict between the European and Indian witnesses. Nonetheless great was the restraint exercised by Congress, which under such trying circumstances tactfully reposed its earnest hope on the dispassionate functioning of the Commission.

English Life for Indian Youths

It was the month of May in the year 1909, just past the Easter week and the flowers started blossoming. Diurnal journey of the earth continued and spring passed over to pleasing summer. The pleasant ambience suddenly heated up with the shockingly harsh news that 'The Evening Standard' announced. The Benchers of Gray's Inn had delayed calling two Indian students to the Bar pending full enquiry as to their involvement with seditious movement. Indian community in England dismayed as subsequent report confirmed that one student had been one of the managers of India House. This Indian student was none other than Vinayak Damodar Savarkar. The other student, however, was called to the Bar a little later on his tendering an apology for his association with the Nationalist Party in London. His Majesty put 'India House' under their prying eyes and tightened the rules for presentation of Indian students.

'India House' was an establishment of only four years' old but its expansion had been spectacular. It was the brainchild of Shyamaji Krishnavarma who migrated to England in the year 1898. He made his debut in Indian politics by publishing the first issue of his English Monthly *The Indian Sociologist* in January 1905. Certain articles in 'The Indian Sociologist' that Shyamaji edited and letters purported to have been written by him to *The Times* drew attention of the Benchers of Inner temple. In March 1909, the sub-Treasurer of the Inner Temple advised Shyamaji to show cause, why he should not be disbarred. Shyamaji cared little beyond submitting a written statement. The result was a foregone conclusion and on 30 April 1905 Inner Temple announced its decision. Shyamaji was disbarred and his name was removed from the books of the Society. *The Indian Sociologist*, through which Shyamaji started his public activity, was preached to be an organ of freedom as well as political, social and religious reform. Shyamaji followed it up by founding five travelling fellowship to enable Indian graduates to finish their education in England. These fellowships were purported to be a tribute to Herbert Spencer, a venerable liberalist for whom Shyamaji had unbounded regards. Valued at £ 135 each a year, the abiding condition of these fellowships was to sympathise with the cause that Shyamaji was fighting for. British rule in India was an anathema to Shyamaji and he could not allow the awardees to accept any office that British India might offer. Shyamaji, thoroughly resolved and unrelenting in his endeavour, expanded his activities with breathtaking speed. Within a month and half in 1905, about 20 Indians met at Shyamaji's new house at Highgate to inaugurate 'The Indian Home Rule Society' (IHRS). Shyamaji was the President of the Society and Vice-President was Sardar Singh Rewabhai Rana belonging to Princely State Limbdi who had settled in Paris with his jewellery business. Shyamaji could not reconcile with moderate elements in Indian National Congress represented by pensioned European Civilians Hume, Wedderburn and Cotton and their Indian collaborators. Shyamaji fixed his aim to secure Home Rule for India and the extremist element of Congress appeared to him to be the viable choice. 'India House' was opened in July 1905 for accommodation of the students availing Indian Travelling Fellowship. Rana supplemented

Shyamaji's initiative by offering another three travelling fellowships for Indian students. These fellowships were valued at Rs 2,000 each and their titles 'Rana Pratap' and 'Shivaji' were symbols of Indian glory and independence. Such was the activity of Shyamaji and his associates that in no time their appeal touched Indian students studying in Great Britain. Pandurang Mahadev Bapat, a Bombay graduate who was studying Engineering at Edinburgh on Government Scholarship became the first convert. Bapat delivered a lecture on 'British rule in India' and in his youthful zeal published it in form of a pamphlet. Bapat's pamphlet and its appreciative notice in *The Indian Sociologist* immediately drew attention of the India Office. Government quickly issued orders depriving Bapat of the scholarship held by him. Bapat's brave act and the harsh Government decision were widely debated in the Indian press. Bapat was acclaimed a hero and martyr. The withdrawal of scholarship so deeply distressed Bal Gangadhar Tilak that he warmly recommended Bapat's case to Shyamaji for extending financial assistance. The other Indian student whom the leader had recommended to Shyamaji was Vinayak Damodar Savarkar. It all started with Bal Gangadhar prompting his youthful disciple, a Bombay University graduate to apply for the scholarship. Vinayak who was editing *Vahari, Bombay* received Shivaji fellowship and proceeded to England.

Almost at the same time, Hardayal, a most distinguished MA of the Punjab University, who proceeded to England in 1905 as a Government of India Scholar, resigned his scholarship. He was studying at St James College, Oxford and found it hard to reconcile his love for country with the favour received from the hands of alien oppressive rule in India. Hardayal wrote an article titled 'A Stirring Appeal' exposing how the English were undermining Hindu character. Imperial educational policy and methods were designed to destroy Hinduism, as Hardayal felt, with the objective of destroying social consciousness and national individuality of Indians. The foreign rule was thus successful with their scheme of perpetuating the political bondage of the Indians. Hardayal corresponded regularly and maintained links with Shyamaji to whom he had been first introduced by Bhai Paramananda in April 1906. His elaborate schemes for expanding the New Society, the India House and *The Indian Sociologist* were taking shape. But before long, Hardayal left for India in January 1908 with his ailing wife. British government sensed danger and intensified vigilance on the activity of Shyamaji. Equally alert was Shyamaji himself who became aware that the mischief was brewing and the political propaganda that he was carrying out would be given a short shrift. He left England during June 1908 and settled down in Paris. Shyamaji, however, did not cut-off himself from the political activities. Subsequent to Muzzafarpur bomb case of 1908 in which two English ladies died, he announced scholarships bearing the names of the Bengal martyrs-Prafulla Chaki, Khudiram Bose, Kanailal Dutt and Satyendranath Bose. His message to the world was 'there are no anarchist in India...what we wish for is to free our lives from the foreign rule that poisons or corrupts us'.[18]

Political activity in England continued and the most untoward event occurred on 1 July 1909. National Indian Association was hosting the anniversary meeting at the Imperial Institute in London. Colonel Sir William Curzon Wyllie, political *aide-de-camp* at the India Office was present at the meeting. Madanlal Dhingra, a relatively unknown Indian student assassinated Colonel Wyllie at the meeting. Dhingra had then been studying engineering at the University College, London for about two years. Though he was not staying at the India House at that time, on many occasions he had stayed in London and had come under the influence of Vinayak Damodar Savarkar. The Association invited Surendranath Banerjea for the meeting, who was in England at that time. He did not attend the meeting as he was feeling tired and sleepy. The astute politician promptly reacted as he realised the need to arrest public indignation spreading from the individual student who had committed the deed to the class. Next day Surendranath drafted a letter and dispatched with his signature to all newspapers throughout the United Kingdom condemning the murder. This was followed up by a meeting of Indian students organised at New Reform Club on 3 July 1909. Surendranath presiding over the meeting disavowed the crime and repudiated it in most explicit terms. Vinayak remained peaceful at this meeting but created a scene in a subsequent meeting by his opposition to the main resolution. British press, *The Times*, particularly supported the Prime Minister that a conspiracy was on in India. The prompt and unconditional condemnation of the murder by the majority of Indian students, notwithstanding, the blot could scarcely be erased.

Equally noteworthy was the reaction of Shyamaji when the representative of *Daily Mail* visited him in his Paris residence in the morning of 2 July 1909. Shyamaji evidently knew nothing of the crime until he was shown a copy of the *Daily Mail*. The representative of *Daily Mail* searched the books containing the address of the sub-editors to *The Indian Sociologist* and of the various political agitators with whom he was associated. Failing to find the name of Dhingra, Shyamaji perhaps heaved a sigh of relief. He concluded that Dhingra did not belong to any Indian political association and had acted on his own initiative. He knew Sir Curzon Wyllie personally and had worked under him for several years. Lady Wyllie was also known to his wife. Shyamaji strongly condemned the crime and feared that the act would further limit the privileges of Indian students in England. Very soon Shyamaji, however, changed his opinion. He wrote to *The Times* refuting the charge that he instigated the murder of Colonel Curzon Wyllie. At the same breath, he frankly admitted to have approved of the deed. Dhingra appeared to him to be martyr in the cause of Indian independence. While making this confession, he was aware that his view would shock many. But high minded publicists in England, Shyamaji hoped, would agree with him in recognising the difference between political assassination and murder.

Surendranath reacting to complaints about the treatment of Indian students in England starting from the first decade of 20th century joyfully remembered his student days nearly four decades old. They were welcome wherever they went and being strangers everywhere they felt a disposition of trust and kindness. Indian students of course were very few in number at that time and they threw themselves largely in the company of Englishmen. Amidst the atmosphere of whole-hearted welcome, it was the English winter with its horrid concomitant that Indian youths perhaps dreaded most. During their two-year probationary period in England, which involved four examinations, Romesh and Behari found time to be called to the Bar. The friends listened to Gladstone and Disraeli in the House of Commons, chatted with John Bright, and attended reading by Charles Dickens. Experience of brother pilgrims Manomohan and Satyendranath was singularly alike. They were pleasantly surprised by the great interest that Edward Ryan, the Civil Service Commissioner was taking in their studies. Sir Frederick Halliday who retired as Lieutenant-Governor one day presented himself to them and talked for a long time. The great man, reaching their residence in London asked the house-maid if his subjects could receive him. Halliday might never have condescend to walk while in Bengal but in London appearing just like an ordinary man with an umbrella in hand, introduced himself to them. He seemed to take interest in the Indian youths who returned his visit a few days after his call. They met many noble citizens of England who conducted themselves quite above the narrow-minded prejudices prevalent in India, heartily wishing their success. Indian students fully utilised the opportunity of studying English life and English Institution at close quarters. By and large, they admired British constitutional freedom which was founded on these great institutions. Many of them adapted themselves pretty quickly to democratic functioning and participated in representative politics. In 1875, the scheme of creating 'Native Civil Service' was being debated along with the proposal of shutting off the doors of 'Covenanted Civil Service' to Indians. Brajendra Nath De, a selected candidate for the Bengal Civil Service, undergoing his probationary period at Oxford protested through a letter to *The Times* which appeared in May 1875. The young Indian manifestly had learnt the art of using newspaper to form public opinion. He disapproved of the nomination system because it discouraged qualified Indians from competing for positions in 'The Covenanted Service,' relegating them to inferior positions. The young Indian displayed absolute conviction and concluded by questioning the efficacy of British system of training young Civilians.

As the Indian students grew in number, the urge to form ethnic societies seized them. 'Indian Society', a discussion club, was established in London by natives of India in 1873. Its main objective was to promote cordiality and sympathy among Indians from different presidencies. Fortnightly meetings were arranged and the society was open to Indian ladies as members. Brajendra Nath De, the successful candidate of ICS in the year, read his paper on the 'Races of India'. As the students swelled up in British universities, more such societies were formed. Cambridge University had all long been preferred by Indian students over its older counterpart Oxford. In the early twentieth century, a government committee under the chairmanship of Sir W Lee Warner examined the conditions of Indian students in Britain. It found in the year 1907 that Indian students at Oxford were happier and more popular than those in Cambridge. At the same time, there were only 32 Indians at Oxford, while 87 were at Cambridge. Oxford's requirement of passing an examination in classical language as undergraduates perhaps discouraged many Indian students. The problems at Cambridge were different in nature, originating from concentration of Indian students at three colleges, in which they formed cliques.

Cambridge rightfully bagged the honour of forming first 'Indian Student Majlis' in the year 1891. It began with an ethnic gathering of Indian students on every Sunday afternoon in the house of Dr Oopendra Krishna Dutt. The doctor was popular among the English working class with his medical practice and aligned himself unmistakably against imperialism. Arabinda, still moderate in his outlook, was one of the earliest associates of the society. Very soon the majlis moved towards nationalism and started preaching against the policies of Indian Government. Oxford University where the Indian students were relatively less in number did not wait for long. Maulana Mohamed Ali while studying at Lincoln's College, Oxford gathered round him a set of Indian students. The society founded was named 'Nauratan' after the style of the Great Mughal. The nine Courtiers were no ordinary folk and represented all races and classes of Indian community. Among its members were Fateh Singh Gaekwad of Baroda scion, Rane of Gujarat and

Bhaba of Bombay. In course of time, 'Navratan' came to be known as 'Oxford Indian Majlis' toeing the line of its predecessor. Cambridge Indian Majlis, on 21 November 1896, gave a complimentary dinner at the University Anna Hotel to Prince Ranjitsinghji and Atul Chandra Chatterji. Hafiz G Sarwir of St John's College, presiding over the meeting, complimented Ranjitsinghji for breaking records in cricket, one of the most difficult games and unarguably an acquired one from the imperial masters. Atul Chunder Chatterji had done the same honour in the most difficult of examinations, topping the list in ICS open competition. Hafiz was palpably happy to share with the audience that Chatterji was going to continue historical studies and harboured great hopes that he would correct the mistake of the past historians. The evening gathering continued in presence of the Hindu spiritual leader Swami Vivekananda. Swamiji had no difficulty in acknowledging that Indians had many things but their past, to learn from the Europeans. The glory of India, which had passed away, Swamiji opined, should constitute even a still greater source of inspirations and instruction. Turning attention to the deplorable state to which the country had plunged, Swamiji hoped that like in past cases India would again triumph and recover its past glory.

Long before the Indian students set out to form societies in British soil, band of philanthropic Englishmen collaborated with Indians as they felt the need to enhance the social intercourse between Englishman and Indians. Dadabhai Naoroji pioneered the initiative as 'The East India Association' was established in 1866, chiefly through his untiring work. His Highness, the Prince of Holkar, observed the great promise of the Association in promoting the true interests of all people and princes of India. Prince believed that the welfare of India and the permanency of British rule chiefly relied on frank, mutual confidence and earnest sympathy of Englishmen and desired spread of better knowledge in England of India's people and their needs and wants. Holkar chief contributed a sum of Rupees 25,000, the interest of which would accrue to the Association as long as it would last.

The National Indian Association (NIA), founded in September 1870, was the next initiative. Mary Carpenter, with the assistance of Keshub Chunder Sen who was then touring England, began this association in Bristol. It started with the objective of encouraging female education in India and gradually expanded its activities to promote social intercourse between Englishmen and visiting Indians. Its London branch was set up in 1871 with Mrs Manning as Joint Secretary and Hodgson Pratt, a retired Bengal Civilian as her collaborator. It turned its attention to the difficulties faced by Indian students who started reaching British shore by growing number. These students proceeded to England, mainly for competing for government services and studying for the learned professions. The association started publishing a monthly journal from 1871, providing information about their activities and also organised public lectures by Indians for spreading the knowledge about India. Surendranath, just before leaving for India after passing the final examination of Civil Service, delivered perhaps one of his earliest public speeches. On 21 July 1871, he gave lecture on 'The Evils of Hindu Society in Bengal'[19] with Professor Goldstucker in the chair. The Sanskrit Professor of University College, London was nearly bemused by the oratory skill of his dear student. In 1880, a sub-committee of the association, the Northbrook Indian Club, was formed to look after for Indian students. The sub-committee became an independent Society under the tutelage of Lord Northbrook in 1884. The purpose of course remained same of befriending Indian students and visitors to London and bringing them in touch with prominent Englishmen interested in India. As long as Lord Northbrook was able to interest himself in the work, the Society was singularly prosperous and successful. Wealthy Indian gentlemen realised the utility of the scheme and provided the Society with endowment of more than £ 10,000. A large number of subscribing members, both English and Indian, were enrolled and a club was opened in Whitehall Gardens which was subsequently transferred to the Imperial Institute. But the Society lapsed into obscurity as Northbrook passed away in the year 1904.

In the election of British Parliament in 1905, Liberals were returned to power. Lord Morley was appointed Secretary of State in December 1905. The time was difficult for Indian students as they were drawn into the whirlpool of conflicting currents. Recent events both in England and in India tended to accentuate the misgivings, exposing the lack of effective provision for promoting the welfare of the young Indians. The seriousness of the issue did not escape the notice of Morley. He constituted a departmental committee appointing two members of his Council, Sir William Lee Warner and Theodore Morrison. Sir Curzon Wyllie, his political ADC, who possessed Indian experience, was the third member of the committee, which was entrusted to take evidence and make recommendation on the subject. The committee laboured hard, examining students as well as their tutors and professors of Oxford, Cambridge and Edinburgh Universities where Indian students were numerically significant. Various societies interesting themselves in Indian students were also consulted and the report was submitted towards the end of the year 1906. Morley reacted fast and started correspondence with the Governor-General in Council. But this did not abate the radical activities which was conspicuous by the gathering of nearly 100 students on 10 May 1907 at India House. Vinayak presided over the determined group of young enthusiasts who assembled to celebrate the fiftieth anniversary of 'National Rising' of the Indian mutiny.

In July 1909, the Government of India announced that the Secretary of State had decided to establish a Bureau in London for the supply of information to Indian students as well as a Standing Committee for general advisory purposes. The Bureau assisted by the committee and in co-ordination with the Board of Education in England, would answer enquiries related to educational facilities in England. It would maintain a list of lodgings and boarding houses suitable for Indian students and of private families willing to receive them. Government of India in its turn established local committees in each Province to disseminate information collected by the Central Bureau to the students or their parents. The detailed arrangement was thus put in place but what it lacked most was the sensitivity. Lord Morley and his Council's good intensions notwithstanding, the Bureau functioned in its characteristic bureaucratic style. Within a couple of years' of its working, the intended beneficiaries started voicing their complaints. The bitterness of feelings and disagreeable experience of Indian students multiplied as they felt that the Bureau was subverting the object which thoughtful Indians and Englishman alike had at heart. The agitation continued and in May 1914, Indian students assembled at Caxton Hall in large number. In presence of two Congress leaders Mohammed Ali Jinnah and Mazharul Haque they demanded total and immediate abolition of Indian Students' Department. Situation might have aggravated further but for World War I which broke out in August 1914. All differences thus sunk temporarily. Indian students under the guidance of Mohandas Karamchand Gandhi offered unconditional service to the war effort of Great Britain. Under Secretary at India office welcoming the move, suggested that an 'Indian Voluntary Aid Contingent' be formed for rendering aid to the sick and wounded. Indians, however, were not allowed to join Territorial establishments. Lord Crewe reasoned that Military duties might harm the students by detaching them from their studies for three years.

Homecoming

The first native Civilian Satyendranath Tagore returned to Calcutta in November 1864, receiving congratulations from nearly all quarters. Hardly a fortnight passed, before which his friends and well wishers formally welcomed him through a public meeting arranged at Belgachia Villa,

Calcutta. The event was attended by eminent persons of the city and displayed a perfect harmony with all the major communities being represented. Among the gentlemen present, three were medical men, one of whom had accompanied his grandfather in his second sojourn to Europe. Rajah Pertaup Chunder Singh, Moulvie Abdool Luteef and Manockjee Rustomjee assisted in introducing him to the assembly. Among others present were venerable Vidyasagur and Reverend Krishna Mohan Banerjee. Neither was Satyendranath asked to perform *prayaschitta* nor did he volunteer the same. He along with his wife Jnanadanandini in no time proceeded to Bombay to join his duty. *Hindu Patriot* wished him 'the same success in his onward career that has attended the labor of his early life'.[20] 'Thus ended a most happy social reunion',[21] the paper remarked, holding high hope that the gathering would prove 'the forerunner of many such gatherings in native society'.[22] By the time Surendranath and his two friends returned to India, Bombay and Calcutta had been connected by railroad. Completing the continental trip, the friends boarded an Italian steamer at Brindsi and arrived at Bombay in September 1871. They came straight to Calcutta, breaking journey only at Allahabad, where Indian Community arranged a reception. When the train rolled in at Howrah, Keshub Chunder Sen and other friends were present to receive them. These early successes roused the whole country and more students proceeded to England. The whole country waited with bated breath for the result of the ICS and accorded warm welcome on their return. The tradition continued to the next century, nearly in all parts of the country. Ghaznafar Ali, the third Mahomedan Civilian returned to Bankipore in November 1899 by the Down Bombay Mail. He was brother to Dr Asdar Ali Khan and a splendid reception was arranged for Ghaznafar at the Bankipore Railway Station itself. Nearly whole of the town elite was at the station to welcome the young Civilian. In the following year, Balak Ram after a brilliant academic career in England returned home. Besides successfully passing the open competition in 1899, he stood fourth at the Cambridge Mathematical Tripos Examination. He reached his home at Lahore, before joining duty at Nasik in Bombay Presidency. Elite of the society nearly 2000 in number were present at the railway platform to embrace him and gave quite an ovation. Once the reception was over, a grand procession accompanied him to his house. The situation was no different in Burma which though a part of British India, varied greatly in customs and conventions from rest of the country. But when Arunachalam Thyagrajan reached Rangoon, the Indian community accorded him a warm welcome on the New Year Day of 1908. Like Balakram, Arunachalam was also a wrangler and successful candidate of the open competition of 1906.

Notwithstanding the varied reception of Indian Civilians, big and small, the welcome of Birendranath De, a Wrangler-Civilian at Kharagpur railway station marked the most controversial event. The young Indian, a Government Scholar hailed from Midnapore, which he found a hot bed of swadeshi agitation on his return. The Wrangler-Civilian was no way familiar with the quick change his motherland had undergone. So intense was the fervour of the movement, originating in the wake of Partition of Bengal that a large assembly, formed of students' majority, braved the cold of late November morning to wait for their countryman Birendranath at the platform. Teachers and pleaders were present in large number in the gathering and the 'conquering hero'[23] got down amidst loud shouts of 'Bande Mataram', being presented an inscription of the same motto. Responding to the popular demand, the England-returned Civilian changed foreign costume to his national dress. This act pleased his countrymen who mustered strong at the station and he was taken to the important temples of the town direct from the station. Anglo-Indian paper *Englishman* came down heavily on Birendranath for engineering such demonstration. It was unable to reconcile the fact that the Government, by the aid of scholarship, helped the Indian Civilian to prosecute his studies in England. The paper certainly overlooked in its indignation the fact that the money came from the scholar's own countrymen. Native press reminded that if allowed the countrymen would ship-off brilliant students to more advanced countries by hundreds instead of one in every twelve month. The incident, the press reminded, Indian Civilians of the position to which the benighted 'Englishman' sought to reduce them.

Family Links

ICS was known as a preserve of several Anglo-Indian families maintaining Indian link for generations. Directors' privilege of nomination indulged the love for Indian service hardly to be affected by competitive examination. A number of Anglo-Indians could boast that both sides of their family had been in India for over a century. William Wedderburn joined in 1860 shortly after his brother and sister-in-law and their child were killed during Sepoy Mutiny of 1857. Sir Henry Cotton's great grandfather was a Director of the East India Company, his grandfather and son both were in Madras Civil Service. Sir Henry Cotton himself was a Bengal Civilian coming out successful in the examination of 1865. The Lyall brothers, Alfred and James, reached the top of the ICS as Lieutenant-Governors. Thirty members of George Loch's male descendants spent their career in India, six in the Civil

Service, many of the rest in Army. David, eldest son of John Beames came out to India with a commission in the Indian Army. But the family link in Civil Service was discontinued as Frederick, their second son, failed in his final examination losing the opportunity to follow his father in a Civilian career in India. The link, however, was not totally obliterated as his youngest daughter Angela was married to a member of Indian Civil Service. Angela's son Cristopher Cooke also served the United Province till 1947 as a member of ICS.

The link in many cases continued through matrimonial side also. Rivett-Carnac married the daughter of Mortimer Durand while Evan Maconochie was the son-in-law of Arbuthnot. Indian stories were no different. Abinash Chunder Dutt, brother of Romesh Chunder competed unsuccessfully but Pratap Chunder, Romesh's nephew was successful. Jyotsna Nath Ghosal, who succeeded in the examination of 1894, was the son of Satyendranath Tagore's sister. Janaki Nath, father of Jyotsna Nath was a prominent Congressman and attended almost all annual sessions of Congress. Ghaznafar Ali selected in 1898 was brother to Khan Bahadur Dr Asdar Ali Khan of Bankipore. Charu Chunder Dutt, eldest son of Kalik Dass Dutt, Dewan of Cooch Behar, was selected in 1898. In the same year was selected Byramji Mehta, son of R D Mehta, eminent public man who served as Sheriff of Calcutta. One of Byramji's compatriots was Manmatha Krishna Dev, a scion of most distinguished Bengali family viz. the Sobhabazar Raj Family. Deprived early of the tender care of father and mother, this young man was brought up and educated by his elder brother, Kumar Anath Krishna. It was, however, chiefly the credit of enlightened young Rajah Binoy Krishna of the same house who overruling the social custom sent his nephew Kumar Mammatha Krishna to Europe.

Satyendranath and Manomohan, when they set out on their mission, were both married. Satyendra's passionate letter urging his beloved Jnanadanandini to come over to England would bring tears. Surendranath and his friend Romesh Chunder left their family in India when they proceeded to England. While Badr-ud-din Tyabji's son Mohsin was the first Mahomedan candidate to be selected in 1885, Abdul Latif Qamruddin Amiruddin Latif selected in 1901 was his son-in-law. Badr-ud-din presided over the third annual session of Congress in Madras and greatly contributed towards the education of Mahomedan youth through Anjuman. The friends of Mohsin gave a dinner in his honour at the Prince's Room in Criterion Restaurant, London in September 1885. Mahomed Ali Rogay presided and in proposing the toast of the evening he stated that the near relatives of Mohsin were the first Mahomedans, who ever occupied the positions of

Barrister, Solicitor and Civil Engineer in India. Many European guests were present in the meeting including Wilfred and Lady Anne Blunt.

The trend slowly changed and successful Civilians returned bachelor were picked up by their senior colleagues in service. Jnanendra Nath Gupta selected in 1892 married the daughter of Romesh Chunder. Brajendra Nath De married off his two daughters to ICS men Sarat Kumar Ghose and Guru Saday Dutt. Birendra Chandra Sen married Labonya, eldest daughter of Krishna Govinda Gupta while Albion Rajkumar Banerjee was Gupta's another son-in-law. But the most gorgeous marriage that took place was that of Jyotsna Nath Ghosal. The ceremony at the Woodlands Alipore in November 1899 was notable for many reasons. Bride was Princes Sakriti Sundari, eldest daughter of H H the Maharajah of Cooch Behar. Whole of Calcutta Society was in attendance to do honour to the occasion of the marriage which was celebrated with Brahmo rites. The civil ceremony that immediately followed was attested with the signatures of three such distinguished personages as His Honour the Lieutenant-Governor of Bengal, the Honourable the Chief Justice and Mr Justice Chunder Madhab Ghose. It was most appropriately remarked that 'the two outstanding sections of the Adi Brahmo Samaj and New Dispensation Church, have been, as it were made one in the royal marriage'.[24] The bride was the daughter of ruling chief and the granddaughter of Keshab Chunder Sen who parted to form 'New Dispensation Church'. The bride groom's mother was the daughter of the venerable Maharshi Debendra Nath Tagore representing Adi Brahmo Samaj. The couple received wedding gifts from Her Imperial Majesty the Queen Empress, H H H the Prince of Wales, and H H H the Duke of York.

Amiruddin Abdul Latif, a distinguished graduate of Bombay University passed the examination in 1901. Latif's father was a leading pleader in Zanzibar and Latif was betrothed to the fifth daughter of Justice Badruddin. Latif studied at St Xavier's College, Bombay. Proceeding to England, Latif pursued his studies with distinction at St John's College, Cambridge, and carried off the Barstow Scholarship. Yet another bigger honour was in store for him. He ranked second in the final examination in 1902 and married Naseema. Next year the Badr-ud-din family presented another Civilian to the nation. Hamid Moizuddin Abdul Ali, the successful candidate, was Badr-ud-din's nephew.

Subsequent native Civilians also reaped the benefit of their free interaction with western society. Mahimohun Ghose and Albion Banerji, the two Indian Civilians went to England to spend their honeymoon and entertained Caine to a dinner at the Reform Club, London. Among the guests invited to meet these gentlemen were Dadabhai Naoroji, Sir William Wedderburn and Parliamentarian Sir John Long and William Woodall.

Unlucky Competitors

Drawing ideas chiefly from his experience of educational and administrative affairs both in India and England, Macaulay formed his scheme of good general education as the basis of open competition. This decision proved neither instinctive nor momentary but withstood temporal progress. Even Republic of India, after independence, continued the same scheme without major alteration. It was greatly beneficial to candidates who plucked to pursue their studies in any stream they liked. An examination on specialised subjects would have led to loss of crucial years for the unsuccessful candidates. Many students, who did not qualify, quickly recovered from initial depression. They could choose from many alternatives, ranging from law at one end to literary and scientific studies at the other and concentrated their energies in equipping themselves. They returned home endowed with western education and benefitted by consorting with English life and its democratic institutions. They were absolutely free in their thought and conduct without any restriction that the government service enjoined. Albeit having great reverence for British democratic institutions, these Indians painfully noted the difference of English sense of democracy and the policies followed by British India. They formed a band of Indians truly emancipated possessing appropriate prospective to contribute to the emerging nationalism. Many of them were active in public life associating themselves with Indian National Congress from its formation. Fewer aligned with the cause of minority as representatives of Indian Muslim League.

Manomohan who tried twice at the open competition but without luck opted for legal profession. He enrolled himself at Lincoln's Inn and was called to the Bar on 6 June 1866. Considering the great hardship to which he had been exposed, the Benches reduced the usual terms as a special indulgence to him and called him to the Bar a year earlier. He returned to India in November 1866 and enrolled at the Calcutta High Court on 8 January 1867. He was the second Indian Barrister at Calcutta High Court, Gyanendra Mohan Tagore being enrolled on 28 November 1865 came first. Manomohan soon distinguished himself as a great criminal lawyer. His practice, however, was largely conducted in the district Courts of Bengal where he became a veritable terror to the justice. Though by 1868, four Indian Barristers had enrolled at Calcutta, only two were in actual practice. Gyanendra Mohan shifted his activity to England and Michel Madhusudan

Dutt never cared for the legal profession. Manomohan and W C Bonnerjee used to sit at a corner in the Bar Library which came to be known as 'Asia Minor'.[25] Manomohan could not join public service but his concern was the service for public. He was persistent advocate of separation of executive and judicial power, attempting to form public opinion for it. He was with Surendranath Banerjea in establishing Indian Association and was deeply involved in the civil service agitation which started against the decision of reducing the maximum age to 19. Manomohan was associated with Indian National Congress from the beginning and as the president of reception committee, welcomed the delegates at the sixth session of Congress in Calcutta in 1890.

Lalmohan's course of life was strikingly similar to his elder brother Manomohan. Being unsuccessful in the open completion of 1870, he returned to India as Barrister. Lalmohan concentrated on his legal profession and was not known for public activity till 1879. He was deputed to England with civil service memorial. In England, Lalmohan impressed the British public with his oratory skills. He became close to John Bright and through him came in contact with Gladstone. During the Ilbert Bill controversy, Lalmohan's service was again called for. He visited England in 1883 to form public opinion in favour of the Bill. In 1886, Liberal Party offered him to contest parliamentary election from Deptford which he accepted. No less encouraged were the Liberal Party supporters of the constituency, with whose help Lalmohan emerged as a strong contender. Manomohan, being in England at that time, was witness to his brother's campaign. But at the final moment Irish question influenced the electorate, ruining the chance of Liberal Party. Lalmohan like many other formidable Liberal leaders could not survive the tempest. Subsequent to Indian Council Act 1892, he was elected to Bengal Legislative Assembly in 1893. In 1903, Lalmohan presided over the annual session of Indian National Congress. In his brilliant address to that Congress, in his inimitable style he ridiculed the wasteful splendour of 'Carzonoration' Durbar which took place at the beginning of that year. His last appearance on the Congress platform was in 1906, when he made his last speech in proposing a vote of thanks to the president Dadabhai Naoroji and eloquently vindicated constitutional reforms against its new critics.

Like Ghose brothers Manomohan and Lalmohan, the Das cousins of Calcutta also remained unlucky in civil service examination. Chittaranjan appeared twice in 1892 and 1893. His cousin Satyaranjan Das competed in 1882, so also did his other cousin Jyotiranjan Das in 1890. Both returned as Barrister. Chittaranjan along with his friend Jnanendra Nath Gupta reached

England in 1890. He soon came into contact with Prof Carveth Reade who taught him Philosophy and Literature. Prof Reade encouraged his student to develop the power of independent thought and expression. Chittaranjan did not take all the papers in the examination of 1892 as he felt that he might not do well. Jnanendra Nath was selected and went to Oxford. Chittaranjan stayed back in London. Meanwhile, the Indian Council Act 1892 generated a lot of controversy in England especially for the remarks of MP, Maclean. During the debate on the second reading of the Indian Councils Bill, Maclean, Member of Oldham among other things said, 'The bacons who could not sign the names to Magna Carta, or simple, unlettered English peasants, were more capable of attending to the administration of their country than the most gifted Bengali -the Bengalis who had been slaves for fifty generations. That was a simple physiological fact'.[26] Chittaranjan along with Dadabhai Naoroji, and few other Indians went down to Oldham, Maclean's constituency, and held a meeting there of the Liberal Union denouncing Indian Councils Bill and Maclean, in particular, for the speech he made in connection with it. Another meeting was held at Exeter and soon came the parliament election of 1892. Chittaranjan spoke strongly for Indian reforms and could draw attention of important Liberal leaders including Gladstone. Liberals won the election but political activity distracted the attention of student Chittaranjan and brought him in rivalry to India Office. After appearing in the examination of 1893, Chittaranjan, however, felt that he had acquitted himself well. News of failure was, therefore, quite disappointing and he wired to his father Durga Mohan 'FAILED. ONE PLACE OUT. JOBBERY'.[27] Chittaranjan ranked fifty-seventh in order of merit in which 56 candidates were selected. All the three positions fifty-seventh, fifty-eighth and fifty-ninth in that year went to Indian students. Durga Mohan was alarmed as he apprehended that his son may resort to some desperate course or refuse to return home. He wired to Chittaranjan imploring him to study law and followed up with a letter stating that family tradition equipped him for the legal profession. A letter from Sir Richard Garth who served as Judge of Calcutta High Court to Bhubanmohan might provide a plausible clue to Chittaranjan's exclusion. 'I tried my best, but the fiery speeches of your son at Oldham have spoiled everything. I could not persuade India Office',[28] communicated Garth. Chittaranjan followed his father's advice and joined Inner Temple. Being called to the Bar, he quietly returned home without drawing notice of his countrymen. On the fiery speech of Chittaranjan, *Hindoo Patriot* commented 'It is however always best to be moderate in tone whether on the English or the Indian platform. It does not appear to be clear who this Mr Das is'.[29]

Subsequent events, however, made Das known to the entire nation as 'Desbandhu'.

In the year of 1873 Abbas Tyabji, a cousin of Badr-ud-din Tyabji, who presided over the third annual session of Indian National Congress at Madras in 1887, also tried his luck. Being unsuccessful, he studied law and became a Barrister. Abbas joined Baroda state as Judge and rose to be the position of Chief Judge of Gujarat High Court. Known for his aversion to criticism of imperial rule, the nation was surprised when he gave up job to join Mahatma's *salt satyagraha*.

Another unsuccessful ICS competitor was Dr Aghor Nath Chattopadhaya. But instead of law, he pursued natural science and obtained DSc from Edinburgh University. He was engaged by Nizam as a tutor of his son and gradually Aghor Nath became the Principal of Nizam College, Hyderabad. Aghor Nath's youngest son Harindranath once travelled with Prafulla Chandra Roy and suppressed his identity for the curiosity of knowing the great chemist's opinion of his father. Aghor Nath, one of the great Bengal geniuses, charmed Prafulla Chandra. In his estimation Aghor Nath was 'One of the greatest Bengal has given to the world'.[30] The young son was so moved with his father's greatness that he could utter no word and wrote 'the most natural way was expressed by my eye which shed a tiny, almost unnoticed tear'.[31]

Virendranath, the eldest son of Aghor Nath passed the Madras Matriculation Examination in the first class from the St George Grammar School, Hyderabad. He did excellently well in the FA Examination having stood second in the list of successful candidates. As he passed BA, his venerable father sent him to England to compete for the ICS examination. Virendranath joined Oxford University in 1902, aspiring for ICS in which to the surprise of his relations and friends he was plucked twice. He enrolled himself with the Middle Temple and started studying law. His contact with Shyamaji Krishnavarma and Vinayak Damodar Savarkar distracted his priorities and induced him to join radical activities. The Benchers debarred him and he was forced to leave the Empire and settled in Paris. The Empire did not stop to haul up his aging father. Soon after Aghor Nath returned from France, a night search was conducted at his Calcutta house in August 1910. British police had the intelligence report that he resided with his son in Paris and swooped down with the hope of securing valuable clues. In course of time, Virendranath shifted his base to Germany where Jawaharlal during his Europe trip in 1927 met 'Chatto' as Virendranath was popularly known. About the Indian students he met in Europe, Jawaharlal wrote 'of the few I met, the only persons who impressed me intellectually were V

Chattopadhyay and M N Roy'.[32] Chatto appeared to Jawaharlal a 'very able and very delightful person'[33] with humour and light-heartedness though 'he was always hard up, his clothes were very much the worse for wear, and often he found it difficult to raise the wherewithal for a meal'.[34] Jawaharlal assessed him as 'not a regular communist',[35] instead rather 'communistically inclined'.[36] His revolutionary work against the imperial power, however, compelled him to go on hiding as 'there was a tempting prize on his head and those who had fixed it were thirsty after his blood'.[37] But he was 'ringed round with a magic',[38] as Harindranath portrayed his brother Viren, 'which death with all its boast and brag could never hope to penetrate or touch'.[39] Virendranath could never return to homeland though sometimes terribly seized by the urge before dying in Moscow in 1934.

Manmatha Chandra Mallick was another Indian who competed on Liberal ticket from St George's (Hanover Square) in 1905. On his candidacy, the Liberals hoped to capture what was commonly known as citadel of Conservatives. But it was the attraction of civil service that brought the young lad to England. Like his attempt in open competition in 1873, he was unlucky in the Parliament election also. He became a Barrister and settled in England, never losing interest in the Indian affairs. While preparing for the civil service in England, he joined the 38 Middlesex Rifle Volunteers, a privilege denied to the native Indians. *Hindoo Patriot* was quick to point out 'The fetters of the Benagali fall as soon as he touches the soil of England. In his own country, he is interdicted from joining the volunteer corps'.[40]

A student of Hare School and Presidency College, Nagendra Nath Ghose was sent to England by his father in November 1873. He joined University College, London and came into contact with James Martineau, the great unitarian philosopher. With barely five months' preparation, Nagendra Nath appeared for the civil service in 1874, in which he did not succeed. He was called to the Bar in 1876 and returning home enrolled as a Barrister in Calcutta High Court. Pandit Ishwar Chandra Vidyasagar persuaded young Nagendra Nath to take up lecturer-ship in literature in Metropolitan College where he eventually became the Principal. He served as fellow of Calcutta University for 20 years. In August 1891, he started the paper 'The Indian Nation' in partnership of D C Samadder and served as editor till his death in 1909. In the year 1901, Nagendra Nath contested for the seat in Bengal Legislative Council as representative of Calcutta University against the candidature of Ashutosh Mukhopadhyay. His claim to the seat was quite justified as he had acquired considerable public experience, having been a Municipal Commissioner of Calcutta for many years. As a public speaker, Nagendra Nath ranked second to none. But even with these rich credentials, he could not stem the enormous influence which his rival exercised in the Calcutta University. Nagendra Nath did not lose heart and contested again in 1903. This time Bhupendra Nath Bose robbed off the honour to represent Calcutta University in the Bengal Legislative Assembly.

Dr Upendra Krishna Dutta is perhaps more widely known as father of Rajni Palm Dutt. He belonged to a branch of Dutt family of Rambagan, the other branch being represented by Romesh Chunder. As Gilchrist Scholar Upendra Krishna reached England and competed for civil service. Having failed in the examination, he studied medical science. Romesh Chunder helped Raj Kissen when his son Upendra faced financial hardship in prosecuting his studies. Upendra settled in England becoming a very popular doctor among the working class people in Cambridge. His residence at Cambridge was the meeting place for Indian students from which originated Cambridge Indian Majlis. Upendra married Swedish writer Anna Palme. Two of his sons Rajni Palm and Clemens were the early members of British Communist Party.

In the year 1896, Atul Chandra Chatterji headed the list of successful candidates but stood second in Sanskrit by scoring 279 out of 500. Shadi Lal scored 280 in Sanskrit and came out first in the subject though he remained unsuccessful. He declined the place in Colonial Civil Service which was offered to him. Before coming to England Shadi Lal graduated from Government College, Lahore in 1894 coming out first in the province. He passed MA in Physics next year and proceeded to England on Government of India Scholarship. Following the attempt in Civil Service, he studied law at Balliol College, Oxford. Shadi Lal topped the examination for Bachelor of Civil Law (BCL) and carried off the Barstow Scholarship. Coming back to India, Shadi Lal enrolled as an advocate of Punjab Chief Court. He joined Law College at Lahore as lecturer and soon became the Principal of the Institute. In 1904, he was inducted in Punjab University syndicate which was followed by his election in Punjab Legislative Council in 1909. In 1911, when the Punjab Municipal Bill was on the anvil, Shadi Lal took great interest in it and fought single-handed for the grant of Local Self-Government to Local Bodies. His strong advocacy of the cause and his debating skill were greatly appreciated in and outside the Legislature. But his most outstanding achievement as a legislator was his persistent effort to raise the Punjab Chief Court to the status of a High Court. He was elevated to the bench of Punjab Chief Court. Interestingly several years later, when the demand was conceded to by the British Government, Shadi Lal himself adorned the Lahore High Court as its first Indian Chief Judge. On his retirement from job, he was appointed member of Judicial Committee of the Privy Council in England, the highest appellate authority of Indian High Courts. Shadi Lal received knighthood also.

Another Indian candidate who declined the offer of colonial service was Harinath De. His father was in legal profession at Raipur. A double First Class Honours of Calcutta University's BA in Latin and English, Harinath did MA in Latin. He secured Government of India Scholarship of £ 200 per year for three years for prosecuting higher studies. Joining Christ's College, Cambridge, he obtained the degree of Bachelor of Arts with first class in Classical Tripos. He was elected member of Royal Asiatic Society of Great Britain and Ireland. Harinath sat for the Civil Service Examination in the year 1900, chiefly to please his father. Though not successful, he displayed proficiency in languages. He secured first place in Sanskrit and fourth place in French. Appointment in Colonial Service was offered to him, which he declined. Returning to Cambridge, he was recommended by the Professor of Arabic for the Allen Research Scholarship (which, however, was awarded to a student of theology), and won the Skeat Prize for English Literature. He continued studies at Cambridge and in the following year secured honours in the English section of Medieval and Modern Language Tripos. Appointment in Imperial Educational Service was offered to him. This was the first occasion since the reorganisation in educational service in 1896 that an Indian was given the distinction. Harinath joined Dacca College as Professor of English. Subsequently, he was transferred to Presidency College, Calcutta and was elected member of the Asiatic Society of Bengal. Imperial library, Calcutta had the first Indian librarian in him.

Not only the Indian National Congress, the all India Muslim League owed its origin and growth in early years to the leadership of 'Plucked ICS.' Maulana Mahomed Ali, the younger of 'Ali brothers' was born in Rampur in 1870. He went to Aligarh Muslim College where he regularly earned a small scholarship every year as one of the best boys in the class. But the real surprise he presented was by standing first in the BA Examination of Allahabad University. This distinction was sure to have secured a nomination to some post in the Provincial Civil Service like his brother Shaukat. But it was not in the nature of Mahomed Ali to be content with this ordinary course of life, more so after achieving such spectacular success. He already had started aspiring, with the indulgence of his elder brother Shaukat Ali, for the prize of higher education in England. Ali family prepared itself to sacrifice all worldly comforts as Saukat with his meagre salary decided to send the younger brother to England. Mahomed Ali was now twenty years old with his horizon filled only with the aspiration of becoming member of the much-coveted Indian Civil Service. He arrived in London in September 1898 and chanced to share accommodation with Mia Fazl-i-Husain who was also toiling for the same cause. After a couple of months, Mahomed Ali left for joining Oxford University. He lived in style at Oxford and enjoyed his stay. He was exuberant and freely exposed himself to University life. Thanks to an English spring, he failed in the Indian Civil Service Examination, a veritable calamity. It was a rude end to all the expectations that Saukat had built around his younger brother. But for her mother's resolute and realistic attitude, Shaukat Ali's disappointment would have been disastrous. Their mother, throughout her life had cared for nothing other than the boys' education. On this occasion, she lifted up the spirit and advised for Mahomed Ali's return, observing that 'His fiancée was waiting for more than three years and it was time that he got married'.[41] Her solution was much in line of simple woman's remedy for all frustrations.

Mian Husain Bakhsh considered ICS the most suitable career for his son and wanted to send him to England to try for it. Considering his resources and his liabilities it was a great sacrifice for him, but he was convinced of the educational benefits and the chance that would be offered of a good career. Fazl-i-Husain applied for admission at Cambridge. Muhammad Said, cousin and brother-in-law of Fazl-i-Husain came to Dera Ghazi Khan to accompany him to England. Within two days of his arrival in England, Fazl-i-Husain went to 'Wren and Gurney',[42] the famous coaching establishment for the ICS competitive examination and got himself enrolled for a year. The ICS examination was a difficult one requiring considerable knowledge of many subjects. Fazl-i-Husain selected as his subjects Arabic, English History, European History, Political Science, English Law, Moral Science, Mental Science and Logic and Elementary Mathematics. He maintained his studies throughout the following year though these were interrupted sometimes by ill-health. Indifferent health always stood in the way of his whole-hearted devotion to work, but it never deterred him from his determination to do as much as was physically possible.

Failing in his first attempt for the Civil Service, Fazl-i-Husain went to Cambridge. He chose the Oriental Languages Tripos, and in his examination at the end of the first year secured a first class. The College authorities recognised his ability and hard work by electing him the Pen's Scholar of the year. Concurrently with his work at the University, Fazl-i-Husain continued his preparation for the ICS examination and sat for it again in August 1900. When the result was declared, he was clearly disappointed to miss his name in the list. Quite puzzling was his observation that read: 'I was not disappointed, because I was never sanguine of success.'[43] The result nonetheless disappointed Fazl-i-Hasain. Very candid was his exclamation

'Little less than two years have I spent in most unsparing hard work. I have denied all comfort, disregarded rest, shunned society, neglected health, dress and everything'.[44] What concerned him was 'simply thirst for knowledge and to afford pleasure to my dear father and those interested in me'.[45] Neither was successful, Muhammad Sharif from Patna or his own brother-in-law Muhammad Said, who was his co-traveller in the voyage on steamship Australia which ferried them to England. Back in India, he got into public life and soon became member of Punjab Legislative Assembly. For a time Fazl-i-Husain even dared to oppose mighty Jinnah's vision of an independent Pakistan and founded Punjab Unionist Party. He carried his non-communal stand and being nominated to the Executive Council of Governor-General, handed over the leadership of the party to a Hindu, Chaudhry Chhotu Ram.

Tragic End

Indian Civilians selected against enormous adversity returned home in exalted state to join service. Not only their own community, entire country welcomed them on return. But untimely death deprived the nation from their service. Pulicat Ratnavelu Chetti was successful in open competition of 1874, being the first man in his year in Mathematics and the second in Moral Science. He then joined Balliol College, Oxford and completed probationary training. Pulicat's father P Rangaswamy Chetti was the second Vice-President of the Madras Municipal Commission. Pulicat reported for service in Madras Presidency on 24 December 1876 and was posted as Assistant to Collector and Magistrate to Salem on 2 January 1877. Subsequently, he served at Arcot and Malabar. In 1879, Pulicat was seriously injured when thrown off while riding and had to undergo treatment at Madras. On 28 September 1881, when he was discharging duties as Acting Head Assistant Collector, Palghat an accident carried him off the earth. On the very day, Pulicat attended office in the morning and as usual returned to his bungalow for lunch. In the evening, after having his dinner Pulicat came out with his loaded double barrelled breach-loader hitting a pigeon with the first bullet. He then proceeded to the valley for his usual target practice. He instructed the servant boy to carry a board painted with a chalk with brick bait at centre. Before proceeding to the valley Pulicat tried a second shot, and shortly thereafter a third shot was heard. The servant reached the valley carrying the board and found his master lying on his back, in a pool of blood, and the gun lying a few feet from him on the left side. On examination, it was found that the bullet penetrated the left chest, and made its way out, through the back. Apparently he held the gun with stock upwards, the muzzle putting to his chest, and in trying to hit something, the barrel went off piercing through the body. Unused ball cartridges were found in deceased's coat pocket. No inquest, however, was held as there was no suspicion. With his death, Madras Presidency lost the first native Civilian.

The year of 1889, snatched away two Indian Civilians, both in their prime of youth. Besides administrative ability, both of them were known for superior intellect and scholastic attainment. In January, the nation grieved the death of Anundoram Borooah from fever and paralysis. Successful in the examination of 1870, Anundoram returned to India in the autumn of 1872, and was appointed Assistant Commissioner of Sibsagar district in Assam. He was the first Indian Civilian to be placed as District Magistrate and Collector, an honour that he jointly shared with Romesh Chunder Dutt. He served in the Noakhali district of Bengal where his health deteriorated in the winter of 1888. Sudden attack of paralysis disabled him and he took leave for three months. Anundoram came to Calcutta and stayed with his friend Tarak Nath Palit. The best medical facilities that the imperial capital could provide, was afforded to him, but to no avail as he passed away in the afternoon of 19 January 1889. None perhaps moaned his death more than the poor natives of Noakhalli district. Annandaram spent Rs 15 every Saturday in giving alms to the poor who flocked by hundreds to his house. He took delight in treating the Vaisnavas with sumptuous feasts. *The Indian Mirror* rightly assessed the national loss as 'Long, long will his memory be cherished with grateful feelings by the people of Noakhalli in whose improvements he took the most lively interest and for whom he laboured with his head and heart'.[46]

Next to fall victim was Sripad Babuji Thakur. He along with Surendranath was disqualified for over age after selection in 1869. The clever youth worried little, calmly watching Surendranath fighting out the battle with Civil Service Commissioners. He was re-instated in service with Surendranath. His was signal instance of a man born of poor parents, raising himself to uncommonly high position in life through sheer force of character and intellectual power. Sripad had the advantage of his elder brother Balji Baloj Thakur, BA preceding him in the university and rising well in life. It was under the guidance of his brother that he got his education in school and college. He graduated as a Bachelor of Arts in the Bombay University in Greek in 1868 and proceeded to England. He returned to India in 1872 and served Bombay Presidency in various capacities of judicial and revenue administration. Surendranath wrote about his friend 'When he arrived in London, Thakur was a vegetarian and used to wear like the rest of his orthodox countrymen. Sir Taraknath soon made him a meat-eater and induced him to dress and wear his hair like an Englishman; and Thakur was never happier than with his new habits and in his new habiliments'.[47] Chess was his favourite diversion. He had a marvellously brilliant memory and a particular commanding facility for learning a new language. No less than fourteen languages including both European and Oriental he could master. Being very modest in dealings, he was full of humours. In 1889, he was working as District and Sessions judge of Shikarpore, Sind. His health suffered from diabetes and in the morning of 21 July he was attacked by paralysis. On the same evening, he breathed his last leaving an old mother, a young widow and a large number of personal friends to mourn the loss. With his death at the premature age of 42, the work of preparation of Sanskrit dictionary which he started remained unfinished. He had the misfortune to lose his only sister which made his mother very much upset. In the year 1886, Sripad went on furlough taking his aged mother and young wife to England, and stayed for a year. The old lady, who had continued to live there in the pure vegetarian way that she had been all her life, returned looking all the better for her trip. Sripad was deeply attracted to his mother, and he afforded a perfect example of filial piety of the most exalted kind.

Lokendra and Satyendra, both the brothers joined Lower Bengal and were proving to be hard working officers. But Satyendra who joined as Assistant Magistrate and Collector, Purnea in January 1894, could not serve long before falling prey to fatal enteric typhoid. He was working in Godda in the Santhal Parganas where he contracted the mischievous illness. The illness deceived Satyendra and he ignored the early symptoms. He stayed back on duty at Godda for fourteen days without much **of** medical assistance. The malady which, ought to have been treated at the earliest stage, finally sent Satyendra to Calcutta for medical assistance. He arrived at Calcutta suffering from fever and all that medical skill could do was done. But before a week passed, Satyendra was carried away in the early morning of 9 September 1895.

Byramji Rustamji Mehta was the son of well-known R D Mehta of Calcutta. R D Mehta was associated with the public work of Indian Association. In 1892, he was appointed Sheriff of Calcutta. The preceding year, Mehta sent his two sons to England. The younger son Byramji passed the competition successfully in 1898, and joined the lower Bengal province. But the young man of great promise could not serve the country even for a decade. When in 1908 Byramji was working as sub-divisional officer of Angul, Orissa, the nation was grieved with news of his untimely death at Cuttack.

John Joseph Platel was one of the two Eurasians selected in the competition of 1892. Born in 1870, a Calcutta boy Platel grew up amidst great adversities, being placed in the Murgihata Catholic Male Orphanage from his tender years. He passed with success through the course of seven standards, gaining a scholarship at middle school examination. Old brother John, the Director of the Orphanage, knowing the lad, pleaded with the Rector, St Xavier's College, Calcutta. John Platel thus was admitted in the entrance class, passed brilliant examination and gained new scholarships at each. On securing a first class, with triple honours at the BA examination, he was chosen for the state scholarship of £ 200 a year at an English university. The scholarship lasted for three years and Platel chose Oxford University and joined Balliol College. He was soon induced to try for the ICS which meant preparing for two examinations at once as he was to cross the upper age limit in that very year. Subsequently, after being successful, he was assigned to the province of Lower Bengal and served mostly in judicial assignments. Platel studied law and despaired for missing a first class in the law school. But everyone who happened to interact with him, men both ordinary and eminent, countenanced his good sense and judgment. His constitution, however, was thoroughly undermined by prolonged adjourn in districts notoriously known for infection of malaria. Ironically when he was once indisposed, the Medical Officer wrote strongly of his deteriorating health, recommending a change of place. No doubt the same was granted but Platel was sent, with absolute lack of concern, to an equally unhealthy place. His health deteriorated fast so much so that he had to undergo surgical intervention at the Darjeeling Sanatorium in the year 1905. The operation put him back to work but Platel really was never himself. Sir Andrew Fraser, the Lieutenant-Governor of the new Province of East Bengal and Assam visited Platel as he lay prostrated in the sanatorium. Sir Fraser, a Civilian himself, regretfully acknowledged the unfair way Platel had been dealt with. This time he was sent to Cuttack, a healthier place, as Judge and he worked as hard as he ever had done, much above what was humanly endurable. Platel went on furlough in the year 1909 with his family and spent a couple of months in England. He then proceeded to Dublin where he breathed his last after a very short illness of high fever followed by failure of heart.

Atul Chunder Dutt also died rather prematurely while in service. He was the son of Charu Chunder Datt, Barrister-at-law of the well-known Christian Dutta family of Rambagan. Atul Chunder served mainly in the judicial branch and was looked upon as a distinguished member of Madras Civil Service. In June 1915, he suddenly died from pneumonia. Dutt passed the Mathematical Honours of the Cambridge University as senior optima. He had a passion for Astronomy and devoted significant time to the study of the subject. He came to Calcutta for brief stay and passed away.

Chapter VI
COVENANT AND COMMUNION

European Response to Indian Selection

The Charter Act of 1853 cleared the path of any natural born subject of Her Majesty for admission into ICS. Queen's proclamation further confirmed the right of Indians of free and impartial admission to the office in the service. British people at that moment were perhaps intoxicated with the charm of expanding the Empire. Little did they expect and much less worry that one day Indian youth would overcome the insurmountable barrier to win the competition. The conquered race, enfeebled by the foreign rule was struggling to come out of age old religious prohibitions. Not only Indians were backward in education, native society fraught with many evils was a strong impediment to improvement in moral character. As there was no cause for apprehension of the native challenge to all-European bureaucracy, the ruling class could happily pretend their nobility. The day seemed far, perhaps not before the dawn of millennium, when the natural hewers of wood and drawers of water would be able to successfully compete with the privileged class. Indian universities at three Presidency towns had just been set up in the same year as that of Mutiny. Benefit of western education was accessible to a very limited class of people, the majority being denied the advantage. Such a backward society could hardly think of producing sons who could match the enlightened British youth. Racial pride perhaps obscured their assessment of the extraordinary capabilities of Indian individuals, as they maintained a sham policy of equality in privileges between the ruling and ruled classes. Few individuals, who were far above the average countryman, exposed the fallacy of the assessment, upsetting the whole scheme. Born in native community, they derived the benefit of both western education and rich oriental tradition. Their zeal was strong enough to overcome racial infirmities and social imperfection. These Indian youths fired with extraordinary determination competed with 'unconquerable' British youths in their home turf in an examination designed purely on English academic curricula. This must have been one of the proverbial 'oriental mysteries' which empowered these young men to tear off family bonds, disregard social customs and face the climatic adversities in an alien land to compete with the privileged class. Furthermore, they had just crossed their teens and were hardly matured enough. But what they lacked in age and maturity was adequately compensated in their conviction of moral duty to their motherland. The young lads, while proceeding to England, were by no means certain of success in their endeavour. Rather the young men were seized with the idea of setting examples to their fellow countrymen. This attitude must have appeared to British people nothing more than youthful adventurism and no way a serious threat to take cognisance of. Set against this background, success of Indian youth within the first decade of competition was a trial to English feeling, certainly far stiffer than the trial to English jaw for pronouncing hideous Indian names. Reality thus rubbed off the sham. The *Friends of India* while declaring the selection of first Indian Satyendranath Tagore was not prepared to reconcile to the reality. The paper expressed reservation about the competence of Indians and remarked 'what sort of Magistrate will Hindoo Civilians make? They must be treated Justice of Peace; how will European British Subjects relish the idea of being liable to their jurisdiction?'[1] One could distinctly hear in this reaction, the first warning of Ilbert Bill controversy, nearly two decades before it actually broke out. 'The political gain to the Empire is great'[2] the paper observed and did not try to suppress disgust saying 'we shall not at present estimate whether the moral loss is greater'.[3] Indian press enjoyed the predicament and in stark contrast was its response 'peradventure some, more passionate, will say has smuggled himself into the reserved seats of the most favoured of the favoured conquerors'.[4]

Civilians were entitled to get rewards for acquiring superior knowledge in classical Indian languages. Regular tests were conducted for Sanskrit, Arabic, Persian and Hindustani. As early as in 1872, Bengal Government was unduly alerted to note the possibility of native Civilians carrying off all the prizes. George Campbell as Lieutenant-Governor of Bengal represented to Government of India that native Civilians should not be entitled to these rewards. It was contended that Sanskrit, Arabic, and Persian, are a Bengalee's mother tongue. Governor-General in Council, however, did not accept the proposal for making any distinction between natives and Europeans. 'The advantage which a native has over a European in acquiring knowledge of these languages is not very important',[5] the Council opined. The case of Hindustani was treated differently. It was observed that Hindustani though not the vernacular language of Bengal, was constantly and universally spoken and understood by the educated classes of natives in that province.

My Dear Mr. Sutherland,

May I ask you to let me have your opinion on the following point. In a case under Chapter 37 of the Criminal Procedure Code (of security for keeping the peace) the defendants in their examination stated that they had no objection to find security in the sum of 500 Rs. They afterwards said that they made this statement through mistake and although they had no objection five hundred Rupees was too much for man in their position. I myself think that 500 Rs. is too much and the statement might have been made through mistake. Is there any objection in finding them down for a less sum than 500 Rupees.

My Dear Mr. Banerjea,

You had better consult the Joint Magistrate to whose legal knowledge you attach so great importance.

Your's sincerely,

(Sd.) H. C. SUTHERLAND.

In order to enable the Hon'ble Court to appreciate fully the meaning of this reply, I would beg to state that while I exercised second class powers, you helped me with your advice although you were then my appellate Court; and that within a week after this reply you wrote officially that I was unfit to exercise first class powers. It will be for the Hon'ble Court to decide whether in a matter like this I was not entitled to have the benefit of your advice, seeing that I have been placed under you for instruction and training and that judicially I am your subordinate, although exercising co-ordinate powers and that in this case you were not my appellate but my revising authority.

Again, on the 25th of April when I sent to you my opinion that in lodging a charge of disobedience of summons, the officer of Court who could depose to the fact of the disobedience and not the officer who could depose to the service of the summons should have been sent from Mr. Deputy Magistrate Mackertich's Court where the offence was committed, the Magistrate gave me the following reply

The Assistant Magistrate could easily have sent for one of Mr. Mackertich's Muharir to give the Izhar. All Courts should assist one another especially in cases when recusancy on the part of defendant or witnesses tends to the unnecessary prolonging of the case. *The Assistant Magistrate will do well to look at judicial work from a larger point of view than such as lawyering would suggest case returned to the Assistant Magistrate.*

H. C. SUTHERLAND.

Government of India, therefore, concurred 'with the Lieutenant-Governor that civilian native of Bengal should not under ordinary circumstances be allowed to receive rewards for passing in Hindustani'.[6]

Within a decade, another seven Indians passed the open competition and few others reached England to join the race. The service, however, remained supremely European. Indian ascendancy was insignificant to pose any threat to Europeans. To many British Civilians, the situation appeared grave enough to react sharply. In August 1873, the subscribers to the Bengal Civil Fund met to discuss the question of admitting native Civilians to the benefit of the Fund. It was resolved that native Civilians who were members of service as on 15 May 1872, should be allowed the privilege. Other Indians joining the service after this date would, however, be debarred from the privilege. The original motion proposing the exclusion of the subsequent candidates was voted with absolute majority. It was indeed an overwhelming victory for the racial superiority, falling just short of unanimity. Westland expressed the strong objection, denigrating the Hindoo social system which produced the native Civilians. Polygamy, seclusion of females, infant marriage and prohibition on widow re-marriage appeared to the Europeans as factors debilitating the moral character of the community. Odd European voices were heard against such strong objection, albeit few in number, sympathising with the cause of native Civilians. One such European Civilian Bernard defended the privilege of native Civilians as 'It was politic to give the native Civilians the advantage of feeling that they belonged in all respects to the honourable service they joined.'[7] Indian Press, even in this humiliation, could derive some learning experience. *The Bengalee* urged the young native Civilians, who felt aggrieved at the decision to 'unite and come forward to support the Hindu Family Amenity Fund'[8] and 'strive at something national in its character'.[9] The fund just started, the paper observed, could prosper with the support of those who by virtue of their position could judge its utility.

Dismissal of Surendranath

European officials never stopped grudging the way Surendranath was re-instated in the service. They continued to insinuate that he did not enter the service with clean hands. This prejudice was so widespread and deep rooted that it seemed to have affected even the Lieutenant-Governor of Bengal, Sir George Campbell. On his return to India, Surendranath as in duty bound, waited on His Honour and at first Surendranath was refused an interview. It was subsequently granted to him but the first question which Sir George asked was about the trial to which he was put in order to prove his age. Eventually, it was Sylhet where the young man in November 1871 was posted as Assistant Magistrate on first appointment. Sutherland was the Magistrate of the district under whom Surendranath was to learn his work as an apprentice. The Magistrate, at the beginning, appeared to be cordial and allocated as much work to Surendranath as he could manage to get through. The other Assistant Magistrate of Sylhet was Posford, a couple of years senior to Surendranath. Both of them appeared for the same departmental examination. Surendranath passed the examination but Posford plucked. This outcome did not please Sutherland and the strained relationship soon became a local gossip, rapidly pervading all corners of the small town of Sylhet. The failure of British Civilian must have bemused native community. Sutherland wrote to the authority and arranged exemption of departmental examination for Posford.

Around the same time, another European Civilian Anderson joined Sylhet as Joint Magistrate much to the chagrin of Sutherland. Anderson and Surendranath soon became friends, thus further alienating the native Civilian from Sutherland. With resentment, Sutherland tightened his control on Surendranath and started examining his work more closely. Soon a case came, in which, a native was accused of theft of boat. Burdened with heavy work of the district administration, Surendranath did not devote any special attention to this case. The office superintendant rather misled him in signing an order showing the accused in the list of absconding offenders. This was a sort of routine practice of subordinate staff to avoid explanation as to the delay in finalising the enquiry. Surendranath, displaying lack of administrative maturity, signed this rather innocuous order put up in a heap of papers. This casual act presented Sutherland an opportunity that he was waiting for. He called for records and demanded an explanation from Surendranath. Sutherland naturally was not pleased with the explanation that Surendranath submitted and wrote to the District Judge. Examining the case, the District Judge acceded to the request of Sutherland and wrote to High Court saying 'this case should be laid before the Honourable Court in order they may determine whether Mr Banerjea should, for the present, be allowed to exercise the power of a Magistrate of the first class'.[9] The District Judge formed this opinion overlooking the fact of heavy workload of the young Civilian.

A three member Commission, obviously all-European, was appointed by the Lieutenant-Governor of Bengal for the inquiry. The Commission investigated into the 14 charges levelled against Surendranath Banerjea and found him guilty of all but one. The Commission was severely critical of two charges. Firstly, Surendranath had conscientiously entered the name of the accused in the list of absconding offenders. The second charge was that in his explanation, Surendranath had pleaded ignorance but the whole incident occurred with his full knowledge. The Commission delighted to have found in him wants of application, accuracy, and conscientious discharge of duty, falsehood and palpable abuse of his judicial powers. In the face of such a finding, the Lieutenant-Governor George Campbell could only recommend removal of Surendranath from the Civil Service. Campbell opined that the high standard of honour and morality laid down for members of the service could hardly be compromised. He recorded that such gross and persistent dereliction from truth and honesty in work and conduct by members of the service would cause disastrous effect on the administration. There was no scope of leniency in such cases, irrespective of the official's race and origin.

Surendranath appealed for transferring the hearing to Calcutta where he could have afforded better legal counsel. He also appealed that the Government may provide him defence counsel. These appeals were rejected and the Commission finalised the inquiry holding Surendranath guilty of charges but without, however, making any recommendation. Surendranath came down to Calcutta where he could obtain a copy of the inquiry report. It was not long before he came to know that Government of India had recommended to the Secretary of State for India for his dismissal from service. He would be provided with a pittance of compassionate allowance of Rs 50 per month. Surendranath followed it up with a trip to England to plead his case before the Council of Secretary of State. Government on this occasion granted him three months' special leave. The response he received in India Office was, however, cold and unsympathetic. It did not delay in delivering the official intimation of his dismissal. Thus a careless act of a novice civilian was made out to be grave offence of 'wilful misuse of judicial powers and dishonest fabrication of record'.[10] The impartial India Office, with no desire to exercise discretion, could think of no other punishment for the young civilian but dismissal. Indian press resented the decision pointing out the disparity of the case of Humprey who had been permitted to resign from the service. The native press questioned about Humprey as to why 'Was he allowed so long to draw subsistence allowance?'[11] To them these two cases appeared identical which prompted them to ask whether 'even handed justice been meted to the white and the black when the one has been permitted to resign and the other dismissed, and when the case of the former has been kept out of public view and that of the other proclaimed to the world'.[12] The Government indeed had neither any answer nor did they bother to provide one.

Clubs and Social Events

The exclusion of native Civilians extended to social occasions also. European clubs, without few exceptions, were not open for the Indian Civilians. Satyendranath Tagore, the first native Civilian, had rather pleasant experience of mixing with the Anglo-Indian society. Normal social customs of English society were extended to him without any discrimination. He had free admission to the European clubs and served as President of Sholapur Club for few years. But while acknowledging his cordial relationship with British Civilians, he observed that the great barrier which separated the two societies was difficult to overcome. Other Indian Civilians were not as much fortunate as Satyendranath and often faced discrimination. Brajendra Nath was an early victim, being placed in rather awkward situation. Sir Ashley Eden, Lieutenant-Governor, visited Durbhanga when Brajendra Nath was posted there. A dinner party was arranged at the Ray House which was Colonel Money's residence. Brajendra Nath was kept out of the guest list apparently as he was not wearing Orthodox English dinner dress. The news, however, reached Sir Ashley and the Indian Civilian was finally invited at the insistence of Lieutenant-Governor. This event, however, marked the benevolence of an individual and could hardly remove racial exclusiveness. Indian members of the ICS were prevented 'from being members of the United Service Club in Calcutta'.[13] Same was the case of other European clubs at major cities and towns. European exclusivity was carefully guarded well into the third decade of twentieth century. Kumara Padmanabha Sivasankara Menon was transferred in April 1927 to Peshwar as Under Secretary to the Chief Commissioner. Menon went down to Peshwar where he was denied full membership of the Peshwar Club. Indians belonging to the Imperial services could become honorary members paying subscription. Right to take part in elections was not extended to the honorary members. Menon declined to accept the prevailing conditions of membership. The discrimination was finally relaxed when an Indianised Cavalry Regiment was posted at Peshwar. They resented this invidious position and refused to let their horses take part in the great annual event, the races. The discrimination continued as usual at other places. R P Noranha who joined service in 1939 was placed in similar situation. Noranha wrote that 'the ICS cadre in the Central Provinces at Nagpur was at the time almost equally divided between British and Indians and I had the first of a long series of experiences of schism, not only between British and Indian, but between Indian and Indian and between British and British officers'.[14] Indian members at that time had refused to be merely tolerated in the Great White Society. Indian Civilians though permitted to join the White Club (C P

Club) were rather in intolerable situation of having no voting right. The response of the senior Indian officers was to get together and raise a loan, with which they built the Gondwana Club. It was purely an Indian Club to which entry of Europeans was banned. With its delightful surrounding, the club surpassed the old and rather bedraggled C P Club in popularity, generating a sense of bitterness amongst British officers. 'Since the two clubs were mutually exclusive',[15] Noranha continued, 'the British and the Indian officers met each other in their offices and sometimes at their homes, but never in their clubs'.[16]

Ilbert Bill

On 9 February 1883, the Law Member of the Government of India, C P Ilbert, introduced a bill in the Legislative Council to amend the Code of Criminal Procedure of the Indian Penal Code. The measure was designed to overcome certain anomalies in the exercise of criminal jurisdiction following the code of criminal procedure of 1872. The code of 1872 had brought European British subjects in the muffasils under the jurisdiction of muffasil Courts. Earlier European British subjects in the muffasils had to be taken to the High Courts in the Presidency towns for trial on criminal offences. Meanwhile, a proposal for amendment had been initiated by an Indian Civilian Behari Lal Gupta. In his proposal, Behari Lal urged that native members of the senior or Covenanted Civil Service, especially native District Magistrate or Sessions Judge, should have the authority to try a European British subject in the muffasil. This glaring anomaly put the native District Magistrate or Sessions Judge in embarrassing situation since his subordinate European Joint Magistrate possessed the same authority. Furthermore, native Civilians, who as Presidency Magistrate could exercise jurisdiction over European British Subjects in the Presidency town, ceased to have the authority on transfer as District Officer in muffasil towns.

Lieutenant-Governor Sir Ashley Eden sent the proposal of Behari Lal to the Viceroy, judging it as a matter of general policy and administrative convenience. Government of India worked on Eden's recommendation and asked the opinion of the Local Governments. At that stage, an overwhelming consensus of opinion emerged among the officials who felt that it was time to reconcile the privileges reserved for the Anglo-Indian in the muffasils by the code of 1872. Dissenting voice was hardly audible. Government thus sent the proposal to amend the Code of 1872 to Secretary of State. Hartington approved the proposal, perhaps forgetting to inform the hostility of some Council Members to the proposed changes. Ripon instructed the Legislation Department to draft a bill incorporating Behari Lal's proposal. The outcome of the exercise came to be known as 'Ilbert Bill' as C P Ilbert, the Law Member introduced it. But the Bill extended the scope of changes beyond what Behari Lal originally proposed by empowering not just natives in the senior or Covenanted Civil Service but various other classes of native Civil Servants as well.

The howl of protest from Anglo-Indian community over the Bill had less to do with the Bill itself, but more as a challenge to the erosion of their privilege. Both the official and non-official Anglo-Indian community were unanimous in protest. The boycott of all the Government House entertainments in Calcutta by the wives of the non-official community proved a great success. With them joined the Anglo-Indian press viz. *The Pioneer*, *Englishmen* and *Civil and Military Gazette*. The protest reached England also where Arbuthnot, a former high ranking Indian Civilian led a protest to Secretary of State. Lord Lytton, the former Viceroy emerged as a staunch opponent to the Bill. Henry Sullivan Thomas, in his speech to the Viceroy's Legislative Council, cited a report written by an Anglo-Indian officer on Satyendranath Tagore. Sullivan's purpose was to illustrate that even exceptional Indians who had undergone the rigours of an examination in England that catered primarily to British candidates could not be expected to conform to the desirable standard of objectivity. The report of A S Borridale, District Magistrate of Broach, had suggested that Tagore, because of his own religious prejudices, had been unable to convict a Hindu zealot for murder in a trial that had come before him.

Ripon was startled at the rapidity with which he was losing support from the heads of Local Governments. Those who stayed with him in the thick of events were really very few. W B Jones, Chief Commissioner of Central Province, contradicted the views of his predecessor, proposing that the jurisdiction be given automatically to all District Magistrate and Sessions Judges. Apart from Jones, only one Head of Government, Aitchison endorsed the principle of the Bill as a positive gain. Grant Duff, Governor of Madras, whom Ripon had counted on firm support and sympathy, disappointed him most. Though Duff privately affirmed the Bill to be absolutely harmless, he never publicly defended the Bill. Crosthwaite, the Chief Commissioner of Burma, declined to effect any change. Thompson, Lieutenant-Governor of Bengal, stuck to his opposition and ascribed the change to 'the sentimental grievances of an infinitesimal minority'.[17] Elliot, Chief Commissioner of Assam, was rather confused. He had endorsed the principle of the Bill, castigating the arguments against it as largely ill-founded, inaccurate and 'tinged with prejudice'.[18] Yet European opposition made him recommend that the Bill be withdrawn. Ripon lost the vital support of two high officials who had supported the Bill on principle earlier but switched their position afterwards. They were J B Lyall, Chief Commissioner of Coorg and John G Cordery, Resident of Hyderabad.

Alongside this official opposition, the controversy generated an interesting dual between a European Commissioner John Beames and his Indian subordinate Brajendra Nath De, Joint Magistrate of Hooghly District. Beames bluntly stated that he had never seen an Indian being fit for any post higher than Deputy Collector. The Bill appeared to Beames as 'last straw'[19] for Englishmen, already humiliated by having 'natives placed on a level with themselves'.[20] He saw in the Bill 'a serious danger to the stability of our rule in India'.[21] The demands of Indians was 'nothing but place-hunting and power-hunting, more or less artfully designed'.[22] Brajendra Nath was equally forthright in his comments and held 'that an Indian was quite capable of understanding and judging a European and no one had shown otherwise'.[23] The issue of Europeans' wish to be tried by European Magistrates only, Brajendra Nath opined, was 'thoroughly imbued with the idea that a European can do no wrong'.[24] Beames sent this comment to the Government of Bengal attaching his remarks that he observed in the opinion of Brajendra Nath 'a tone of dislike to Europeans and almost disrespect to Government'.[25]

Brajendra Nath's fearless reaction cost him dearly as later on he found his expected promotions were mysteriously blocked. The brave man never rose to pucca Commissioner-ship and his tenure as temporary Commissioner of Burdwan division in Lower Bengal was very short. In course of time, Brajendra Nath came to know that adverse opinion given by superiors blighted his prospect. The connection of course was not far to relate. His brave expressions delighted the countrymen as much as these annoyed the Government. Brajendra Nath finally retired from service in September 1910. He was extremely popular with all classes of people, with whom he happened to come in contact during his term of office. Native press bemoaned the injustice done, by denying him the office of a permanent Commissioner which he rightfully deserved by virtue of his seniority, ability and successful track record. The final attempt to promote him was made just before his retirement by Satyendra Prasanna Sinha who was then the Law Member of the Governor-General Council. He advocated the candidacy of Brajendra Nath for appointment as the Indian member in the Executive Council for Bengal. Provincial Government defiantly pointed out his lack of competence. An officer who had not been considered fit to be appointed permanently as a Divisional Commissioner, the Government argued, was certainly not fit to be a member of the Executive Council. Interestingly die hard Anglo-Indian paper *The Pioneer* on this occasion shed all reservation and paid him a well merited compliment.

The Indian community, however, was taken aback by the writings of another native Civilian Kavasjee Badshah. In unison with his European contemporaries in Bengal, Badshah held strong opinion against the Ilbert Bill. Badshah's powerful and well-argued minute, setting forth his reasons for opposing the measure belied the native sentiment, as he considered the changes, dangerous and uncalled for experiment. The Ilbert Bill controversy presented emotional crisis for the Beveridge family, exposing their difference in opinion to public. Annette Ackroyd came down to India propelled by her zeal for education of Indian females. Keshub Chunder Sen during his England trip in 1870 profoundly influenced Annette. Keshub Chunder's speeches convinced her of the need of elevating influence of education for Indian women. In October 1872, Annette embarked at the steamer Xantho heading for India with most hopeful plan for the social regeneration of India through education of the women. She reached Calcutta in the middle of December, two days after she had reached the age of 30. She was not totally alone in the city and was hospitably received by her old acquaintances Manomohan Ghose and Krishna Govinda Gupta. Her characteristic devotedness coupled with the assistance of her friends enabled her to start Hindu Mahila Bidyalaya (Hindu Ladies School) on 18 November 1873. That was the day on which Annette, having at last collected a Pundit and a second mistress to share her labours, moved into 22 Bania Pookar Lane, Calcutta with some dozen people. The school was founded on principles of theological neutrality teaching Indian women modern subjects like physical and political geography and elements of physical science. The school was wound up on her marriage to Henry Beveridge, a Bengal Civilian in April 1875. The ugly controversy roused her passion and Annette could not help suppressing her feeling. She addressed a letter in *Englishman* calling Indians uncivilised people for caring about stone idols, child marriages and seclusion of its women. She reminded her countrymen of the Mutiny calling the murderers of women and children 'savages'. Her letter full of diatribe must have been a rude shock to her Indian friends whose number was not insignificant by any measure. Her husband Henry was stronger in his conviction and wrote plainly to Annette, 'I have been pretty faithful to the Bengalees for a quarter of century and am too old to change it now'.[26] With Annette in England, Henry was too emotional to feel comfortable at Calcutta. He had barely any support among his colleagues and prevailing circumstance pushed hard against remaining neutral or impartial.

When Annette reached London in the spring of 1883, she was taken to task severely by Miss Manning of the National Indian Association and friends of her pro-Indian past. Her letter to the *Englishman* against the Bill had brought her in public opposition to her husband Henry. Poor Henry tried hard to come out of the controversy, defending her letter as temperately worded. Henry anonymously presented a proposal in the columns of *The Statesman*, Calcutta that would excuse white woman from appearing in Court before a native Judge. With his experience in judicial work, Henry argued for special concession to be provided for white women in the Ilbert Bill, similar to the concessions already provided to record testimony in cases involving *purdanashin* Indian woman. Henry's proposal recommended exclusion of non-Asiatic woman in the extension of jurisdiction of native Magistrates over European British subjects. But Anglo-Indian emotion by this time had certainly reached a level of animosity to quickly dismiss this simplistic proposal as absurd. The proposal nonetheless was an indication of the importance of the involvement of white woman agitating against the Bill. Henry felt helpless and was manifestly unable to endure the crisis at Calcutta. His letter to Annette teemed with supplication 'I hope and trust that you and I will not fall out on the native question.'[27] The controversy, however, was infinitely bigger than a domestic crisis. Growing opposition both in India and home, marginalised Ripon no more than the passivity of Gladstone disappointed him. Circumstances changed rapidly forcing reconciliation on half-hearted Viceroy. Beveridge family narrowly averted a major crisis and heaved sigh of relief. Annette, however, was not to mend her way. Five years later she wrote to her husband from Darjeeling where she was vacationing with children, 'There are things and classes in India, which have brushed out all my poetry about her people; Still dear! If the sentiment still glows in you, I can appreciate it'.[28] Annette's youthful aspiration had manifestly dried but did not infect Henry who retained old allegiance with India burnt in him.

Henry Harrison and Henry Cotton were the two Civilians in mould of true paternalist. Surendranath regarded them as men of high intellectual eminence and twins in their political views on India. Harrison was a student of Mathematics at Christ Church and President of the Union at Oxford. He also won for himself a reputation at cricket and racket, and came to Bengal in 1860. As Chairman of Calcutta Municipality, he achieved the distinction of advancing important reforms. His modifications were singularly important as he did not attempt to work against the opinion of the majority of Municipal Commissioners or in opposition to their wishes. He thus succeeded in gaining the confidence of the popular representatives of the city which no one before him could attain. Cotton was junior to Harrison in the service by nearly a decade but received a brotherly affection from him. 'They were twins in their political views as regards India'[29] and the dark days of Ilbert Bill could not shake their conviction and the love for their adopted country. At that time Harrison was serving as Chairman of Municipal Corporation of Calcutta and Commissioner of Police of the city. Henry Cotton was the Secretary, Board of Revenue of the Bengal Government. Together they got up a dinner in their house in Kyd Street, in which were invited the leading Indian and English gentlemen. Cotton made a speech propounding the spirit of equality between Europeans and Indians. Regrettably racial emotion by that time had reached a level of animosity which the valiant and noble effort of Harrison and Cotton could hardly allay. Nonetheless Cotton bluntly admitted that he was ashamed to see that members of his own service headed the opposition to the Ilbert Bill. Cotton observed 'practical unanimity of opposition to that measure was as complete among Civilian Magistrates and Judges as it was among planters, merchants and members of the legal profession'.[30] He felt for the harassment of Ripon in an inconceivable degree by the bigotry and race feeling of his own countrymen. In Cotton's assessment neither Ripon nor any man in his position, single handed, could have overcome the dead wall of antagonism by which he was confronted. Ripon finally agreed to compromise much to the delight of his opponents. John Strachey, a leading opponent rejoiced by defining the reconciliation as 'the virtual though not avowed abandonment of the measure proposed by the Government'.[31]

On the basis of modifications approved in the Secretary of State's dispatch, European British subjects were given the privilege. When brought for trial before a District or Sessions Judge, they were entitled to claim trial by Jury, as provided for by Section 451 of the Criminal Procedure Code, subject to the following conditions:

1. No distinction was to be made between Native and European District Magistrate and Sessions Judges.
2. Powers of District Magistrate, under Section 446 of the Code, to be extended to imprisonment for six months or fine of Rs 2,000, or both.

Ripon retreated from his original scheme through settlement reached with 'Defence Association' protecting European privilege. The timing of the Bill, perhaps, was importune. The Anglo-Indians were upset at the larger trends of the liberal programme. The Judges of the Calcutta High Court had two particular grievances. Their salaries had just been reduced by the Home Government to the level of other High Courts. When the Chief Justice, Sir Richard Garth had gone on leave, Ripon had named his senior most colleague as Acting Chief Justice. This happened to be the only Indian on that Bench, Romesh Chunder Mitter. This upset Richard and Ripon heard he had spent his leave 'getting up a Tory conspiracy against the government'.[32] The Chief Justice, he wrote 'is now at open war with the Government, and doing all mischief he can in regard to the Bengal Rent Bill'.[33] Racial animosity did not abate so easily and the European boycott of Viceroy continued till arrival of Lord Dufferin as successor of Ripon. Arrival of new Viceroy sent jubilation to European community both at official and non-official levels. Herman Kisch, a Bengal Civilian, was so elated that he went with his wife to Bengal Secretariat where a great many people assembled to see the new Viceroy arrive. The unofficial English residents, who for two years kept themselves away from Government House and all its entertainments, were delighted with this change of head of Government. They could again 'enjoy the hospitality of the Viceroy without in any way retreating from the position they have taken up with regard to Lord Ripon'.[34]

Inconvenient Transfers

Satyendranath had no qualms against his Anglo-Indian colleagues and admitted to have been honourably accepted in the English society. Indian press, however, never relented to point out his postings as 'they have been kicking our worthy Native Civilian like a football from hole to hole and corner to corner, giving him no rest'.[35] It all started when he was posted as Assistant Judge at Dhulia. Charles Prichard, Magistrate of Dhulia, produced four accused in his Court on the charge of false witness. Interestingly, Prichard was both prosecutor and witness in the case. Satyendranath did not budge from his official position and released the accused persons, considering the unilateral witness as not fully reliable. This refusal was adequately strong to enrage Prichard who lodged complaint with the Government. The reaction of the Government was absolutely predictable. They not only transferred Satyendranath from that place, but appealed to High Court against his order of releasing the accused. High Court fortunately upheld his order and after a series of appeals, Satyendranath could get transfer to a relatively better place of Poona. He was quite happy at that moment but bigger surprise was in store for him. The local people stirred by the incident arranged a farewell function for him in which an address was presented to him. This time Government reacted very sharply and issued order prohibiting government officials to accept address without its prior permission.

Frequent transfer at short notice did not end with this incident. *Indian Spectator* observed, 'Mr Tagore has adorned his position wherever he has gone and won general popularity, both with the natives as well as Europeans'.[36] In November 1874, Satyendranath Tagore was again shifted to Shikarpore, Sind. This order was unexpected for Satyendranath as he had already served the province and the climate did not suit his health. Before leaving Bombay for Shikarpore, he called on the Governor and one of the Secretaries placing before them his difficulty. The Secretary assured Satyendranath of a quick transfer and obtained the choice of places where Satyendranath would prefer to work. Satyendranath joined Shikarpore expecting an expeditious transfer as the places would fall vacant. He, therefore, was greatly relieved on being appointed Judge of Surat. But his misery did not end as on arrival at Surat, Satyendranath found another Civilian McPherson had already been appointed Judge. Native press criticised the move as 'certain English people can't bear to see an English assistant under an Indian Judge'.[37] As the native opinion was getting restive, Government finally sent Satyendra to Poona.

Sripad Babaji Thakur, the other native Civilian of the Bombay Presidency, on his arrival in India in December 1872, was posted as Assistant Magistrate and Collector at Surat. Hardly had he completed a year in that post when he was expelled from the Baroda state by order of the Resident. Gaekwar State at that time was in thick of controversy and the incident was linked to the suspicion of Sripad being involved in it. Soon thereafter Sripad was transferred from Surat to Carwar. Native press appropriately ridiculed the decision as 'If every assistant that goes to Travancore without previously obtaining the permission of Mr Ballard is to be transferred, the Fort, St George gazette will become really interesting business'.[38] With such coverage, the news of expulsion of Sripad from Baroda state by the Resident reached England. Some of the Indian authorities and independent persons were shocked to a degree palpably short of prompting them to act.

Many Civilians had to move out as they lacked the confidence of the Anglo-Indian business community. Imperial Government in their attempt to attract British capital was not prepared to ignore their demand and often acted without proper appraisal of the situation. Anundoram joined at Chittagong, and had to move out to Jessore only after a few weeks. The truth was that his presence was not liked by the business owners. Tea-planters and the Anglo-Indian community held a meeting at the Chittagong Club House and memorialised the Government of Bengal for the transfer. The prayer was granted transferring Anundoram to a relatively insignificant district. Brajendra Nath likewise was shifted out of Raneegunge Sub Division

Sir Krishna Gobinda Gupta K. C. S. I.
The First Indian Member of the Council of the Secretary of State for India.

as the European colliery owners and managers were not happy with him. Brajendra Nath lamented 'Every effort was made for hustling me out of the place, and there was an opportunity before long for doing so'.[39] Even the native states Cochin and Hill Tippera could not utilise his rich experience and ability. When Cochin Government asked Government permission to engage Brajendra Nath as Diwan, they were told that there was no reason why one Bengali should succeed another in the position. A Bombay Civilian was selected to succeed Albion Rajkumar Banerjee. The State of Hill Tippera offered him a post of Manager but the Bengal Government objected to his appointment.

European Civilians were not either absolutely free from the hardship of frequent transfer. What worked behind the scene was the shadow fighting between Secretariat and the district Civilians. John Beames attributed it to 'the Secretariat mind'[40] which he felt 'that if a man is left too long in a district he gets into a groove'.[41] Secretariat never wanted to afford a Civilian the opportunity to acquire real insight into the condition and needs and wants of the people, discovering the vanity of fine theoretical cobwebs which the Secretariat mind was artfully spinning. District experience might even equip the Civilian to administer inconvenient pricks to Secretariat windbags, ultimately exposing their emptiness. Secretariat, therefore, perpetually wanted men new to the district who would swallow all their nostrums.

Coveted Posts-European Exclusivity

Even when the rules of examination were altered, the selected Indians were kept out of executive branch and were put mostly in judiciary work. Gokhale as a member of the Islington Commission put a question to Jnanendra Nath Gutpa of the Indian Civil Service who appeared before the Commission as to why most of the Indians in the service were in the judicial branch. Jnanendra Nath said in reply that they preferred the judicial line because in the executive branch they stood the risk of not having their services duly appreciated and their claims superseded. Brajendra Nath also observed that several European members of the service suggested that Indian members of the service should do well to join the judicial branch. Brajendra Nath further felt that 'there was perhaps an implied hint in this, that we were not by nature and capacity fit for executive work'.[42] The response of Indian Civilians was just the contrary as 'it was perhaps in reply to such suggestion',[43] Brajendra Nath asserted that nearly all his Indian colleagues joined the executive branch.

Indians were again barred as a rule out of the precincts of the Secretariats. Even man of such outstanding abilities as Romesh Chunder and Krishna Govinda were not even thought worthy of being appointed to the responsible office of the Chief Secretary and only very few were raised to the position of a Secretary. Indian officers were appointed now and again to the Board of Revenue but were debarred as a rule from the superior offices in the Secretariat. In 1891, the Anglo-Indian paper, *The Pioneer* recommended the appointment of Satyendranath to the Bombay Governor's Executive Council. This recommendation followed a rational assessment finding him the most senior of the District Judges in Bombay, and that he belonged to a high Brahmin family. But fortune ordained otherwise and Satyendranath never got the recognition he deserved. He retired prematurely in 1897 still having a couple of years more to serve. Very candid was the expression of Bengali member of the ICS about his British colleagues. He told a French administrative expert that 'They treat me as an inferior and patronise me. The only man who has really treated me as an equal is an Irishman'.[44] The Irish feeling especially after 'Home Rule' agitation sometimes echoed with discrimination of Indians. In 1883, O'Donnell, the Irish member, called the attention of the House of Commons to the supersession of Behari Lal in the appointment of the Senior Magistrate of Calcutta. On the temporary absence of Chief Presidency Magistrate of Calcutta, Behari Lal, the Magistrate next in rank, 'was passed over in favour of English Barrister',[45] Handerson. The Member of Parliament, in possession of detailed information, accurately established both seniority and competence of the native Civilian over the British Barrister. O'Donnell by his pointed query startled the House to which the Secretary of State blushed to reply, much to the delight of Indians. Source of such intimate information could not be hidden for long and the search zeroed on his Civilian brother.

Ilbert Bill was purported to remove the limitations of native Judges extending their judicial authority over European citizens. Resistance both in India and Home left Ripon in lurch and forced compromise. A 'revolutionary change' however occurred around the same time appointing Romesh Chunder as Officiating District Magistrate and Collector of Balasore in May 1882. Rivers Thompson, Lieutenant-Governor, bitterly opposed the Bill but was significantly the first to send a native Civilian to head the district administration. Thus the event was as much out of 'ordinary course of things'[46] as it occurred 'without anybody knowing about it'.[47] Native press was jubilant over the honour bestowed on Indian to occupy such onerous post. It was persuaded to hope that disinclination of Europeans to serve under natives was gradually wearing away. Anglo-Indian paper, *The Pioneer*, missed the occasion and perhaps noted the appointment only when

Romesh completed his term of three months. It acknowledged the competence of native Civilian holding charge of a district without provoking any disturbance among the administrative staff. Romesh deserved the honour and conducted himself without misusing authority. Subsequent events disappointed native sentiment and the solitary appointment could hardly remove distinctions between European and Native Civilians. History recorded the event as a benevolent act of Lieutenant-Governor known for his racial arrogance.

Again in the year 1884, Romesh was appointed Officiating Magistrate and Collector of Backergunge. On this occasion, an Indian Civilian was allowed to head the district for a whole year. When their fitness to properly manage the affairs of a district was repeatedly questioned by the authorities, the favourable opinion of Lieutenant-Governor of Romesh's conduct gratified the whole nation. Administrative ability and the capacity of natives for successfully dealing with the complex machinery of district affairs were established through Romesh while discharging the duties of the troublesome district.

Krishna Govinda Gupta whose official career among the native Civilians had been the most spectacular, entered Bengal Secretariat in 1887. Lieutenant-Governor, Stewart Bayley, appointed Krishna Govinda as Junior Secretary to the Board of Revenue of Bengal. The selection was done strictly following the rule of seniority, the senior Civilians having declined the appointment. On this occasion, native paper *Indian Mirror* was thankful to Stewart Bayley for rewarding the aspirations of a young Bengali. Sir Stewart though made no departure from the rule, deserved the credit for breaking 'the official tradition of prejudice against Native members of the Covenanted Civil Service in the bestowal of Secretariat appointment'.[48] Anglo-Indian paper, *Englishman*, was rather unhappy with this appointment and vainly attempted to treat the selection of Krishna Govinda as a routine affair. At the time when the Presidency was slowly recovering from the Ilbert Bill controversy and European discontent soon becoming public, British Civilian W C Macpherson who joined as under-Secretary in the Revenue Department of the Bengal Office was an applicant for the post of Junior Secretary to the Board of Revenue of Bengal. Macpherson before joining Bengal Secretariat had served in the Assam Secretariat. He left Assam in disappointment in consequence of having been overlooked for his claim to the post of Director of Agriculture by the Chief Commissioner, Elliot. Sir Stewart's brave act bitterly disappointed him. Krishna Govinda's good luck, however, did not continue for long. On the next occasion, he lost his claim to a European Civilian. Krishna Govinda was passed over in 1891 by appointment of C W

Bolton, as Senior Secretary of the Board. Bolton entered the Board's Secretariat much later than Krishna Govinda. The convention of promoting Junior Secretary to the Senior Secretary of Revenue Board was conveniently ignored on this occasion. Krishna Govinda was removed to the collectorship of Nadia to extinguish his claim to the Senior Secretary-ship of the Board. An Irish Civilian, Nolan, was also axed at the same time. Native press helplessly enquired of the presence of 'any Irishman in the Viceregal Cabinet or in that of the Secretary of State for India'.[49] Nothing could disarm Secretary of State, Lord Cross, to utterly disregard the reality, pompously announcing that 'Justice is the great key-stone of British policy in the country'.[50] Nor could anybody question the underlying principle of 'British justice'. By the turn of the century, *Indian Mirror* highlighted another act of overlooking the right of Krishna Govinda. With dispassionate assessment native press supported the justified claim of Krishna Govinda for the post of Chief Secretary to the Government of Bengal. Though there was 'not a more talented and sober officer in the whole of Bengal Civil Service',[51] Krishna Govinda was not allowed to rise beyond Excise Commissioner. At the same time, Behari Lal who was serving as a District Judge was passed over for elevation to the High Court Bench. Their denial was attributed to the crime of colour. In order to make people believe that the native Civilians had not been ignored because of colour, another grave injustice was done to a highly meritorious officer of English birth. Knox-Wright, District Judge of Patna, was ignored when after 28 years of zealous service, an opportunity turned up of rewarding his contribution by promoting him to the High Court Bench. Native press felt sorry when his rightful claim was axed to maintain sham pretence of British justice. Knox-Wright, the upright and distinguished District and Sessions Judge, was unable to adjust with the slight. Finding no other course open to him in consonance with his judgment and self-respect, he resigned from the Civil Service. Knox-Wright missed the berth in High Court Bench but nonetheless commanded the respect and affection of Indian community.

Brajendra Nath could never recover from the official displeasure he incurred during Ilbert Bill controversy. His untiring initiative to improve the condition of his countrymen was never recognised in full. Expectations swelled up in Bengal as John Woodburn, the Lieutenant-Governor promoted two native Civilians. Behari Lal was elevated to the Officiating Bench of the Calcutta High Court and Krishna Govinda got a Divisional Commissionership. Native press while congratulating the Lieutenant-Governor reminded how Brajendra Nath had served with honour and distinction in numerous districts. Despite having an unblemished record, the deserving Civilian was supplanted by at least half a dozen European juniors. Countryman urged that a Divisional Commissionership be awarded to Brajendra Nath who was serving as District Magistrate and Collector of Bankura. His administrative ability unfortunately could hardly erase the blot attached to him.

Appointment of Indian Civilians in Foreign and Political Department was practically delayed till the third decade of 20th century. The Indian Princes did not like their 'own countrymen to lord it over them as Resident or Political Agent'.[52] Southern states viz. Cochin and Travancore, figured as isolated exceptions where Rajagopala Chariyar, a Statutory Civilian served as Diwan of Cochin for five years and then again Travancore for three years. Albion Rajkumar Banerji succeeded Rajagopala Chariyar and was appointed Diwan of Cochin in 1907. Albion was in the post for seven long years. The legacy continued and Joseph William Bhore, another Indian Civilian replaced Albion. The issue of Indianisation of the Political Department could not, however, be shelved forever. In 1924, the Lee Commission on the Superior Civil Services of India recommended that 25 per cent of the Indian Political Service should be Indianised. It was under this scheme that K P S Menon was taken into the Foreign and Political Department in 1925, in the third year of his service. The recommendation of the Lee Commission, however, was complied more in breach than its observance. In 1939, out of a total of 172 officers in the Political Department, only 12 or 7.5 per cent instead of 25 per cent were Indians. Out of them only two or three were from ICS and eight or nine were Mahomedans.

The doubt on the ability of Indian Civilian and the official deprivation they were subjected to, remained debatable forever, occasionally getting animated by cases of deprivation. The untimely retirement of Abdullah Yusuf Ali at the time when World War I was diverting all attention, afforded one such occasion. *The Pioneer*, more in an attempt to tease the Indian public, paid ungrudging tribute to the Indian Civilian, retiring after service of only 15 years. 'The humdrum routine of district work',[53] it pointed out banteringly, did not please the intellectual interests of the Cambridge man. It appeared strange to them that an Indian official should find life and work in this country distasteful. Native press joined the debate stating that the Civilian was compelled to resign the service because the service did not provide sufficient scope for his talent and ambition. It was the fault of the service which barred Indians to the higher ranks in the service. Romesh, one of the ablest Indian members of the Civil Service, did not even rise to the position of a 'pucca' Divisional Commissioner. Krishna Govinda was more fortunate to become a Member of the Board of Revenue. Thereafter, he was shunted off to the Fisheries Department and had to do special work. Being the senior officer, at the time when a temporary vacancy occurred in the Lieutenant-Governorship of Bengal, he was passed over. Krishna Govinda's appointment as Member of the India Council was due to the reform scheme and the initiative of Lord Morley. Indians though qualified by seniority and service to become Divisional Commissioners were assigned 'special work'.

Fareedpore Experience

In the year 1888, the district of Fareedpore in Lower Bengal had the taste of all-native administration. Brajendra Nath joined as the Officiating Magistrate while Behari Lal Gupta officiated as District and Sessions Judge. The District Superintendent of Police for a short period was Mahendro Nath Hazra, another native gentleman. The Indian Civilians proved their competence and equally happy were the residents. At the departure of District Judge, Behari Lal, the local press reported that the little town was agog with only one topic and Behari Lal's transfer was almost on every man's mouth. It was a rare occasion which presented genuine reason to be flushed with nationalist fervour. On his transfer, Behari Lal left behind a career, extending over three years, which was not only free from any taint or blemish, but was a subject of universal admiration. The conclusion recorded was more feverish, 'It is certain that he leaves the district with the sincere blessings of the million'.[54] Starkly in contrast was the European response which resented this administrative arrangement. Nonetheless, they distorted public opinion as in his letter in March 1888 H M Kisch wrote about his Fareedpore trip: 'The Judge is a native, and the District Superintendent is also a native. Until recently, the Magistrate-Collector was also a native, for Government apparently wanted to see how a district would get on administered entirely by natives. There was no serious breakdown, but I doubt if the experiment pleased anyone. The officers themselves naturally prefer to have a few European with them and not to be left alone as if unfit to associate with Englishmen. The non-official natives, too, far prefer Englishmen as their rules to natives, too, whatever views they may express in speaking or writing in public. My friend told me that when he went to Fareedpore to relieve a native Collector, he was most warmly welcomed, and one after another of the native residents and officials asked him why Fareedpore had been selected for an experiment in native administration, and what crime the district had committed thus dishonoured.'[55]

Physical Assault

The incident which surpassed all other events in barbarity occurred on the last day of the year 1898. Sheikh Ashgar Ali, a native Civilian posted as Assistant Commissioner, Hissar was travelling from Lahore to Kasur. When the train arrived at Lahore, Ashgar found that the first class compartment of the composite carriage was occupied by two passengers, one of whom was C M King, Deputy Commissioner of Ferozepur. The composite carriage was literally packed with luggage with a lot many waiting to be shoved in. Ashgar waited on the platform till he saw King coming up with several other Europeans. He then wished the European Civilian. To his polite enquiry of the possibility of attaching another coach at Lahore, King curtly indicated his ignorance. Another carriage was soon attached, and Ashgar put his things in a compartment of the new carriage. King and all the Europeans were together, and they were apparently friends. The European passengers were military personnel stationed at Ferozepur. When the train was about to start, King went up to Ashgar and asked him to go to the other carriage as all of them wanted to occupy the newly attached carriage. Ashgar had no objection, but there were no coolies to shift his luggage and the train was about to start. King then went back to his friends and had a consultation with them. King and one other passenger returned to the composite carriage while two Europeans came into Ashgar's compartment. Shortly after they had entered, they asked Ashgar not to put his feet upon their clothes. Ashgar had done no such thing and he said so. Then three men left the compartment and soon came back with their dogs. They left the dogs in Ashgar's compartment to which Ashgar protested and decided to report the matter to the guard. As the train approached next station and Ashgar was about to get out of the coach, the military officers beat him severely injuring his left eye and causing a swelling on the head. Some fellow passengers took Ashgar to the intermediate class compartment, in which he travelled to Kasur. At Raiwind, Ashgar personally reported the matter to King who took no cognisance of it. The assailants refused to give their name to police, the Station Master or the guard. Thus a native member of Indian Civil Service, himself a first class Magistrate was assaulted by European in presence of a European member of the elite service. Government evinced little interest in probing or penalising the assailants.

Imperial Administration-Oppressive European and Indian Cowardice

20th century marked the beginning of violent form of Indian agitation against the invidious policies of Imperial rule. Two decades of Congress politics of representation had produced very little but cold assurances. Discontent among Indians grew stronger, often changing from the characteristic mildness of previous century. At the same time concurrent world events engendered an urge for nationhood in the minds of educated Indians. Lord Curzon's plan of dividing Bengal in 1905 might have been a measure of administrative convenience. To Indians, it was, however, another manifestation of the devious scheme of promoting religious division. Public agitation spread far and wide and became more broad-based. Imperial administration invoked repressive measures and in many places ruthlessly crushed the agitation. At the same time, many seditious activities were reported to have taken place in different parts of the country. Quite a few riots targeted against the administration also broke out during this time. Guntur Riot added a new dimension to the heightened controversy that was rocking Indian public life. On the *Sivaratri* day in 1909, a serious unrest occurred at Kotappakunda in Guntur District. On that day, large number of people flocked to visit the local temple of Siva. The crowd was suddenly enraged with the news of prodding of a bullock by a constable with his bayonet. The crowd got provoked and venting their fury, began to assault the constable. Other constables came to the rescue of their colleague and a general fight between the crowd and the police ensued. The crowd surged in no time and a mob of five thousand assembled at the temporary Police Station and started pelting stones. The Inspector ordered the police to fire; two rioters were killed and a number wounded. One constable and one salt peon were killed and the temporary police station was burnt. Other constables felt endangered and dispersed in the face of angry mob. Dadacharji Kershasp, a Parsee Civilian who joined the service in 1895 was the Divisional Officer and Magistrate of Narsaraopet. District Superintendent of Police was also an Indian, Arun Subba Rao. Kershasp, when he became aware that the riot was in progress, arrived on the scene without any delay. After arrival, he tried to pacify the mob by making few promises into the alleged grievance that the rioters delivered through the Sub-Magistrate. Kershasp felt limitation with the local vernacular Telegu and the Sub-Magistrate had to act as an interpreter. It impacted his confidence in contending the crowd and Kershasp was perhaps momentarily unnerved when he saw his duffader hurtled in his presence. The District Superintendent of Police who arrived later at the scene, was severely wounded in his attempt to quell the riot. It was reported that both Kershasp and Arun Subba Rao decamped in the guise of pilgrims. Madras Government deputed Member of the Board of Revenue, Horne William Ogilvie, ICS, to make an on the spot investigation into the circumstances leading to the riot. Both Kershasp and Subba Rao were placed under suspension as Horne initiated his inquiry. Horne laboured hard and completed the investigation in a couple of months. Around the time when he submitted the report, the suspension orders for both Kershasp and Subba Rao were revoked. They were posted as Assistant Collector and Deputy Superintendent of Police respectively. Kershasp, with his sensibility, could hardly endure the ignominy and went on leave for six months.

Government agreed with the investigation report and held that Kershasp entirely failed to realise the responsibilities of his position. As an officer of the Indian Civil Service and Magistrate, he was found quite unfit for measure of responsibility which devolved upon the Magistrate in independent charge of the division. He was reduced to the rank of passed Assistant Collector and Magistrate without independent magisterial responsibilities. Government, though recognising the difficult situation that Subha Rao confronted, did not deal with him leniently. The police officer who in face of the danger had been found wanting in nerve and personal courage, the report opined, could not again have sufficient influence with the force to be useful as Superintendent. He would not inspire confidence if similar trouble would occur while he was in charge. Punishment for Subba Rao was equally severe as he was reduced to the post of first grade Deputy Superintendent of Police. Divisional Inspector General of Police was advised to appoint Subba Rao as personal Assistant to the District Superintendent of Police.

The Government decision neither triggered any sympathy for the penalised Indian officials nor did the press disapprove the act. Government after all possessed the right to punish the officers who behaved disgracefully and deserted their duty when they ought to have stuck to their guns. Europeans successfully triumphed in their campaign as the incident presented to support what they all along propounded. Degenerate race was not capable of producing young man with adequate moral strength required for such high official job. A careful examination of Kershasp revealed that he was not a weak soul to submit to the European notion of race superiority. Native press comforted itself by publishing many virtues of Kershasp, specially his disavowal of western contribution to world advancement. Through his many studies in Persian History which were published in 1905, Kershasp depicted the attempts of European historians from the earliest times to distort facts to the disadvantage of Asiatics. By a close examination of the statements of different historians and the circumstances, Kershasp attempted to prove that the stories intended to exalt the Greeks at the expense of the Persians, were of pure mythology. He opined that the Greeks had been overrated a good deal and that Asia had done much more in every direction than Greece for human progress. Kershasp presented the contemporary archaeological discoveries which converged to the same conclusion. East appeared to him to be the home of civilisation. He believed that but for their political experiment and the cultivation of fine Arts, the Greeks of the classical period did not distance some eastern nations in the race.

The Indians did not despair for long and their subtle mind could soon detect inconsistencies in Government action. It drew a parallel between cases where officers instead of proving inefficient in the way they did in Guntur case of deserting their duty, proved oppressive and tyrannical. British Civilians in different parts of the country, committed grave irregularities, tampered with documents and harassed innocent men. The 'vigorous despots' ceased to remain pure 'benevolent' and paternalist class became a vanishing tribe. The native press opined that an officer had acted contrary to discipline not only when he had deserted his duty. Government, on more occasions than not, treated the 'despots' with avuncular indulgence. The officials by overstepping the limits of fairness, humanity and justice were interfering with elementary rights of the subject. The grave offences committed were overlooked as the European officials were guarding the Empire. The Government, therefore, did little justice by treating two forms of misdemeanour in different manner. Manifestly the Government could not rid itself of the double standard and opened itself to just condemnation. The issue did not subside for a long time and was raised even in the House of Commons. Secretary of State had to clarify of the practice of appointing officials in charge of division, and the issue was subsequently referred to the notice of the Government of India. The controversy continued and five years down the line Sir Ralph Benson, as witness to Royal Commission, pointed out the incidence as an instance of Indians lacking requisite strength of character for holding high executive posts. In 1914, Sir Ralph, the senior most Civilian in India, was serving as Judge of Madras High Court. He informed the Commission of Kershasp's degradation for showing cowardice in the face of a very serious riot. Kershasp instead of running away, Sir Ralph opined, ought to have sallied forth and held his ground. No member could possibly bring to Sir Ralph's notice of the letter which appeared in British newspaper in 1907. It was an aggrieved English parent's denial to allow his son to compete for ICS. The attacks on English officials in India dispossessed (successfully!) the parents of their valour. They were seriously thinking against the choice of an Indian prize for their sons.

Official Reprieve and Native Communion

Satyendranath, the first Indian Civilian, was often subjected to inconvenient postings and despaired a lot. But while moving out of Dhulia, he had nothing particular to complain. He was certainly going to a better place, Poona. What pleased him immensely more was the unprecedented honour conferred on him by an assembly of 500 local people. They gathered under the guidance of G A Mankar, acting Head Master of Dhulia High School, to present him a farewell address. The address itself threw light on the progress of opinion in India, more so on the position occupied by Satyendranath in his own community. The ceremony started with an address of Mankar followed by addresses in Sanskrit, Marathi and Hindustani. The meeting was conducted in pure Marathi tradition with customary distribution of nosegays, goolab, atar and supari and display of fireworks. But the most touching moment of the meeting was when Satyendranath rose to reply to the honour bestowed on him. His words, 'Although my dress and manner may appear foreign to you, I can nevertheless assure you, and even proud to say, that I am the same flesh and blood as yourselves'[56] convulsed the crowd. Satyendranath, the organiser of Hindu Mela, was perhaps wondering how the national feeling was progressing across the country. While in service, Satyendranath took part in the second Chaitra Mela held at Calcutta in 1867. It was on this occasion that he composed and set to music the patriotic song 'Gao Bharater Jai'.[57] The mela was perceived to be the forerunner of Indian National Congress and the song remained the *de facto* national anthem for nearly a quarter of the century until it was replaced by his brother Rabindranath and the rebel-poet Kazi Nazrul Islam. Satyendranath did not serve the full tenure and retired early from the service. Immediately after his retirement, he presided over the 10th annual session of the Bengal Provincial Conference held at Natore in June 1895. Satyendranath addressed the assembly in English which his brother Rabindranath translated into local vernacular Bengali. Satyendranath's first-hand experience made a wholesome effect on his understanding of Indian affairs. His address was felt to be a masterpiece in the exposition of the problem facing the people of Bengal and of India at that time.

Brajendra Nath served as the Magistrate of Hooghly devoting his initiative in organising Local Self Government in the district. When the merit of this young but experienced and worthy officer was being recognised, Brajendra Nath was transferred to Fareedpore in 1888. The people of the district regarded his transfer as a heavy loss and met him in a large number. The Municipal Commissioner passed a resolution to name a road after Brajendra Nath and to keep his oil painting in the Municipal Office. Brajendra Nath, who had difference of opinion with his European Commissioner, was supremely gratified by the deep appreciation of his work by his own countrymen. Another Civilian Romesh Chunder, while serving as District Magistrate, Mymensingh earned so much of goodwill of local people that the 'Town Hall at Tangail' opened on 1 January 1891 was named after him. In the previous year, his friends and admirers made an offer of annual medal to be given to the first student in Sanskrit at the University Entrance Examination which was accepted by the District Board of Mymensingh. Krishna Govinda Gupta, the popular Commissioner on his visit in 1903, found Bhadrak bustling with popular enthusiasm. When he arrived at the Railway Station, which was 3 miles away from the town, at 9 pm, a torch light procession followed him, and as soon as he reached the town, 20 bombs were fired. This was followed by grand display of fireworks in the bank of the river Salindi. Next day, Commissioner inspected the offices, dispensary, jail and granted interviews to gentlemen, having kind word for one and all. Amidst another display of fireworks, and followed by a torch light procession, he left the station at 7 pm. Native press was teeming with commendation: 'We had never before such a kind and popular commissioner in Orissa.'[58]

Anundoram Borooah was the first Indian to be appointed as District Magistrate and Collector joining Noakhally in 1884. This invoked a public demonstration of joy in that town. In public meeting, a resolution was passed to illuminate the town and firework display was arranged by public subscription in honour of the Indian Magistrate. The celebration was all the more noteworthy as Noakhally with predominately Bengali population rejoiced the elevation of Anundoram, an Assamese. National feeling was certainly spreading far and wide, melting the regional barriers. Large hearted, amiable in disposition, affable in manners, Anundoram was accessible to everyone who wished to see him and represent his wants. He lost no time in directing his initiative in addressing numerous wants of the district population. Steam communication was opened between Noakholly and Burrisaul, bringing the district in easy reach of the imperial capital Calcutta through Burrisaul, Khulna and Jessore. This link immensely facilitated the growth of trade in the district. Anundoram realised the need for improving the river communication facility of Noakhally town. His proposal to deepen and widen the Noakhally Khal so as to make it navigable throughout the year was accepted by the Government. Sadly enough, Anundoram did not live long to witness the developmental work being undertaken. His concurrence with the public demand of a telegraphic line, undeniably displayed his urge for native development. Anundoram backed up the demand and successfully moved the Government for sanction of the line. Histireless soul must have exalted at the time when Mail connection between Chandpore in Tippera and Ranigunge in Noakhally was opened through his initiative.

Another Indian civilian who was appointed District Magistrate round about the same time was Romesh Chunder Dutt. Through his letter published in *The Statesman*, Romesh criticised different policies of Ashley Eden, the retiring Lieutenant-Governor of Bengal. Rivers Thompson, who succeeded Ashley, was not at all perturbed by the young Civilian's forthright exposition and quietly appointed Romesh as Officiating Collector of Balasore under the cover of Ilbert Bill controversy. Subsequently, Romesh was appointed as District Magistrate of a troublesome district Backergunge. His competence was keenly testified through his conduct of administration in the onerous charge. Romesh passed brilliantly combining tact with proficiency. Next he was transferred to Pubna where he served for a short period. His performance nonetheless was far above ordinary as the Chief Executive of Pubna district. Though the transfer of Romesh Chunder to Mymensingh fell like thunder-bolt upon the people of Pubna, Lieutenant-Governor Stewart Bayley was lauded for his matchless identification of native competence. Romesh was diligent and untiring in his work and maintained extremely cordial relation with his subordinates. His adept management of police affairs merited special credit. His cordial relation with District Superintendant of Police did not allow a single case of oppression or high handedness to take place during his regime. The local self government institutions, both Municipal and District Board, were invigorated in their activity with the sagacious counselling of District Magistrate. Romesh was perhaps aware of the complaint of heavy official interference and displayed characteristic restraint in management of self-government affairs. Romesh appreciated the need for expanding the scope of education and directed his initiative in the cause of it. Pubna Zilla School rightfully boasted as its own student was appointed as District Magistrate. Thus with a heavy heart Pubna bade farewell to the deserving native Civilian.

Krishna Govinda as Magistrate and Collector of Jessore won the admiration of the district people. On his transfer in 1887, a farewell dinner was arranged at the premises of Babu Umesh Chunder Ghose, a local advocate. The gathering was attended by a number of native gentlemen. All present expressed satisfaction and admiration of the ability with which Krishna Govinda had worked for the district. Some speakers said that in point of administrative ability he stood second to very few of his predecessors. His courtesy and affable manners won for him a lasting name. When Krishna Govinda in his subsequent assignment served as District Magistrate of Nadia, a leading Zamindar of Krishnanagar Babu Nuffer Chander Pal Chowdhury, gave an evening party. The party turned out to be a public gathering. Bengal Government took notice of the occasion and did not sit idle. Krishna Govinda received a reprimand as Lieutenant-Governor promptly asked him to submit an explanation for attendance at the party.

Loken with his soft temperament aided by intelligence and ability became immensely popular among the native community. As District Judge of Fareedpore, he exhibited the rare characteristic of absolute fearlessness and independence. Loken possessed the courage and during his tenure of office, disposed of numerous civil appeals against the decisions of Subordinate Judges which had been pending for long period. During the unrest of 1905, Loken sympathised with native sentiment prompting *The Bengalee* to record that 'the public of Fareedpore will be ever grateful to him for his sympathetic attitude towards the people during the Partition agitation'.[59] Loken made substantial grant for procuring the equipment of the Fareedpore Hospital and endeavoured hard for betterment of the Girls' School.

Sripad Babaji Thakur as Sessions Judge of Shikarpur had a tiff with the District Collector. Sripad was fond of playing chess and used to invite all sorts of people, including humble shopkeepers from the town, to come and play chess at his bunglow. Sometimes when out, riding on a camel through the town of Shikarpur, there men would meet him and beg him to honour them by resting at their shops. Sripad enjoyed their company and unless pressed for time, he would comply with their request. The Collector of Shikarpur, who resided at Sukkar, was a military man, Colonel Mayhem by name. Colonel nurtured a very big notion of his own importance and disliked such mixing with common man. He reported to Government that the District Judge of Shikarpur was in habit of mixing with common people on terms of family unity, thereby lowering the importance of district officers and the Government. A copy of the report was sent to Sripad, who promptly applied for sanction to prosecute Colonel Mayhem for libel. The upshot was that the gallant and indignant Colonel had to apologise and withdraw his offensive remarks. The facts though not published became folklore.

Emerging Nation – Civilians' Concern

By the first decade of 20th century, Indian public opinion started losing faith in the benevolence of imperial administration. People, by and large, realised that their country had been subjugated to colonial interest. On many a sensitive mind, worked the urge to recover the oriental glory. Western education, expanding rapidly and by its sense of liberality, inflamed the desire for the emancipation from foreign yoke. The outcome was obvious and manifested in growing extremism. The great awakening heralded the golden moments for the nation to feel the need for development of education, agriculture and industry. Indian Civilians, by their education and training, possessed just the elements, needed to judge the course of action. Many of them could not forget their ethnicity and origin, overtly aligning with the developmental needs. Mass education naturally became the priority area for them. The word 'swadeshi' was rather inspirational as the movement led to the formation of the society 'Advancement of Technical Education in Bengal'. Pramatha Nath Bose, a Cambridge man, formed the society at the behest of Calcutta Barrister Taraknath Palit. Pramatha Nath, in his endeavour, received worthy counsel of eminent scientists viz. Nilratan Sircar, Jagadish Chandra Bose and Prafulla Chandra Ray. Taraknath and his Civilian son Loken were among the principal donors for the cause.

Jnanendra Nath Gupta, Loken's junior colleague, came up with a scheme of vocational industrial school evolving a form of instruction and training which would equip Indian youth to earn a moderate living. With an untiring soul, he visited Kalimpong Industrial School as well as Santiniketan and Surul with an objective of formulating a practical scheme. Agriculture with allied food production and dairy farming appeared to Jnanendra Nath to be one of the most promising areas for development. It afforded vast opportunity of employment generation, supporting the vital link between development of agriculture as well as industry. He attempted to popularise it among native people, orienting his institution to focus on elementary engineering, practical agriculture and training in cattle breeding, poultry rearing and dairy farming. Carmichael College at Rangpur in Eastern Bengal owed its establishment to the relentless effort of two native Civilians, Kiran Chandra De and Jnanendra Nath Gupta. Kiran Chandra De, while serving as Magistrate and Collector of the district, interested himself with the popular demand. He was successful in securing an assurance of significant donation from leading aristocracy of the district. Bengal Governor on his visit to the district was approached with the prayer to sanction the establishment of the College. His Highness deferred the decision till an on the spot enquiry was made. The Director of Public Instructions carried out the enquiry to ascertain the practicability of the scheme. Jnanendra Nath, who succeeded Kiran Chandra, pursued with an unfailing sense of attachment. The college, finally established in 1916, was named after the Governor of Bengal. Kiran Chandra had the company of equally worthy spouse whose perspectives were deservedly enriched by her Civilian father. The lady tirelessly contributed to the functioning of Rangpur branch of National Indian Association. Lady Carmichael, Her Excellency attended the annual session of the Association in the year 1913. She bestowed fulsome praise on expansion of women's education that was taking place under the tutelage of the Indian Civilian and his wife.

Similar interest for educational purposes was taken by Abdulla Yusuf Ali. Quite early in his service in 1903, he addressed the Mahomedan Educational Conference at Delhi, advising his countrymen to study the classical Hindu literature and learn the ennobling teaching of Hindu heroes. When in December 1910, he was invited to preside over The All-India Mahomedan Educational Conference held at Nagpur, Yusuf had gathered adequate practical experience. He conducted the proceedings with remarkable competence. The conference was attended by eminent Mahomedans of all parts of the country and deliberated on the spread of English education among the community. The event acquired credence by securing the presence of the Chief Commissioner of Central Province and the Director of Public Instructions. As the officials showed sympathy for ameliorating the condition of the indigent and backward community, the demand for Mahomedan University was revived by Aga Khan.

Abject poverty of the rural population and working class distressed the sensitive minds of the Indian Civilians to the point of restlessness. They despaired the way alien rule was designed to ruin the indigenous industry and attempted to revive the same with equal vigour. Lokendra Nath nurtured an innate passion for developing indigenous industries and felt the need for state protections at the early stage. He was greatly influenced by his predecessor Romesh exposing the economic drain of the nation. In October 1901, when touring England, Loken read a paper at Carlyle Society on 'Creation of Industries in India'.[60] Lokendra Nath was pleased with England prospering on industrial development and observed: 'It is well for England who sells her skill and labour on the markets of the world to preach free trade.'[61] But at the same breath, he pointed out that the success of England to emerge as manufacturing nation was not through free trade. The imperial power began to preach the eternal truth of free trade, Loken continued, 'when she had developed qualities that enable her to fear no competition'.[62] Lokendra Nath threw up all official trammels on his conduct and objected to the preaching of industries developed in England, inviting India with incipient industrial growth to compete on perfectly even terms. Exposing the sham policy of the Empire, he opined, 'The true remedy for famines is to be found in the revival of our industries'.[63] Government's attempt to tactfully conceal the fact agitated Loken's sensitive disposition and it turned absolutely irreconcilable. Swadeshi movement following in the wake of Partition of Bengal in 1905 successfully revived the demand for home made products in many cases. Birendra Chandra Sen, serving as Magistrate of Jessore, gladly watched the development and the prevailing conditions were appropriately captured in his report to Government on the progress of the Swadeshi in his district. Birendra Chandra observed that the movement had spurred the demand for country made clothes. Handlooms were working in full swing in many places and equally active was the sugar industry at Koda-Chandpur. The mattresses of Narail were doing well in the market and the factory itself was thriving. 'Jessore knows how to work patiently in silence, without fuss or parade whatever'[64] Birendra Chandra proudly concluded.

The year 1907 heralded occasions for Indians to rejoice as Atul Chunder Chatterji was appointed by the Government of United Province to carry out an industrial survey. Eastern Bengal followed the example and nominated Jnanendra Nath Gupta for the same job. Atul Chunder spared no effort and studied in details the existing industries of the province, the cause for their decay and possibilities of revival. In course of the survey, he visited Presidencies of Madras and Bengal as well as Punjab to update his knowledge of production processes and need for modernisation. Atul Chunder identified the manufacture of carpet, leather, brass and copper items and dairy production to be very promising to engage rural population productively and in large number. In weaving industry, in order to solve the scarcity of imported synthetic dye, he insisted on reintroduction of vegetable dyes by concerted action on part of the large dealers. Being trained in the process of mixing of the synthetic dyes with vegetable dyes, Atul Chunder felt, the weavers could overcome the problem to a great extent. Availability of fibrous grass and wood pulp from the numerous forests in the province made it an ideal location for paper mill. No less important to the province was the spread of sugar industry with easy availability of sugarcane. The export of raw seed to England did not escape his notice as his inquisitive mind felt the desirability of processing seed in the country to produce oil and cake. Export of finished product certainly provided value addition and concomitant employment generation. Atul Chunder became acutely aware that sugar produced in his province cost more than imported variety from Java and Mauritius. He advocated as much the need for change of production line and scale of production to make indigenous product economically competitive as the expansion of co-operative credit to rescue the weavers and artisans from their impoverished condition. His endeavour to invigorate native industry did not end with submission of the report. Addressing the second industrial conference of the province in 1908, Atul Chunder regretted that no substantial step had been taken to realise the resolutions taken a year back.

APPRECIATION OF MR. A. C BANERJEE'S SERVICES BY THE COCHIN GOVT

The following has been published in the "Cochin Government Gazette," Extraordinary of March 6:—

His Highness the Raja desires to place on record his high appreciation of the valuable services rendered to the State by Mr. A. R. Banerjee, M.A., C.I.E., I.C.S., during the tenure of his office as Diwan

2. In every branch of the administration his influence is manifest, and the present prosperous financial condition of the State is greatly due to his policy.

3. His versatile genius, untiring energy and indomitable courage in the introduction of reforms were only equalled by his sincere love of the people and devotion to the best interests of the State, and in recording his appreciation of his work, His Highness desires to thank Mr. Banerjee for his great services to the State

The places he visited all over the country, witnessed the dawn of genuine industrial enterprise with most hopeful sign that the educated and professional classes were permeated with the true industrial spirit. Atul Chunder urged his countrymen to utilise the splendid opportunity and to begin to work with real earnest, with a view to falling into line with more advanced industrial communities. Jnanendra Nath identified the potential of paper manufacturing in Assam. The state was abundant with availability of soft wood and bamboo which could replace the raw materials hitherto utilised. The idea of utilising river Dhanseri for water transport of raw material, bear the marks of characteristic ingenuity of the Civilian.

Abdullah Yusuf Ali, best known for his public speech than any other endowments, captivated many an audience in India and England alike. A Barrister himself, Abdullah studied at Bombay University and St John's College, Cambridge and succeeded in the ICS competition of the year 1894. Abdulla possessed the uncanny ability to consort with the gentry and common man with equal ease. He served as Deputy Commissioner, Sulatanpur in 1909 and was invited to preside at the Provincial Industrial Conference at Agra. Abdulla analysed the industrial needs of the country with clinical precision, both practical and academic.

A couple of years later Albion Rajkumar Banerjee as Dewan of Cochin inaugurated the Second Annual Exhibition of the Arts and Industries. He observed that the Exhibition was begun by the Cochin Durbar with the objective of rousing the enthusiasm and interest of the people in the matter of agricultural and industrial progress. The improvement in the indigenous industries, Albion felt, could not take place without co-operation and enterprise amongst capitalist of the country. Durbar, under his guidance, considered extending concessions such as exemption from commercial taxation, stamp duty and registration fees. He hoped that these measures would encourage firms and enterprises in developing the resources of the state by launching new industries. The hereditary aversion of Indians to invest capital in business appeared to Albion to be aiding monopoly of European capital and agency in the commercial activity in this country. But the task of developing the country's resources should legitimately be undertaken by the sons of the soil, the Civilian concluded. Native press sided with the Dewan in his endeavour to stir up the capitalists of Cochin to start new industries utilising their surplus wealth and the resources of the country. Krishna Govinda Gupta while deputed to inquire into the prospects of fisheries in Eastern Bengal, conducted a detailed study. So long as man only refrained from interfering with their normal growth by indiscriminate or untimely slaughter, Gupta was sure of a good supply of fish.

Another vital issue, the importance of which Indian Civilians readily realised, was the utility of agricultural banks. The idea of establishing co-operative banks was propounded by their illustrious colleague William Wedderburn, a Scotsman. While serving as Magistrate of Maldah, Jnanendra Nath convened several meetings for starting agricultural banks in selected villages. He persevered hard for the success of the scheme largely by associating people of all classes. Government started co-operative credit societies and the post of Registrar of the department was also reserved for Civilians. Statutory Civilian Perungavur Rajagopala Chariyar of Madras Presidency served as the Registrar of the department. In the year 1907, he attended the co-operative conference at Simla and followed it up by visiting different parts of the Presidency. In order to ascertain the practicability of founding rural or urban banks, Rajagopala interacted with leading townsmen, merchants and even the money lenders whose activity the society intended to substitute. With unfailing patience and earnest eagerness to popularise the co-operative banking, Chariyar explained the advantages and the rules governing the functioning of the banks and shared the experience of similar institutions in other centres. He was successful in impressing the public of the utility of such institutions. So profound was his ground work that the path for his successor was well laid. Panamalai Ramchandra Rao, the next Registrar, possessed intimate knowledge of the conditions of the agricultural population supplemented by untiring enthusiasm. The membership, paid-up-capital, deposit and loans, all went up under his tutelage. Government report on this occasion did not err on the assessment of the functioning of the department. It remarked that co-operative activity had well sustained the rate of progress shown in previous years and the year's performance was regarded as nearly brilliant. Ramchandra understood the working so minutely as to conclude that but for central banks, Government assistance was unnecessary and by its favourable terms tended to obscure the real business of the Societies. His conviction was well supported by increasing confidence of the non-members in the functioning of the societies. They unhesitatingly invested their money at a time when co-operative credit movement was just in its infancy covering a very small portion of the agricultural population of the country. The progress was, however, spectacular and held out the hope of solving the problem of agricultural indebtedness by a great measure with spread of co-operative movement in the country.

The experiment undertaken in Eastern Bengal and Assam added another dimension to the utility of the society. Kiran Chandra De as Registrar succeeded in forming two weavers' co-operative societies in the new province. One of them at Jaffrabad in Tipperah was registered as an ordinary rural society. The weaver-members were granted cash loan for purchase of yarn and they sold the stuff they produced in open market repaying the society in cash. The other society was at Bharenga in Pubna and was registered as an urban society. The society started buying yarn wholesale and supplied it to the members on credit. Business was brisk in the very first year and promised to be successful. Members weaving cloth sold them in the open market. After repaying their debts to the society, they could borrow more yarn. In order to clear weavers of their old debts, Kiran Chandra attempted to raise capital and made an application to the Government for an extraordinary loan. Pitfalls, notwithstanding, the example of Jaffrabad and Bharenga became model for spread of the co-operative movement in the whole country.

Freedom struggle in its extreme intensity could not shut the eyes of Jnanendra Nath to the wide gulf that separated the educated and advanced sections of Indian people from the great mass of the rural population in miserable poverty. He could realise that all political ideals would be meaningless and hollow as long as they represent the aspiration and demands of a numerically negligible section of the people only. The democratic form of Government being introduced into the country raised his hopes for transfer of the political power into the hands of the people, empowering them to improve their own position. Jnanendra Nath's British experience taught him the efficacy of District Boards and Village Union Boards which only could address the need of national regeneration.

Call of Motherland - Covenant and Conduct

At the end of probationary year in England, K P S Menon who succeeded in the open competition of the year 1921 received a summons from India Office. He presented himself and was interviewed by two Members of the Council of the Secretary of State for India. The senior of the two read extracts from *The Indus*, a magazine then published in England, in which Menon was stated to have made a speech, asserting that India could not long remain in the British Empire. This conviction of the candidate, the Member pointed out, was inconsistent with the covenant he had executed. As a member of ICS, Menon had avowed to remain loyal to King George V and his heirs and successors forever. With characteristic reasoned argument, Menon, however, could clarify his stand and avoided the risk of losing the appointment. But keeping with the covenant, he had to lead double life in the ICS, both 'heaven born' and 'earth-bound', a sahib and a native, a sun-dried bureaucrat and a man of the people.

Lokendra Nath Palit was a good friend of great poet Rabindranath Tagore. Together they enrolled at the University College of London in the year 1880. Rabindranath did not continue his study for long but his friend carried on and passed the open competition four years later. A man of rich intellect and poetic temperament, Loken freely consorted with European classmates, never feeling any difference. Anything British appeared novel to him till he heard his friends singing

> 'Rule Britannia! Britain rules the waves
> Britons never shall be slave'[65]

From that day, never did Loken's heart beat in harmony with his friends.

Romes Chunder Dutt retired from service in the year 1897. Ananda Mohan Bose, in his presidential address at fourteenth Indian National Congress held at Madras in December 1898 congratulated his friend Romesh on his being 'un-muzzled'. Ananda Mohan trusted Romesh, unfettered of the trammels of office, would be in a position to render even greater service to the Government he had served so long and so faithfully. Subsequent activities of Romesh did not belie the trust his friend had reposed. Romesh with his informed exposition of the effects of Government policy addressed open letter to Viceroy Lord Curzon. The real benefit of the exposition was the spread of awareness of economic exploitation among countryman and the nation keenly watched Government setting up a committee to examine the issue and prepare a reply. Romesh had been quite adept in using the press in ventilating his opinion even when he was in service. At the time of departure of Ashley Eden, the Lieutenant-Governor of Bengal, Romesh craved for the indulgence of the Editor of *The Statesman* to state a few words that majority of his educated countrymen thought of the great man. 'A native of Bengal'[66] represented the 'impartial opinion'[67] of countrymen, whose identity soon poured out to be none other than the covenanted Civilian Romesh. Brushing aside the sweeping strictures of *The Bengalee* and the fulsome flattery of the *Hindoo Patriot*, Romesh remembered Sir Ashley for his support to the oppressed ryots against the planters and concern for thousands of traders with small income whom he exempted from the operation of income tax. He was thankful to the great man for the draft of the Bill about landlords and tenants, in which Ashley had boldly proposed to confer the right of occupancy on the majority of cultivators of Bengal. Ashley appeared to him to be free from race prejudice and a man of strong conviction. The good qualities of Ashley of course did not blind Romesh of his great blunders. Romesh resented his fondness of abusing patronage and old class of patriarchal rule, and cool indifference to new feelings and the growing aspiration of the educated people. Ashley greatly annoyed Romesh for his opposition to the Calcutta Municipality and attempt to crush the vernacular press. As Romesh retired from service, the nation bestowed the greatest honour, inviting him to preside over the annual session of the Indian National Congress in the year 1899. Romesh accepted the offer and was most argumentative in exposing the colonial policies designed for economic exploitation. His subsequent association in national politics, both in India and England, helped in forming public opinion against the drain of wealth.

Kavasjee Jamasjee Badshah as member of ICS served postal department for a long time and introduced many wholesome reforms. Badshah, however, was heavily criticised by Indian press for his opposition to Ilbert Bill. He served as Excise Commissioner and retired early to settle down in England. Very soon nationalist emotions appealed to him. Along with other members of House of Commons, he joined 'The India Civil Rights Committee'.[68] Formed by the liberal members of the House of Commons, the committee was agitating against the deportation of Krishna Kumar Mitra and Aswini Kumar Dutta. Lord Curzon's decision of dividing Bengal sparked strong opposition in the entire country. Krishna Kumar was the maternal uncle of Arabindo, who strongly criticised the decision in his paper *Sanjivani* while Aswini Kumar was organising the public agitation in East Bengal. The Government deported them and Indian Courts refused to admit Writ against the action. 'The Civil Rights Committee' decided to move the King's Bench and Badshah actively associated himself with the move.

At a time when Badshah was raising public opinion in England against illegal deportation, a native District Magistrate in Pubna clashed with the British authorities in India. Serajgunge subdivision of the district, which Satish Chandra Mukherjee headed, was an important centre of agitation against the Partition of Bengal. The people in the district were roused, rallying to the slogans of 'Bande Mataram' and 'Swadeshi'. Just before Satish Chandra had taken up his post, there was an incident when the police had assaulted lawyers, students and others with leather thongs. Cases of assault were brought before the British Sub-Divisional Officer who dismissed them. Satish Chandra thought this to be unjustified and insisted that an apology be made by police. The apology was offered and the cases were withdrawn. This apparently did not please the Superintendent of Police who complained to the provincial authority. The Commissioner, accompanied by Lieutenant-Governor Bampfylde Fuller, came to investigate. At that time some students of the district school at Pubna, where Satish Chandra was president of the school managing committee, were calling out 'Bande Mataram' and chalked this on the doors. He considered the event to be a trifling matter and let the students off. Satish Chandra perhaps could convince his Commissioner that instead of letting down the prestige of British Government, he was enhancing it by his policy of conciliation. But the Chief Secretary and others were not satisfied. Satish Chandra later found that a Deputy Magistrate had been appointed to spy on his activities. Shortly thereafter Bengal Provincial Conference was held in Pubna in 1906 at which Rabindranath Tagore presided. Though the meeting went off without any incident, the authorities were further incensed with the native District Magistrate. His promotions were stopped and many years later when the regime was more relaxed, Satish Chandra came to know that he was branded an anarchist at heart. The deprivation hardly changed later activities of Satish Chandra. As District Magistrate of Nadia, he generously donated to Krishnagar Public Library and associated himself with its working. Mahespur Agricultural and Industrial Exhibition interested him as much as Krishnagar Working Men's Institute, the forum he utilised to spread the importance of mass education. Restoration of Krittibash Memorial Fund was undertaken by Satish Chandra with missionary zeal. The medieval poet Krittibash was a resident of Fulia in the district of Nadia and composed the classic of Ramayana. The resolution to erect a suitable memorial to the great poet perhaps symbolised the recapitulation of Indian glory, a hallmark of Swadeshi movement.

Satish Chandra palpably enjoyed his stay as the premier of the district and turned its protector. Even when in 1914, the World War I broke out, the distress of famine stricken countrymen appealed to him more than the war need. The Empire was engaged in the fiercest tussle with its enemy but the covenanted Civilian was fighting a separate battle. Colonial authority did not countenance the fearless conduct of the native Civilian. His family, however, stood by him and his own children participated in charity shows organised for raising funds for famine relief. Such brave effort and open defiance could not go unnoticed. The local press promptly drew public attention to his uneven struggle and applauded the humane consideration of the Indian Magistrate. Their overenthusiastic praise further infuriated the British authority and closed his fate. Satish Chandra never recovered from the imperial condemnation and stagnated in the service.

Rather uncanny, beyond the ordinary comprehension, was the conduct of the successful Indians who passed the open competition in the year 1890. They displayed remarkable variety and it was certainly more than a mere coincidence that a number of them ignored the British authority. Arvind Akroyd Ghosh, a compatriot of Satish Chandra, was the first rebel. Arabinda did not bother to appear for the mandatory riding test and was denied appointment. He returned home unperturbed, joining Baroda State Service, which his well-wisher Henry Cotton had arranged for him. The nation scantly noticed the nationalist appeals that the young man started publishing. Arabinda could not rest himself in peace and soon started revolutionary activities. Through his journalistic disposition, he emerged as the leading representative of extremist element of nationalist group which culminated with Alipore Bomb Case. He appeared more like a whirl-wind and his role in national politics was disproportionately short to his contribution in the great awakening across the country. His younger brother Barin was more restive and continuously urged him to adopt the policy of violence. British officials who perpetrated oppression in crushing the Swadeshi movement, the young man felt, deserved reciprocation. The bomb that had been thrown at Kingsford, missed the target and set the administration on prowl. Arabinda by that time had changed his name as Aurobindo but was quickly detected and implicated in the famous 'Alipore Bomb Conspiracy' case. He was imprisoned and set free after captivity of nearly a year. While in prison, Arabinda had started getting heavenly summons. He responded to the calls and settled in Pondicherry with divine undertaking. It is not clear whether he at all influenced the lesser mortals like Satish Chandra, his compatriot. But the nationalist urge certainly appealed to his other compatriot Govind Dinanath Madgavkar. The Maharatta youth served in Burma for short time before falling ill. Subsequently, he was transferred to Bombay Presidency. In December 1905, Arabinda brought Barin with him when he went to Bombay to talk revolution with this 'sympathetic ICS officer'.[68] The principal order of business was a proposal to send Madhavrao Jadhav to Japan for military training. Govind Dinanath agreed to contribute Rs 1,000, quite a large amount by the prevailing standard, towards the expenses. The men also discussed the forthcoming session of the Indian National Congress which was to be held that year in Ahmedabad. The group successfully enticed prince Gaekwar of Baroda to address the industrial exhibition which preceded the annual Congress at the city.

The service continued to produce rebels of whom Charu Chandra Dutt emerged as the leading example. His father Kalikadas Dutt was the Dewan of the Cochbehar state and was obsessed with the idea of his son joining the ICS. The son was equally against the idea of joining the service and pleaded helplessly with his father. Even before proceeding to England, he was engaged in secret activities against the Empire. At his father's insistence, he sailed, still with the hope of joining the Royal Army as preparation of his bigger plan. The authorities replied to his appeal and expressed their limitation to engage Indians in Royal Army against the wishes of India

Office. Charu Chandra turned to his father, seeking approval to pursue study of law and profession of journalism. His supplication could not budge Kalikadas from his plan. Charu Chandra cleared the open competition at the first chance and completed the training. But India Office came to know of his connection with secret societies for which the Indian Civilian was reprimanded. He returned home and joined the Bombay Presidency. In the service, he, however, found ample opportunity to start revolutionary activities. Charu Chandra came in contact with Arabinda and associated himself with the activities of the group. Charu Chandra's involvement in the secret society was active, much more than the generous donations he made. In association with the group members, he planned to kill Andrew Fraser, the Lieutenant-Governor of Bengal. The plan did not succeed but he was implicated in the 'Alipore Bomb Conspiracy' case. Witnesses named him and the link was exposed. Parliament member Odonell's question in the House of Commons, enquiring to know whether the Indian Civilian was unreasonably harassed by the police, embarrassed the Secretary of State. Secretary on this occasion chose to remain silent but the Government of India was infuriated without bound. Father's influence saved Charu Chandra of the dismissal from the service. Nonetheless, he was interned for a couple of years and later on kept under subsistence allowance. Charu Chandra was prepared for the tribulations and displayed uncommon indifference. His convictions were firm as much as his zeal for the nationalist activities. His master, Aurobindo, however, immeasurably depressed the ardent follower through his withdrawal from active politics. Governor-General reinstated him back to the service in the year 1913. Charu Chandra never had great ambition of his role in the service and passed another 12 years in the service without any major attrition. His emotions and inclinations during the time greatly distressed his conscience which he unburdened through his voluntary retirement. The emancipation thus achieved, remarkably differed from the induction, which was thrust on him by filial obligation. The rebel mind comforted itself in the public work that he could pursue thereon. None shared his sensibilities as much as Rabindranath who appointed the retired ICS as the Chancellor of Viswa Bharati.

The attitude grew with the increasing number of Indians in the service. Hassamal Baharmal Shivdasani who came from Sindh, succeeded in the open competition of the year 1914. He was a scholar of St John's College, Cambridge and took a first class in both parts of Mathematical Tripos. He briefly served as the Assistant Collector of Surat in Bombay Presidency quitting the service just before the Council Election of 1923. Elected as a *swarajist*, Shivdasani continued to expound the ideal of obstruction in principle. He pestered the governments' ministers with endless questions, which usually had to be sent off to various departments of the Government for answers. He made long tirades on the budget and other issues that came before the legislature. A couple of years' senior in service to Shivdasani was Yeshwant Anant Godbole. A resident of Poona, he served in the newly created provinces of Bihar and Orissa. His progress in the service suffered for his nationalist views, but that made no difference to his attitude. He freely comingled with native-folk and took great pains in their development.

CONCLUSION

Competitor and Collaborator

Introduction of competitive examination opened the path for Indian youths to join the ruling aristocracy of British India. This radical change took place at a time when India was ruled by the Company. Through transfer of power to the Crown, India became a part of the Empire. There was, however, no change in the scheme of open competition which was conducted only at London. Very small number of Indian students, therefore, could compete, and much less did actually succeed. What held them back were the racial superstition and the prohibitive cost that the travel to England entailed. Adversities were great, but greater was the determination of the extraordinary individuals. With uncommon resolve, they defied social prohibition and left Indian shore rather at tender age. Separated from their family in an alien land, they struggled and lived a hard life. They came in touch with English life and gradually became imperial citizens. But such Indians were really very few in number. For others, the prevailing conditions were insurmountable, destroying the ambition of meritorious young men. On the other hand, the Indian prize was quite favourite with the British youth. Attracted by the privilege and prospects, they joined the service in large number. The trend continued till the World War I. Even the few Indians, who were selected, were denied admission to the core of the administrative activity of their own country and were kept at the periphery. Imperial administration did not consider them competent for executive assignments, big or small. Indian Civilians by and large were consigned to judicial line. Their European colleagues often advised them to shun the more attractive executive line. A sense of dejection was thus born among the native Civilians. Their first brush with British democratic institutions, in prime of youth, often impressed their tender mind which later on blossomed into reverence. Demand for equality in the service was justifiably right for them as they won places by beating the 'un-conquerable British youth'. When the successful Civilians returned home, the Indian society embraced them whole heartedly. By and large, they were given welcome reserved for the conquerors. Acutely conflicting was, however, their experience in serving imperial bureaucracy. European reaction to Indian selection was retributive and the discrimination in the service was glaring. Dejected sons turned to their own community which was on its way to become more aggressive. A strange communion thus originated in the native soil. Indian Civilians had the benefit of both education and training to figure out the need for the emerging nation. Along with places secured, they derived immense confidence from their success in the competition. Their independent conduct embarrassed the authority who further tightened their attitude. Large majority of native Civilians performed two roles. One of these was as a member of Indian community and the other as that of imperial bureaucracy. They juggled the priority of one role over the other and skilfully walked between the two ropes. Imperial authority closely watched the activities of the Indian Civilians but rarely acknowledged their ability and demand for equality. Deprivation notwithstanding their fascination for western world did not diminish. Continent in general and Great Britain in particular remained a favourite haunt for them. Indian Civilians made liberal use of furlough and took their families to Europe. These visits opened up a new front on women liberation in Indian society questioning eternal conservatism.

Still few acquired tact and collaborated wonderfully well with imperial authority. Their progress in the service was unmistakably smoother. Krishna Govinda Gupta was the first Indian who could sit with the Counsellors of the Secretary of State. His selection did not please the retired Civilian Henry Cotton who had the distinction of presiding over Indian National Congress. A member of House of Commons, Cotton felt that Krishna Govinda was by no degree representative of the progressive Indian opinion. To him the nominee appeared to be a 'retired Hindu Civilian who is saturated with officialism'.[1] Nonetheless, Lord Morley appreciated his merits and Krishna Govinda had no small share in shaping the reform scheme with its liberal policies that were introduced into the Indian administration. Apart from his immediate duties in the India Office, Krishna Govinda vastly interested himself with the Indian young men who stayed in England for education. Krishna Govinda was conspicuous in his absence at the farewell held in honour of Dadabhai Naoroji in the year 1907. Many felt Krishna Govinda, considering his official position, gave the gathering a miss for being of a political or semi-political character. But the same man never erred to protest against the English game of belittling the educated Indians and casting wanton aspersion on their motives. At the time of introducing reform,

Charles Crosthwaite, a retired Civilian felt that the system of election which was to be introduced was far in advance of the state of the country. The unrest in India, Crosthwaite continued, was caused by the small educated class who were discontented not because they wanted self-government but because they wanted to supplant English officials and administer the country. Krishna Govinda could no longer restrain himself and reacted sharply. 'Loyalty to the Government and patriotism to help his countrymen in the path of progress and prosperity are most conspicuous in him',[2] was what a native paper remarked on his conduct. Crosthwaite, who served India as member of Governor-General's Legislative Council and Chief Commissioner of Central Province, was certainly not a minion. But so forceful and convincing was Krishna Govinda's argument that Crosthwaite had to apologise unconditionally in an attempt to bury the controversy.

Krishna Govinda did not stop at this point. The war intensified further and his acute sense could make out that India, for its role, would claim its rightful position in the Empire. He collaborated with William Wedderburn to prepare a note on charting the course of Indian reform to attain self-government within the Empire. Wedderburn, an Indian Civilian, himself was associated very closely with Indian National Congress and was a Liberal member in the House of Commons. They agreed that a gradual, but persistent development of representative institutions in every grade of legislative and administrative authority was the most crucial requirement. At the same time it was urged to restore self-government both at village and district level. Members of permanent civil service dominated Supreme and Local Governments, the note observed, thus ensuring absolute bureaucratic control. It was suggested that a fundamental change be made so that representative men, both Indian and British, could be appointed in the Executive Councils. Deliberations continued and reforms were introduced at the end of the war. It was singularly interesting that the reform contained many schemes which were actually delineated in the joint note.

Rather strange was the fascination of the leading nationalist for the service. Many of them shared the passion and sent their sons to compete for ICS. Badr-ud-din Tyabji, Manomohan Ghose and Janaki Nath Ghosal were leading nationalist of their time. They associated themselves with the activities of Indian National Congress from the very beginning. Love for the motherland united them but the commonality did not end there. Manomohan did not succeed in the open competition but the attraction of the service did not leave him. He sent his brother Lalmohan and thereafter his son Mahimohun to sit for the open competition. Badr-ud-din endured the pang of parting with his son when he dispatched Mohsin to England at a very tender age. The sons came out successfully in the open competition for the ICS. No less obsessed was Motilal Nehru by the same bug as he sent his son and brothers to England for education. Sridhara Nehru, who succeeded in the year 1912, was the first member of the family who joined the 'heaven-born' service. At many places, the community came forward to fund the expenditure of the England trip. As early as in the year 1873, the Hindus of the North-Western Provinces established a society called 'Hindus National Improvement Society'. The object of the society was to enable certain number of Hindus to go yearly to England to compete for the Civil Service. Secretary of the 'Anjuman-i-Mirzapore' was Pundit Indra Narayan who co-ordinated the activities. Syed Ahmed Khan of the Aligarh fame did not lag behind. He started a scheme for the establishment of a Society in Punjab for sending promising Mahomedan youths to England. The society known as 'The Mahomedan Civil Service Fund Association' desired the young men to compete at Civil Service Examination. In the midst of growing demand for appointment of Indians in the service, Indian National Congress started its maiden session at Bombay with resolution passed for simultaneous examination of ICS in England and India. For the next two decades, civil service issues were regularly deliberated at the annual sessions of Congress. At the same time, Indian demands consistently featured in the Congress resolutions.

Success in open competition boosted the native morale. The selection of four native Indians in 1869 prompted jubilant press to remark that the success 'affords one more proof that the Hindu yields to no native in the face of the globe in intellectual capacity'.[3] At the end of final examination, Indian Civilians returned home with great hope and supreme confidence derived from their England residency. This confidence perhaps spurred Brajendra Nath to argue with his European superior. At the time of Ilbert Bill controversy, John Beames questioned the competence of Indian Civilian to which Brajendra Nath gave a fitting reply. Thereafter his progress in the service was tangibly affected. But that did not deter his successors to take up just causes. Apathetic imperial rule tormented their conscience. Jnanendra Nath Gupta while presenting the condition of Indian Civilians before the Royal Commission displayed the same courage. European witnesses both official and non-official insinuated that Indian Civilians generally had been found to be lacking in force of character, in organising power and in readiness of resources when confronted with an unforeseen emergency. Not a single case was cited to substantiate the charges. A rising Civilian Jnanendra Nath was not prepared to accept the accusation lying down and fought back pluckily. Anglo-Indian papers felt that such independent attitude was a breach of the covenant that he had executed at the time of joining service. The covenant was designed to secure the crucial loyalty of the Civilians to the Crown. The members of the service who breached the covenant were not spared the consequences.

Educational curriculum at Indian universities under colonial administration was designed in line with the British universities. European teachers abounded at these universities and taught the Indian students. Learning, therefore, was conducted with imperial perspective. Alongside this, even the local newspapers regularly published the events taking place at different parts of the Empire. Being so surrounded, Indian students, imbibed imperial perspective not by a small measure. Judged against this backdrop, their readiness to join even the Home Civil Service (British) and Eastern Cadetship was nothing uncommon. At normal time, they were keen to establish their just right in the service and struggled hard. When the war broke, the same folk buried their differences and pledged their loyalty to the Empire. Being administrative head of district or sub-division, they raised 'War Fund' at many places. Yusuf Ali, who resigned from the service quite early, read a paper on 'India's Rally Round the Flag'[4] at a meeting of the East India Association held at Caxton Hall, Westminster.

The epithet 'heaven-born' aptly described the service as much as the other title 'sun-dried'. European Civilians laboured hard under the tropical sun. In small district towns, they could scarcely get the company of English society. Separated from family, they lived alone for better part of their stay in India. Very few identified themselves with the development of India and served for full term of 35 years. A large majority retired early just after being entitled to earn family pension. They went back home and lived happily in English society. For Indians, the service afforded an opportunity for serving their motherland. That attraction itself ought to have motivated them in their work. Apparently there was no reason for Indian Civilians to retire prematurely. Their resignation from service, therefore, surprised many. The first native Civilian Satyendranath resigned from service in January 1896. He could have continued in service for three more years. *Prima facie* the service did not provide sufficient scope for his talent and ambition. In the year 1891, few years before his resignation, Anglo-Indian paper *The Pioneer* recommended that Satyendranath be considered for the appointment to the Governor's Executive Council. At that time, he was the most senior of the District Judges in Bombay Presidency. Indian community was elated but only for a short while. Government paid little heed to the recommendation and countrymen resented the way Satyendranath was deprived of the honour he justly deserved. This was one of the occasions when he suffered the misfortune of serving his own country under the foreign rule. He remembered the old adage 'he who loses liberty loses half his virtue' and could not afford to wait lest he lost it completely. Even thereafter the native Civilians found that promotion to the higher ranks in the service was more or less barred. The service did not satisfy the aspiration of the ablest and the most ambitious. Romesh Chunder, unquestionably one of the most capable Indian Civilians, did not even rise to the position of a 'pucca' Divisional Commissioner. He resigned from service in 1897 and the trend continued. Kavasjee Badshah, Lokendra Nath Palit and Yusuf Ali all followed suit. Romesh utilised his administrative experience in attempting to expose the invidious policies of the Government. People both in India and England gradually became aware of the economic exploitation of colonial rule. Shivdasani with a short stint in service got elected to Bombay Legislative Council. By that time he had familiarised himself with the functioning of the Government. He engaged himself in embarrassing the Government with endless queries in the Council meetings. Both Satyendranath and Romesh, through their example, transmitted undying aspiration to the posterity for securing a place in the service. Their untimely retirement did not diminish the attraction. Barely a couple of years passed since Satyendranath resigned, that Jyotsna Nath Ghosal, son of his sister joined the service in Bombay Presidency. By the time Romesh resigned, his nephew Pratap Chunder Dutt, was a Civilian in Madras Presidency.

Indian Civilians' demand for equality in service remained a far cry. The need for Indianisation of superior service was not recognised before constitution of Lee Commission in 1923. Starting from the end of 19th century, socio-economic condition in the country under British rule was changing fast. None felt it more than the Civilians who through their work came into close contact of the harsh reality. Abject poverty of the mass, the need for education, improvement of agriculture and industry appealed to them. They could no longer remain aloof in the glasshouse and unhesitatingly expressed their concern. Some of them could defy the implications and openly criticised the Government policies. Others worked more subtly and figured out the need of the motherland working untiringly for its improvement. The scene was certainly warming up during the first decade of 20th century and the enquiry of Royal Commission presented a perfect battle field. Both sides utilised the forum in which officials could say what they liked without fear of censure. Europeans wanted to establish the moral weakness and general incompetence of their Indian colleagues. Notwithstanding the small number Indians resisted fearlessly. But for the War, the conflict would have aggravated further. As the Empire was attacked, a wave of loyalty to the allied cause swept the country. The nation stood behind the Empire and Civilians temporarily buried their misgivings to work for it. Eventually the Empire triumphed but the constitutional reforms introduced subsequent to the War, fell immeasurably short of Indian expectation. Next three decades, therefore, recorded the bitter struggle and the transformation from diarchy to democracy. The Empire followed a dual policy of repress and reform to contain the Indian agitation for self rule. The supremacy of the Empire was again questioned during the World War II. Unlike the previous occasion, Indian support was not at all forthcoming during this crisis. Indian Civilians by this time had significantly grown in number. Their hearts were throbbing with the nationalist aspirations and the inevitable event took place with the separation of the Nation from the Empire. The republic became a reality and the Civilians were relieved of the predicament of living two lives. Thereafter, it was only the Nation that requisitioned their service.

Notes

Chapter I

1 *Calcutta Review* (September – October) 1924: Letters of Satyendranath Tagore

2 *Ibid*

3 Michael Madhusudan Dutt adoringly called Satyendranath Indra, the king of Hindu Gods, partly because he was very handsome and partly because his second name was 'Indra' (Satya + Indra)

4 Ghulam Murshid (Ed): *Heart of a Rebel Poet - Letters of Michael Madhusudan Dutt*, OUP, 2004 – pp 199

5 *Ibid*

6 *Hindoo Patriot*, 29 August 1864

7 Meenakshi Mukherjee: *An Indian for All Seasons: The Many Lives of R C Dutt*, Penguin, 2009 – pp 4

8 Surendranath Banerjee: *A Nation in Making: Being the Reminiscences of Fifty Years of Public Life*, OUP, 1925 – pp 9

9 *The Bengalee*, 23 August 1890

10 *Ibid*, 16 February 1898

11 Surendranath Banerjee: *A Nation in Making: Being the Reminiscences of Fifty Years of Public Life*, OUP, 1925 – pp 17

12 *Ibid*

13 *Ibid*

14 Edwin Hirschmann: *White Mutiny*, South Asia Books, 1980 – pp 25

15 Surendranath Banerjee: *A Nation in Making: Being the Reminiscences of Fifty Years of Public Life*, OUP, 1925 – pp 72

16 A common epithet for ICS *The Bengalee*, 25 December 1909

17 *The Bengalee*, 25 December 1909

Chapter II

1 Akshoy Kumar Ghosal: *Civil Service in India under the East India Company: A Study in Administrative Development*, University of Calcutta, 1944 – pp 13

2 *Ibid*

3 *Ibid* – pp 14

4 *Ibid*

5 *Ibid* – pp 233

6 Bankey Bihari Misra: *The Bureaucracy in India: An Historical Analysis of Development up to 1947*, OUP, 1977 – pp 66

7 Sisir Kumar Das: *Sahibs and Munshis: An Accountant of the College of Fort William*, Rupa & Co, 1978 – pp 4

8 Phiroze Vasunia: *The Classics and Colonial India*, OUP, 2013 – pp 196

9 *Ibid*

10 *Ibid* – pp 197

11 *Ibid*

12 *Ibid*

13 *Ibid*

14 A Lawrence Lowell: *Colonial Civil Service: The Selection and Training of Colonial Officials in England, Holland and France*, Macmillan, 1900 - pp 285

15 George Campbell: *Memoirs of My Indian Career*, Macmillan, 1893 - pp 7

16 *Ibid*

17 *Ibid*

18 *Ibid* - pp 8

19 A Lawrence Lowell: *Colonial Civil Service: The Selection and Training of Colonial Officials in England, Holland and France*, Macmillan, 1900

20 *Richard* Temple: *Men and Events of My Time in India*, John Murray, 1882 - pp 19

21 *Ibid*

22 *Ibid*

23 Ralph Braibanti: *Asian Bureaucratic Systems Emergent from the British Imperial Tradition*, Duke University Press, 1966- pp 138

24 George Campbell: *Memoirs of My Indian Career*, Macmillan, 1893 - pp 8

25 *Ibid*

26 G R Elsmie: *Thirty five Years in Punjab*, David Douglas, 1908 - pp 16

27 *Ibid*

28 Akshoy Kumar Ghosal: *Civil Service in India under the East India Company: A Study in Administrative Development*, University of Calcutta, 1944 - pp 307

29 George Campbell: *Memoirs of My Indian Career*, Macmillan, 1893 - pp 10

Chapter III

1 Sir George Otto Trevelyan: *The Life and Letters of Lord Macaulay*, Vol II, Longmans, Green & Co, 1923 - pp 586

2 A Lawrence Lowell: *Colonial Civil Service: The Selection and Training of Colonial Officials in England, Holland and France*, Macmillan, 1900 - pp 15

3 Sir George Otto Trevelyan: *The Life and Letters of Lord Macaulay*, Vol II, Longmans, Green & Co, 1923 - pp 612

4 *Ibid*

5 *Ibid*

6 *Ibid*

7 A Lawrence Lowell: *Colonial Civil Service: The Selection and Training of Colonial Officials in England, Holland and France*, Macmillan, 1900 - pp 330

8 Sir George Otto Trevelyan: *The Life and Letters of Lord Macaulay*, Vol II, Longmans, Green & Co, 1923 - pp 609

9 *Ibid*

10 *Ibid*

11 Lord Beveridge: *India Called Them*, George Allen & Unwin, 1947 - pp 314

12 Malti Sharma: *Indianization of the Civil Services in British India (1858-1935)*, Manak Publications, 2001 - pp 18 - 19

13 *Seventeenth Report of Her Majesty's Civil Service Commissioners, 1872*

14 P Woodruff: *The Men Who Ruled India: The Guardians*, Vol 2, Jonathan Cape, London, 1963 - pp 78

15 G K Fry: *Statesman in Disguise: The Changing Role of the Administrative Class of the British Home Civil Service*, Macmillan, 1969 - pp 69

16 R P Masani, (Rustom Pestonji): *Dadabhai Naoroji, The Grand Old Man of India*, Kavyalaya Publishers, 1957 - pp 29

17 Bradford Spangenberg: *British Bureaucracy in India: Status, Policy, and*

the ICS in the Late 19th Century, South Asia Books, 1976 - pp 25

18 C Y Chintamani: *Indian Politics since the Mutiny*, George Allen & Unwin Ltd, 1940 – pp 28

19 Surendranath Banerjee: *A Nation in Making: Being the Reminiscences of Fifty Years of Public Life*, OUP, 1925 – pp 48

20 *Ibid* - pp 49

21 *Hindoo Patriot*, 22 September 1884

22 Naresh Chandra Roy: *The Civil Service in India*, Firma K L Mukhopadhyay, 1958 – pp 133

23 N B Bonarjee: *Under Two Masters*, OUP, 1970 – pp 9

24 Ghulam Murshid (Ed): *Heart of a Rebel Poet - Letters of Michael Madhusudan Dutt*, OUP, 2004 – pp 213

25 S Satthianadhan (Containing contribution from A C Dutt & C Krishnan): *Four Years in an English University*, Lawrence Asylum Press, 1893 – pp 139

26 P Woodruff: *The Men Who Ruled India*: The Guardians Vol 2, Jonathan Cape, 1963 – pp 78

27 *Ibid*

28 Richard Symonds: *Oxford and Empire: The Last Lost Cause?*, Macmillan, 1986 – pp 190

29 *Ibid*

30 *Hindoo Patriot*, 8 January 1872

31 *The Behar Herald*, 29 January 1899

32 *The Englishman*, 31 October 1899

33 *Ibid*

34 *The Behar Herald*, 28 September 1898

35 *Twenty Sixth Report of Her Majesty's Civil Service Commissioners, 1882*

36 *Indian Mirror*, 21 January 1891

37 Peter Heehs: *The Lives of Sri Aurobindo*, Columbia University Press, 2008 – pp 28

38 *Ibid*

39 *Ibid*

40 *Ibid* – pp 31

41 *Ibid*

42 *Ibid*

43 *Ibid*

44 *Ibid*

45 *Ibid* – pp 30

46 *Ibid* – pp 32

47 *Ibid*

48 *Ibid*

49 *The Bengalee*, 14 February 1902

50 *Ibid*

51 *Ibid*

52 Kewal L Panjabi ICS (Retd): *The Civil Servant in India By Ex-Indian Civil Servants*, Bharatiya Vidya Bhavan, India, 1965 – pp 30

53 K P S Menon: *Memories and Musings*, Allied Publishers, 1979 – pp 84

54 *Ibid* – pp 41

55 Charles Wallace Cross: *Selection and Training of the Candidates for Indian Civil Service 1870-1880*, Michigan: The University Microfilm International, 1983 – pp 66

56 *Ibid* – pp 106

57 *Ibid* – pp 107

58 *Hindoo Patriot*, 20 November 1882

59 *The Bengalee*, 2 December 1893

60 Brajendranath De: *Reminiscences of Indian Civilian* in Calcutta Review, January 1954

61 Sir Edward Blunt: *The ICS – The Indian Civil Service*, Faber & Faber, 1937 – pp 198

62 *Ibid*

63 *The Times*, 8 August 1898

64 Charles Wallace Cross: *Selection and Training of the Candidates for Indian Civil Service 1870-1880*, Michigan: The University Microfilm International, 1983 - pp 102

65 Evan Maconochie: *Life in the Indian Civil Service*, Chapman and Hall, 1926 - pp 12

66 *The Friends of India*, 3 June 1877

67 *Ibid*

68 *Ibid*

69 *Ibid*

70 Malti Sharma: *Indianization of the Civil Services in British India (1858-1935)*, Manak Publications, 2001 - pp 72

71 Lord Beveridge: *India Called Them*, George Allen & Unwin, 1947 - pp 314

72 *Indian Mirror*, 24 July 1887

73 *Ibid*

74 *Reis and Rayett*, 1895

75 Annie Besant: *How India Wrought for Freedom: The Story of the National Congress Told from Official Records*, Kessinger Publishing Co, 1915 - pp 71

76 *Ibid*

77 *Ibid* - pp 93

78 *Report of the Public Service Commission, 1888*

79 *Ibid*

80 Richard Symonds: *The British and Their Successors*, Faber & Faber, 1966 - pp 103

81 Malti Sharma: *Indianization of the Civil Services in British India (1858-1935)*, Manak Publications, 2001 - pp 223

82 *Ibid* - pp 149

83 *Indian Mirror*, 30 March 1901

84 Naresh Chandra Roy: *The Civil Service in* pp 133

Chapter IV

1 P Woodruff: *The Men Who Ruled India: The Guardians*, Vol 2, Jonathan Cape, London, 1963 - pp 77

2 Henry Cotton: *Indian and Home Memoirs*, T Fisher Unwin, London, 1911 - pp 205

3 B D Basu in collaboration with Phanindra Nath Bose and Nagendra Nath Ghose: *India Under the British Crown*, R Chatterjee, Calcutta, 1933 - pp 56

4 Sir Edward Blunt: *The ICS - The Indian Civil Service*, Faber & Faber, 1937 - pp 120

5 *Ibid*

6 L S S O'Malley: *The Indian Civil Service 1601 - 1930*, Murray, London, 1931 - pp 160

7 Michael O'Dwyer: *The India I Knew It*, Constable & Company Ltd, London, 1925 - pp 150

8 *Ibid*

9 Richard Symonds: *The British and Their Successors*, Faber & Faber, 1966 - pp 25

10 Lord Beveridge: *India Called Them*, George Allen & Unwin Ltd, London, 1947 - pp 50–51

11 Evan Maconochie: *Life in the Indian Civil Service*, Chapman and Hall 1926 - pp 3

12 Henry Cotton: *Indian and Home Memoirs*, T Fisher Unwin, London, 1911 - pp 278

13 *Ibid*

14 Lord Beveridge: *India Called Them*, George Allen & Unwin Ltd, London, 1947 - pp 391

15 *Ibid*

16 *Ibid*

17 *Indian Mirror*, 30 March 1901

18 E N Mangat Rai: *Commitment, My Style: Career in the Indian Civil Service*, Vikas Publishing House, Delhi, 1973 - pp 84

19 John Beames: *Memoirs of a Bengal Civilian*, Chatto & Windus, London, 1961 – pp 223

20 *Ibid*

21 *Ibid*

22 *Ibid*

23 *Ibid*

24 Annie Besant: *How India Wrought for Freedom: The Story of the National Congress Told from Official Records*, Kessinger Publishing Co, 1915 – pp 407

25 *The Bengalee*, 17 October 1914

26 Bankey Bihari Misra: *The Bureaucracy in India: An Historical Analysis of Development up to 1947*, OUP, 1977 – pp 104

27 *Ibid* - pp 137

28 *Report of the Public Service Commission, 1888*

29 *Ibid*

30 *Ibid*

31 Annie Besant: *How India Wrought for Freedom: The Story of the National Congress Told from Official Records*, Kessinger Publishing Co, 1915 – pp 155

32 *Report of the Royal Commission of the Public Service in India*, London, 1916

33 *Ibid*

34 *Ibid*

35 K P S Menon: *My Life and Work in the ICS: The Civil Servant in India*, Kewal L Panjabi (Ed), Bharatiya Vidya Bhavan, Bombay, 1965

36 Richard Symonds: *The British and Their Successors*, Faber & Faber, 1966 – pp 44

37 *Ibid*

38 *Ibid*

39 *Ibid*

40 J Wilson: *The Indian Civil Service as Career for Scotsman*, David Douglas, Edinburgh, 1885

41 J H Rivett-Carnac: *Many Memories of Life in India, at Home, and Abroad*, Elibron Classics Edition, 1910 – pp 34

42 *The Bengalee*, 13 June 1874

43 Military man appointed in civil posts

44 John Beames: *Memoirs of a Bengal Civilian*, Chatto & Windus, London, 1961 – pp 125

45 *Ibid*

46 *Ibid*

47 Charles Wallace Cross: *Selection and Training of the Candidates for Indian Civil Service 1870 –1880*, The University Microfilm International, 1983 – pp 91

48 *Ibid* – pp 95

49 *Ibid* – pp 94

50 *Indian Mirror*, 21 January 1891

51 *Ibid*

52 Bradford Spangenberg: *British Bureaucracy in India: Status, Policy, and the ICS in the Late 19th Century*, South Asia Books, 1976 - pp 30

53 *Ibid*

54 *Report of the Royal Commission of the Public Service in India*, London, 1916

55 N B Bonarjee: *Under Two Masters*, OUP, 1970 – pp 277

56 *Indian Mirror*, 18 October 1871

57 *Ibid*

58 *The Bengalee*, 22 May 1897

59 *Ibid*

60 *Ibid*

61 B K Nehru: *Nice Guys Finish Second, Memoirs*, Viking, India, 1997 – pp 11

62 *Ibid*

63 *Ibid*

64 Jawaharlal Nehru: *An Autobiography*, John Lane The Bodley Head, London, 1941 – pp 154

65 *Ibid*

66 Vijaya Lakshmi Pandit: *The Scope of Happiness- A Personal Memoir*, Crown Publishers, New York, 1979 – pp 29

67 Rajendra Prasad: *Autobiography*, Asia Publishing House, Bombay, 1957 – pp 52

68 Subhas Chandra Bose: *An Indian Pilgrim*, Thacker, Spink & Co. (1933) Ltd, Calcutta, 1948 – pp 37

69 *Hindoo Patriot*, 1 October 1883

70 *Indian Mirror*, 11 February 1905

71 L S S O'Malley: *The Indian Civil Service 1601 – 1930*, Murray, London, 1931 – pp 84

72 *Eighth Report of Her Majesty's Civil Service Commissioners, together with Appendices*, London, 1863

73 Herbert Thirkell White: *A Civil Servant in Burma*, Edward Arnold, London, 1913 – pp 7

74 *Ibid* – pp 8

75 *Ibid*

76 Subhas Chandra Bose: *An Indian Pilgrim*, Thacker, Spink & Co. (1933) Ltd, Calcutta, 1948 – pp 133–134

77 *Ibid* - pp 126

78 C D Desmukh: *The Course of My Life*, Orient Longman, New Delhi, 1974 – pp 51

79 Badr-Ud-din Tyabji: *Memoirs of an Egotist*, Vol 1, Roli Books, New Delhi, 1988 – pp 35

Chapter V

1 *The National Paper*, 7 July 1869

2 *Ibid*

3 J N Gupta: *Life and Work of Romesh Chunder Dutt, CIE*, E P Dutton & Co, New York, 1911 – pp 22

4 *Ibid*

5 *Ibid*

6 *Ibid* – pp 23

7 Sushma Sen: *Memoir of an Octogenarian*, Anjali, Simla, 1971 – pp 4

8 J N Gupta: *Life and Work of Romesh Chunder Dutt, CIE*, E P Dutton & Co, New York, 1911 – pp 37

9 *Ibid*

10 *Ibid* – pp 38

11 *Eminent Orientalists, Indian, European, American*, G A Natesan & Co., Madras, 1922 - pp 286–287

12 Husain Badruddin *Tyabji: Badruddin Tyabji: A Biography*, Thacker & Co. Ltd, Bombay, 1952 – pp 150

13 *Ibid* - pp 112

14 *Journal of the National Indian Association*, August 1871

15 *Amrita Bazar Patrika*, 8 January 1900

16 K P S Menon: *Many Worlds: An Autobiography*, OUP, 1965 - pp 68

17 *Queen's Proclamation* available on eu.wikisource.org/wiki/Queen_Victoria's_Proclamation

18 I K Yajnik: *Shyamaji Krishnavarma: Life and Times of An Indian Revolutionary*, Lakshmi Publishers, Bombay, 1950 – pp 258

19 *Journal of the National Indian Association*, August 1871

20 *Hindoo Patriot*, 14 November 1864

21 *Ibid*

22 *Ibid*

23 *Amrita Bazar Patrika*, 4 December 1906

24 *Indian Mirror*, 1 December 1899

25 Sadhona Bonnerjee: *Life of W C Bonnerjee - The First President of Indian National Congress*, Calcutta University, 1944 – pp 23

26 *Hindoo Patriot*, 23 April 1892

27 Hemendranath Dasgupta: *Desbandhu Chittaranjan Das*, Publications Division, Ministry of Information and Broadcasting, Delhi, 1960 – pp 6

28 *Ibid*

29 *Hindoo Patriot*, 18 May 1892

30 Harindranath Chattopadhyay: *Life & Myself*, Nalanda Publications, Bombay, 1948 – pp 26

31 *Ibid* - pp 27

32 Jawaharlal Nehru: *An Autobiography*, John Lane The Bodley Head, London, 1941 – pp 154

33 *Ibid* – pp 153

34 *Ibid*

35 *Ibid* – pp 154

36 *Ibid*

37 Harindranath Chattopadhyay: *Life & Myself*, Nalanda Publications, Bombay, 1948 – pp 208

38 *Ibid* – pp 212

39 *Ibid*

40 *Hindoo Patriot*, 23 December 1872

41 Afzal Iqbal: *Life and Times of Mohamed Ali*, Idarah-i Adabiyat-i, Delhi, 1978 – pp 34

42 Famous Coach at London

43 Azim Husain: *Fazl-i-Husain: A Political Biography*, Longmans, Green & Co. Ltd, Bombay, 1946 – pp 24

44 *Ibid* – pp 23

45 *Ibid*

46 *Indian Mirror*, 25 January 1889

Chapter VI

1 *The Friends of India*, 3 September 1863

2 *Ibid*

3 *Ibid*

4 *The Bengalee*, 16 September 1863

5 *Hindoo Patriot*, 26 August 1872

6 *Ibid*

7 *Ibid*, 11 August 1873

8 *The Bengalee*, 16 August 1873

9 *Ibid*

10 *Hindoo Patriot*, 4 May 1874

11 *Ibid*, 2 November 1874

12 *Ibid*

13 Richard Symonds: *The British and Their Successors*, Faber & Faber, 1966 - pp 78

14 R P Noronha: *A Tale Told by An Idiot*, Vikas Publishing House (P) Ltd, New Delhi, 1976 – pp 1

15 *Ibid* – pp 2

16 *Ibid*

17 Hirschman Edwin: *White Mutiny: The Ilbert Bill Crisis in India and Genesis of the Indian National Congress*, Heritage Publishers, New Delhi, 1980 – pp 171

18 *Ibid*

19 *Ibid*

20 *Ibid*

21 *Ibid*

22 *Ibid*

23 *Ibid*

24 *Ibid*

25 *Ibid*

26 Lord Beveridge: *India Called Them*, George Allen & Unwin Ltd, London, 1947 – pp 249

27 *Ibid*

28 *Ibid* – pp 313

29 Surendranath Banerjee: *A Nation in Making: Being the Reminiscences of Fifty Years of Public Life*, OUP, 1925 - pp 83

30 Henry Cotton: *Indian and Home Memoirs*, T Fisher Unwin, London, 1911 – pp 180

31 *Ibid*

32 Hirschman Edwin: *White Mutiny: The Ilbert Bill Crisis in India and Genesis of the Indian National Congress*, Heritage Publishers, New Delhi, 1980 – pp 27

33 *Ibid* – pp 28

34 Hermann Michael Kisch: *A Young Victorian in India: Letters of H M Kisch of the Indian Civil Service*, Jonathan Cape, London, 1957 – pp 202

35 *Hindoo Patriot*, 13 December 1880

36 *Ibid*

37 *The Bengalee*, 30 May 1875

38 *Ibid*, 6 December 1873

39 Brajendranath De: *Reminiscences of Indian Civilian* in Calcutta Review, April, 1954

40 John Beames: *Memoirs of a Bengal Civilian*, Chatto & Windus, London, 1961 – pp 244

41 *Ibid*

42 Brajendranath De: *Reminiscences of Indian Civilian* in Calcutta Review, April, 1954

43 *Ibid*

44 Ralph Braibanti: *Asian Bureaucratic Systems Emergent from the British Imperial Tradition* , Duke University Press , 1966 – pp 60–61

45 *Hindoo Patriot*, 18 December 1882

46 *The Bengalee*, 6 November 1882

47 *Ibid*

48 *Indian Mirror*, 12 May 1887

49 *Ibid*, 19 December 1891

50 *Ibid*

51 *Ibid*, 15 July 1900

52 K P S Menon: *My Life and Work in the ICS: The Civil Servant in India*, Kewal L Panjabi (Ed), Bharatiya Vidya Bhavan, Bombay, 1965 – pp 34

53 *The Bengalee*, 17 October 1914

54 *Ibid*, 15 March 1890

55 Hirschman Edwin: *White Mutiny: The Ilbert Bill Crisis in India and Genesis of the Indian National Congress*, Heritage Publishers, New Delhi, 1980 – pp 226

56 *Journal of the National Indian Association*, June 1871

57 Song in the form of National Anthem

58 *Amrit Bazar Patrika*, 26 October 1903

59 *The Bengalee*, 22 March 1905

60 *Ibid*, 28 November 1901

61 *Ibid*

62 *Ibid*

63 *Ibid*

64 *Indian Mirror*, 4 December 1907

65 Sarala Devi: *Jibaner Jharapata* (Bengali), Sisu Sahitya Sansad, Calcutta, 1879

66 *The Statesman*, 22 April 1882

67 *Ibid*

68 *The Bengalee*, 23 February 1909

Conclusion

1 *Indian Mirror*, 20 November 1907

2 *The Bengalee*, 17 November 1912

3 *Hindoo Patriot*, 10 May 1869

4 *The Bengalee*, 27 December 1914

Candidates appeared and succeeded in the open competition during 1855-1914

Year	Lower Age (Years)	Upper Age (Years)	Total Number of Candidates	Candidates Selected	Number of Indian Candidates	Indians Selected	Sucessfull Indians in the Open competition
1855	18	23	105	20	0	0	
1856	18	23	56	21	0	0	
1857	18	23	60	12	0	0	
1858	18	23	67	20	0	0	
1859	18	23	119	40	0	0	
1860	18	22	154	80	0	0	
1861	18	22	171	80	0	0	
1862	18	22	171	82	1	0	
1863	18	22	189	60	2	1	Satyendranath Tagore
1864	18	22	219	40	2	0	
1865	17	22	284	52	2	0	
1866	17	21	242	52	0	0	
1867	17	21	279	50	1	0	
1868	17	21	272	51	4	0	
1869	17	21	325	50	8	4	Romesh Chunder Dutt, Behari Lal Gupta, Surendranath Banerjea, Sripad Babaji Thakur
1870	17	21	332	40	7	1	Anundoram Borooah
1871	17	21	229	37	5	1	Krishna Govinda Gupta
1872	17	21	199	36	4	0	
1873	17	21	203	35	9	1	Brajendra Nath De
1874	17	21	209	40	11	2	Pulicat Ratnavelu Chetti, Rustomjee Cursetjee
1875	17	21	198	38	6	0	
1876	17	21	202	31	5	0	
1877	17	21	202	31	3	2	Kavasjee Jamasjee Badshah, Gustasp Ardeseer[1]
1878 (April)	17	21	69	13	3	0	
1878 (June)	17	19	134	13	0	0	

1879	17	19	174	29	1	0	
1880	17	19	182	27	2	0	
1881	17	19	147	31	3	0	
1882	17	19	140	40	3	1	Mancherji Pestanji Kharegat
1883	17	19	150	42	1	0	
1884	17	19	185	39	4	2	Arthur Goodeve Chuckerbutty, Lokendra Nath Palit
1885	17	19	211	43	5	1	Mohsin Badruddin Tyabji
1886	17	19	205	38	4	0	
1887	17	19	199	46	6	2	Basanta Kumar Mullick, Atul Chunder Dutt
1888	17	19	236	47	4	1	Vengal Venugopal Chetty
1889*	17	19	233	50	6	0	
1890	17	19	205	47	10	5	Aravind Ackroyd Ghose[2], Muhammad Yusuf, Satis Chandra Mukherjee, Mahimohun Ghose, Govind Dinanath Madgavkar
1891	17	19	148	33	4	2	Satyendra Nath Palit, Birendra Chandra Sen
1892**	21	23	69	33	8	3	Kiran Chandra De, Jnanendra Nath Gupta, Francis Xavier D'Souza
1893	21	23	107	56	11	1	Barzore Jamshedji Dalal
1894	21	23	131	62	14	6	Yusuf Ali Abdullah IBN, Pirozeshah Kershasp, Tek Chand Diwan, Jyotsnanath Ghosal, Albion Rajkumar Banerji, Ali Ahmed Hussanally
1895	21	23	154	68	9	1	Sheikh Asgar Ali
1896	21	23	193	63	14	3	Atul Chandra Chatterjee, Cama Ardesar Kaikhoshru, Satyendra Chandra Mallik
1897	21	23	237	68	26	3	Pestonjee Sorabjee Patuck, Joseph Vas, Jnanedra Nath Roy
1883	17	19	150	42	1	0	
1898	21	23	185	66	22	8	Manmatha Krishna Deb, Byramji Rustamji Mehta, Pratap Chandra Dutt, Charu Chandra Dutt, Jotindra Nath Roy, Gokal Chand Badhwar, Ghazanfur Ali Khan, Jotindra Nath Roy[3]
1899	21	23	213	57	18	4	Jotindra Nath Roy[3], Jogindra Nath Paul, Rajappaya Narayana Aiyar, Balak Ram
1900	21	23	213	52	17	2	Erachshah Maneckji Nanavutty, Hariganpat Rao Gharpurey
1901	21	23	203	47	20	4	Joseph William Bhore, Camaji Byramji Navroji Cama, Cama Byramji Navroji[4], Abdullatif Qamruddin Amiruddin Latif

Year	Lower Age (Years)	Upper Age (Years)	Total Number of Candidates	Candidates Selected	Number of Indian Candidates	Indians Selected	Sucessfull Indians in the Open competition
1902	21	23	200	54	25	2	Kumar Jagdish Prasad, Sarat Kumar Ghose
1903	21	23	173	51	23	3	Abdul Ali Hamid Moizuddin, Vontatkre Pandrang Row, Mahim Chandra Ghosh,
1904	21	23	175	52	13	3	Guru Saday Dutt, Indu Bhusan Mundle, Alfred McGowan Coomarasamy Tampoe
1905	21	23	148	50	11	4	Sankara Balaji Dhavle, Vinayak Nand Shankar Mehta, Birendranath De, Joseph Nissin
1906	22	24	166	61	16	3	Mahadeva Vishnu Bhide, Arunachalam Thyagrajan, Panna Lal
1907	22	24	192	58	19	4	Ardeshir Rustomji Dalal, Dhirajlal Dayabhai Nanavati, Prabodh Chandra De, John Ratnam Krishnamma
1908	22	24	161	52	15	3	Janardan Atmaram Madan, Nowrojee Jehangir Wadia, Jagannath Luxmon Sathe
1909	22	24	181	52	18	1	Benegal Narsinga Rau
1910	22	24	184	60	20	1	Ameer Ali Warris
1911	22	24	202	53	25	3	Hiranand Khushiram Kripalani, Sontivenkata Ramamurty, Gurunath Venkatesh Bewoor
1912	22	24	188	47	31	7	Benegal Rama Rau, Ram Chandra, Birendra Kumar Basu, Yeshwant Anant Godbole, Satyendra Nath Roy, Shri Shridhara Nehru, Kshitis Chandra Sen
1913	22	24	163	45	25	3	Kannanthot Padmanabhan Padmanabha Pillai[5], Pheroze Merwan Kharegat, Savaksha Dunjisha Dhondy
1914	22	24	182	53	24	7	Girja Shanker Bajpai, Hassamal Baharmal Shivdasani, Vithal Sivaram Bhide, Shankar Pandurang Desai, Balchandra Krishna Gokhale, Sudhindra Kumar Halder, Nanlal Chamanlal Mehta

1 – Rejected in medical test after probation

2 – Denied appointment for not appearing in riding test

3 – Same candidate rejected twice in the medical test in the year 1898 & 1899

4 – Died in riding accident before final examination

5 – Denied appointment due to age controversy

* – One candidate of Indian descent Alfred William Goodeve Chuckerbutty was ** selected

** – Another Eurasian John Joseph Platel was also selected